Polygamy on the Pedernales

Polygamy on the Pedernales

Lyman Wight's Mormon Villages in Antebellum Texas, 1845 to 1858

Melvin C. Johnson

Utah State University Press
Logan, UT

Utah State University Press
Logan, Utah 84322–7800
www.usu.edu/usupress/

Manufactured in the United States of America
Printed on acid-free paper

Library of Congress Cataloging-in-Publication Data

Johnson, Melvin C., 1949-
Polygamy on the pedernales : Lyman Wight's Mormon villages in antebellum Texas, 1845 to 1858 / Melvin C. Johnson.
p. cm.
Includes bibliographical references and index.
ISBN 0-87421-627-3 (hardcover : alk. paper) – ISBN 0-87421-628-1 (pbk. : alk. paper)
1. Church of Jesus Christ of Latter-day Saints–Texas–History. 2. Wight, Lyman. 3. Texas–Church history. I. Title.

BX8615.T45J64 2006
289.3'764–dc22
2005035650

Contents

	Introduction The Wild Ram of Texas	1
1	Militant Mormonism on the American Frontier	9
2	The Wild Ram Strays from the Fold	32
3	Gone to Texas	54
4	Frontier Mormonism in the Texas Hill Country	70
5	Bishop George Miller and Zodiac: 1848–1849	90
6	Cutting the Wild Ram from the Flock	109
7	Independent Mormonism in Antebellum Texas	124
8	Polygamy and a Temple on the Pedernales	136
9	The Mormon Millers of Hamilton Valley	161
10	The Mormon Cowboys of Bandera County	177
	Conclusion The Way of All Flesh	192
	Bibliography	208

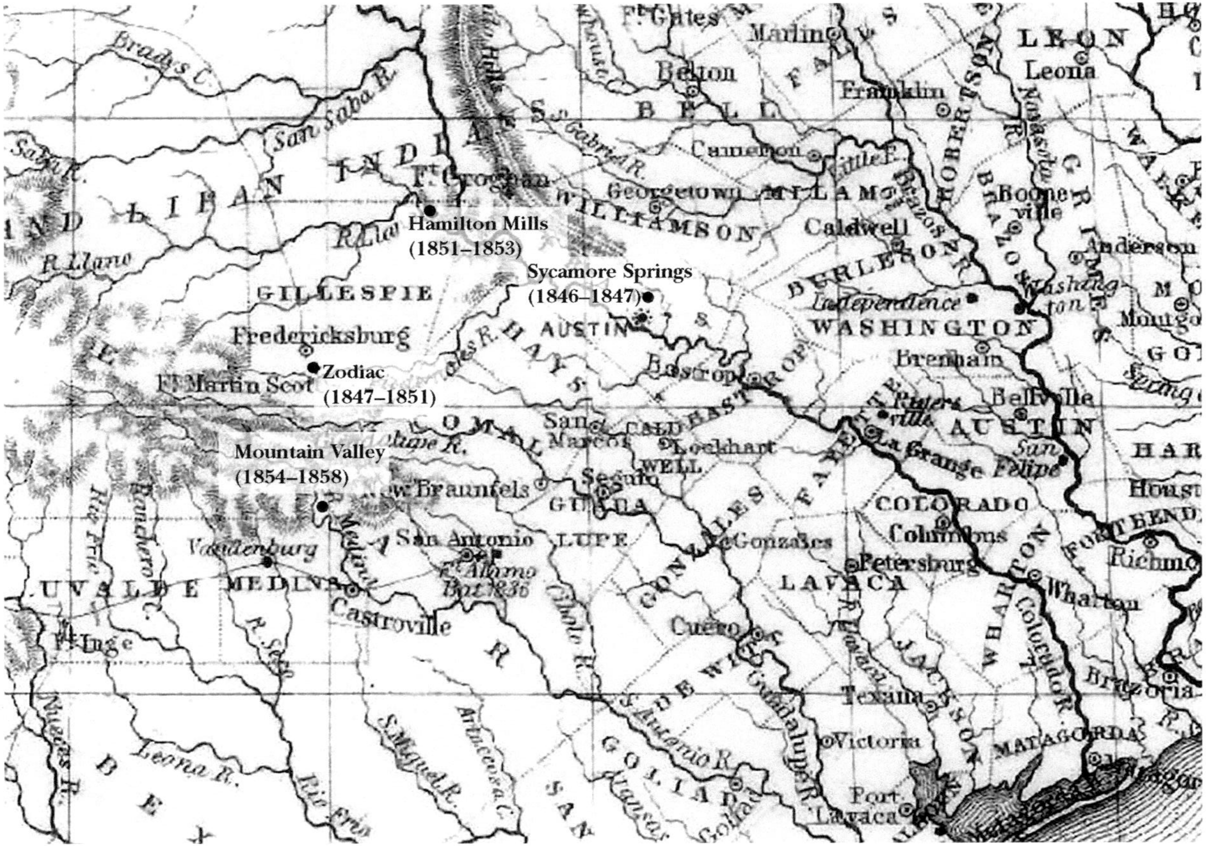

Map of Wightite Villages

Introduction

The Wild Ram of Texas

good history is not magic—and not given to an elite few
—Herschel Harry Dixon Jr.

The history of the Wightites and the polygamous villages of the Texas Hill Country are relevant and timely today. Such stories as headlined in the *Eldorado (TX) Success*, "Arizona Man Says Prophet Stole His Family," in July 2005, catch attention. The *Dallas Morning News* reported a year earlier about the Fundamentalist Latter Day Saints' new compounds "in tiny Eldorado, where fire-and-brimstone religion may be welcome but multiple wives tend to rankle." Once again, more than 140 years later, the American issues of "fringe religions, moral relativism and separation of church and state" have come to Texas. Texas and Texans have seen many unusual denominations, but the Mormons always spark contention when they settle among those who have never been around them. Those Texans who call Eldorado and the Lone Star state home are concerned: "it's because of worries . . . the group's reclusive and powerful spiritual leader, Warren Jeffs, will move in permanently with a few thousand followers and take over the local government. Others say that is too alarmist, and the general consensus is that the polygamists' arrival means life here will never be the same again."[1] Whatever the outcome at Eldorado in West Texas, Texans cannot escape their history.

---

1. "Arizona Man Says Prophet Stole His Family," *Eldorado (TX) Success*, 3 July 2005; Karen Brooks, "Polygamist Group Irks W. Texas Town," *Dallas Morning News*, 14 August 2004.

Let me explain why by beginning at the end. This is an examination of Lyman Wight and his Texas colonists. As their community ended in 1858, this small group of Mormon religionists, led by their indomitable chieftain, had influenced frontier affairs far beyond their numbers. A much, much smaller group than the Latter-day Saints of Utah Territory, they were also fewer in number than other Mormon sects, such as the Strangites of the Great Lakes region and the Cutlerites of Iowa. Yet these Texas polygamists blazed the way for other settlers into the Texas Hill Country, building wilderness mills that became the cornerstones for frontier communities, creating buffer zones between the settlements and the native tribes, and erecting the first practicing Mormon temple west of the Mississippi River. They practiced the precepts of their unique religion without giving in to their neighbors and without going to war with them. Those former colonists who stayed in the Hill Country after their leader's death continued to help to change the region into the dynamic part of modern Texas that it is today.

Known as the "Wild Ram of the Mountains,"[2] Lyman Wight was a rebellious apostle of the Church of Jesus Christ of Latter-day Saints (LDS), who led his polygamous community to the Republic of Texas in 1845. Historian Richard E. Bennett describes Wight's mission as one to "teach Indians, attract southern shareholders to the Mormon cause, raise money, and in other ways hasten and facilitate the return of the Church to the believed staging site of Christ's millennial return in Independence, Missouri."[3]

The history of Wight and his frontiersmen (described as Wightites[4]) is little known. Their many journeys began at Kirtland, Ohio

---

2. The *New York Sun* records the first non-Mormon description of Wight as the "Wild Ram of the Mountains," according to the LDS Journal History of the Church, 45:6 August 1845, 1 (hereafter cited as Journal History of the Church), Church Historical Library, Church of Jesus Christ of Latter-day Saints, Church Office Building, Salt Lake City, Utah. The Journal History of the Church is an unpublished collection of scores of volumes containing many thousands of entries pertaining to nineteenth-century Mormonism. These sources include newspapers, diaries, letters, records of church meetings, etc. Other sources for the LDS church are located in its various libraries, museums, and archives in the Salt Lake City area. All will be cited as the LDS archives.
3. Richard Edmond Bennett, *Mormons at the Missouri, 1846–1852: "And Should We Die . . ."* (Norman: University of Oklahoma Press, 1987), 237n35.
4. The reader should understand that such terms as *Wightites, Rigdonites, Josephites, Brighamites,* etc., are used informatively, not pejoratively. They accurately reflect the wording and definitions of the times.

and moved through Missouri, Illinois, Wisconsin Territory, the Republic and State of Texas, Indian Territory, Utah Territory, Iowa, and California. This study is rooted in local and family history, and it focuses on the time and place as well as the family/kinfolk relationships of the Wightite colony. Larger issues associated with the history of the West, Texas, and the Mormon movement, in general, flow from these relationships.[5]

Lyman Wight's character is important in understanding his community's odyssey. The autocratic frontier leader, increasingly addicted to his alcohol and opium as time passed, still inspired others to follow him for more than fifteen years, in situations often grim and troubled, across America's borderlands in pursuit of their common faith. To understand Wight is to understand that his persona characterized the dedication, the strength, and the personality of early Mormonism and its converts.

A true believer in primitive Christian practices, Wight replicated their rituals in latter-day Mormon communities unusual on the Wisconsin and Texas frontiers. He believed unreservedly in millennial Mormonism and in its founding martyr, Joseph Smith Jr. He literally believed Smith to be a prophet of God. Wight was unswervingly committed to establishing an American Zion in Jackson County, Missouri, and later in creating a gathering place in Texas for the faithful. In sanctified communities of Mormondom, Wight and others believed, the Kingdom of God would be created to prepare them for the Second Coming of Christ. Wight believed that Christ would come soon to Zion and establish an end-time millennial reign amidst His chosen people.

During the formative years of early Mormonism in Missouri, many of its leaders and followers grew to respect Wight, this religious chieftain who waged literal warfare against the enemies of Mormonism. Because of his martial dedication and steadfastness in support of Joseph Smith Jr., he rose to membership in its leading councils. Charismatic, intensely personal, and often domineering in his dealings with others, the Wild Ram became influential with Joseph Smith.

5. For a good discussion about the growing recognition and worth of regional and local history writing, see Randolph B. Campbell, "Family History from Local Record: A Case Study from Nineteenth Century Texas," *East Texas Historical Journal* 29, no. 2 (1991): 13–23.

Primary source materials, public and private, reveal previously unknown details about the Wightites. Material artifacts of their sojourn in Texas are almost nonexistent. Sycamore Springs (1846), north of Austin, is now under water. Only a wheat field with a state marker commemorates Zodiac (1847–51), and decayed, deteriorating cemetery ruins mark the village at Hamilton Creek (1851–53). Medina Lake covers Mountain Valley (1854–58), the final Wightite village.

The colony's population never reached more than 175 at any given time,[6] yet Zodiac and its descendent communities were unlike anything ever seen before in the Texas Hill Country. Although the Wightites opposed Brigham Young's rule in Nauvoo and Utah Territory, they still practiced those tenants marking them as a sect of nineteenth-century Mormonism: temple ritual, economic communitarianism, and polygamy. Polygamy, which here means polygyny, a relationship of one husband with more than one concurrent wife, is used as a neutral description in this work.

The Wightites were the first sizeable party of Mormons to enter the Republic of Texas. Smith Jr. had earlier dispatched an emissary, Lucien Woodworth, in the spring of 1844 to meet with President Sam Houston. Houston and Woodworth discussed establishing a large Mormon colony in the buffer zone between the Anglo-European settlements, the roving tribes of Native Americans, and the northern states of Mexico. Houston, expressing enthusiasm and preliminary approval, counseled Woodworth that the Texas Congress,

---

6. Estimates are based on research into the personal journals, diaries, and memoirs of the colonists; various private and public archives in the states of Iowa, Missouri, Utah, Wisconsin, Nebraska, and Texas; and the records and schedules of several federal censuses. The author has created several databases recording, collating, and identifying the writings, beliefs, and behavior of more than 300 individuals who played roles during the six eras that define the Wightite period: the Black River Lumber Company on the Black River Falls in Wisconsin (1841 to 1845); the trek to the Texas frontier and the wintering at Fort Johnston, Grayson County (March 1845 to March 1846); the trek to Austin and settlement at Sycamore Springs, Travis County (April 1846 to May 1847); the community of Zodiac, Gillespie County (May 1847 to the early spring of 1851); Mormon Mills or Hamilton Mills, Burnet County (late spring of 1851 to December 1853); and the trek to and establishment of Mormon Camp and Mountain Valley, Bandera County (December 1853 to March 1858).

meeting later that fall, would have to approve the Mormon request. Woodworth returned to Smith in Illinois. The Mormon leader, after discussing the matter with his advisers (known as the Council of Fifty), ordered Wight to take a small colony to Texas and make smooth and ready the path for a major migration of the LDS church to Texas.

The murders in Illinois of Joseph Smith Jr. and his brother Hyrum on a warm, muggy June evening, however, changed Mormon church history forever, and led to the intermixing of the histories of Mormonism and Western Americana. The Twelve Apostles gained the joint leadership of the largest group by far among the several factions of antebellum Mormonism. Within the Twelve, the senior apostle, Brigham Young, was the true leader. Young's growing preference for moving the church to the Rocky Mountains inevitably frustrated Wight's plans.[7] Today, more than 160 years after the murders of the Smiths, the LDS church, with headquarters in Salt Lake City, Utah, has a membership in excess of eleven million people.

Wight and his followers travelled fourteen months across the western borderlands from the Wisconsin pineries to the Texas Hill Country. They overcame the cool reception initially given them at Austin, and the next year (1847) moved further west to the Pedernales River, a few miles from Fredericksburg. Here the Mormon community of Zodiac and its mechanical mills became a valued asset. Frontier Texans appreciated the Mormons' hard work and industrial skills and Zodiac's possession of the only mechanical mill west of Austin. They also appreciated the peace the Mormons and the Texas Germans maintained with Comanche chief Buffalo Hump and his tribe.

Wightite socio-economic dynamics fused the sacred with the profane, which made the colony's success possible. Their community

7. B. H. Roberts, *History of the Church of Jesus Christ of Latter-Day Saints*, 7 vols, 2nd ed. (Salt Lake City: Desert News, 1948–52), hereafter cited as *History of the Church*. For incidental details of LDS interest in Texas, see 1:176n; 3:289–90, 315, 420, 445–49; 4:341; 6:260–61, 356, 377; 7:250–52, 254–55, 261. Young was undoubtedly correct in eventually choosing the Rocky Mountains as the church's destination, where it was able to grow with almost no federal influence or opposition for more than ten years. Those years were critical to the survival of the religion.

practices reinforced the union of individuals and families into a cohesive body of believers who maintained a separatist society distinctively aloof from fellow Texans. Communal strength and social cohesiveness were bedrocked on principles of polygamous kin relationships; thus, the individual desires were subjugated to needs of the whole. The socio-economic result was Mormon commercial domination of the Texas Hill Country by 1850. This came with a cost. Wightite socialization created powerful opposition in Gillespie, Burnet, and Bandera counties, based on the excited jealousy of their non-Mormon neighbors. However, unlike other Mormon controversies in antebellum America, the Wightite-Texan conflict never led to bloodshed.

The Wightites built the first Mormon temple west of the Mississippi. Clothed in holy garments, the celebrants performed sacred rituals singular to their faith. These rites included marriages for time and eternity; baptisms for the salvation of their dead; the anointing of religious priests, kings, and queens; and adoptions that bound families and members in time and eternity. The Wightite ceremonies were intended to link eternity with the present and past, creating a continuum of family structures that extended beyond the veil of death. These facets of their history are almost completely unknown today.

The Wightites in Texas did not function in complete isolation from their neighbors. They, like most Mormon groups, proselytized among the Texas communities. Many Texans did not want Mormons (Wightites or other kinds) in their land; thus the missionaries faced much opposition, and, on occasion, violence. Memoirs of both LDS and Wightite missionaries recorded kidnappings, mobbings, and beatings in East Texas and along the Gulf Coast. Polygamy and its practice were the normal excuses for attempts to drive Mormon missionaries from the field. Homer Duncan, an LDS missionary from Utah Territory, thought the Texans' outcry about polygamy hypocritical, because "every negro quarter" in Panola County, Texas, "is filled with blue-eyed children." Despite resistance from many Texas religious leaders and churches, more than 800 Texans converted to Utah Mormonism during the 1850s, particularly in the region of Grimes, Harris, and Montgomery counties. Other preaching successes were recorded in the piney woods of Panola and Rusk counties in deep East Texas. Most of the converts journeyed to Utah Territory as soon as they were able to outfit and travel.[8]

Lyman Wight and his followers, after leaving Zodiac in 1851, continued to establish settlements on the frontier. These included Mormon Mills in Hamilton Valley, Burnet County, and after debts and schism forced them out, the final settlements at Mormon Camp and Mountain Valley, in Bandera County, from 1854 to 1858. Depredations and raids by the Comanches, as well as internal pressures, whittled away the community's vitality and numbers. Wight, growing old and wanting to return to Jackson County, Missouri, declared in February of 1858 that he had received a revelation directing his return there. His movement, reduced to about eighty individuals, struggled only a short distance before he died on 30 March 1858 near Dexter, Bexar County.

His followers dispersed, and their history became fragmented. One group continued north to Iowa, some returned to the Texas Hill Country, and others emigrated to California to escape the coming war. Those living in the Hill Country served the Confederacy and Texas. Ezra Alpheus Chipman, the final polygamous, patriarchal male of the original Wightite colony, died at Bandera City, Texas, in 1913.

An overwhelming majority of the Texas Wightites joined the newly established Reorganized Church of Jesus Christ of Latter Day Saints (RLDS), formally organized in 1860. The movement, also known as the Reorganization, drew its members from dissident Mormon congregations in Iowa, Missouri, and eastern Nebraska. Their opposition to Brigham Young and the primacy of the LDS Church led the RLDS to accept Joseph Smith III, the son of Mormonism's slain founder, as its prophet and priesthood leader for millennial Mormonism. Disagreements between the LDS and the RLDS concerning succession, polygamy, and other theological issues have continued for more than 140 years. The RLDS movement has evolved

8. Diary of Morris J. Snedaker (1855, 1856), 39, 79, LDS archives; John Hawley, "Autobiography of John Hawley" (original and typescript of the handwritten manuscript, 1889), 8, 9, Historical Department archives, Reorganized Church of Jesus Christ of Latter Day Saints (Community of Christ), Independence, Missouri (hereafter cited as RLDS archives); Homer Duncan, *Deseret News* (Salt Lake City), 2 April 1856, also quoted in the Journal History of the Church, 119:2 April 1856, 4.

into what is now known as the Community of Christ, centered at Independence, Missouri.

This history then is a reconstruction of the life and times of Lyman Wight and his followers. To appropriate the words of a local Texas historian, creating a history of the Hill Country Mormons is possible only with a careful "sifting and weighing [of] the raw material for fruitful historical pursuit." For example, Wightite records have been found in the Bandera County courthouse; those dusty registers describe the collapse of Lyman Wight & Company's economic collective and serve as a witness to the ongoing dissolution of the colony itself. Other documents have been located in Texas, Iowa, Nebraska, Wisconsin, California, and Utah.

The story of the Wightites and Lyman Wight is the story of human perseverance in the face of adversity. An old man's manuscript noted that the trek from Wisconsin to Texas was for him, in part, always framed in the stark memory of near starvation—he remembered a little boy so hungry that the discovery of a discarded biscuit in a rat's nest became a wondrous treasure. Such matters bring alive the words "that good history is not magic—and not given to an elite few with the knack, but it is available and there for the taking for anyone who is willing to get to his or her hips in sleuthing."[9]

The history of Lyman Wight and his followers on the American frontier continues in the next chapter, and it has been "there for the taking." Whatever error that exists in this work, of course, is my sole responsibility.

---

9. Herschel Harry "Dick" Dixon Jr., "Charles Louis Klein (Kelty)" (unpublished manuscript, 1995), East Texas Research Center, Ralph Steen Library, Stephen F. Austin State University, Nacogdoches, TX.

1

Militant Mormonism on the American Frontier

That God would Damn them & give us pow[er] to Kill them
—Lyman Wight

Lyman Wight was born in 1796 to Levi and Susanna Wight in Fairfield, Connecticut. The future Missouri militia colonel served as a teenager in the War of 1812, and later he and his wife, born Harriet Benton, settled, by 1826, in the Western Reserve, Cuyahoga County, Ohio. They joined the communitarian movement of Sydney Rigdon,[1] an ex-Baptist minister and convert of Alexander Campbell, in 1829. Wight founded a Rigdonite community styled "the Family," a self-contained, common-stock economy based on New Testament principles of Christian primitivism, in which members shared all possession universally.

Wight wrote later that "the doctrines of the apostles" regarding having "all things in common" led him to enter, with eight others, "a covenant to make our interests as one as anciently." The Family "prosecuted with great vigor" agricultural and mechanical interests, its

1. Sydney Rigdon, a follower of the leading "blue light" minister Alexander Campbell, was second in influence only to Joseph Smith Jr. in early Mormonism. He influenced Mormon doctrines with his teachings on early apostolic Christianity, particularly concerning communitarianism and separatism. Rigdon became the First Counselor in the Quorum of the First Presidency to Joseph Smith. After Smith's murder in 1844, the Twelve Apostles defeated Rigdon and others in a succession-crisis battle for the leadership of the Nauvoo church and directed the fate of a slight majority of those Latter-day Saints after Smith's death. Richard S. Van Wagoner, author of *Sidney Rigdon: A Portrait of Religious Excess*, published in 1994, is Rigdon's leading biographer.

members beginning "to feel as if the millennium was close at hand."[2] Later Wightite communities in Wisconsin and Texas were founded on common-stock foundations. About the time the Family prepared to combine with several other separatist groups at Mayfield, Ohio, intending to begin a communitarian farm and several mills, LDS missionaries, including Oliver Cowdery and Parley P. Pratt, brought the restoration message of Joseph Smith Jr. and the Mormon gospel to the Family. These Rigdonite and Wightite communitarians, 127 of them, converted en masse. Almost another thousand followed shortly, doubling the size of the church and eventually bringing Rigdon (who also converted) to a position only secondary to that of Joseph Smith Jr. Rigdon himself became one of Joseph Smith's prime advisers, quickly reaching high positions in the growing church's governing councils.[3] Smith came to know and trust Wight well, despite some initial reluctance.[4] During the next thirteen years, Wight committed himself to Joseph Smith Jr. and Mormonism. As a mark of Joseph Smith's growing awareness of Wight's potential, the Mormon prophet ordained Wight in 1831 as the first high priest of the church. Wight then ordained Smith to the high priesthood.[5]

---

2. Heman Hale Smith, "The Lyman Wight Colony in Texas" (unpublished manuscript, 1920), 1–3, prepared for the Reorganized Church of Jesus Christ of Latter Day Saints, RLDS archives; Lyman Wight journal, quoted in Joseph Smith III, Heman C. Smith, and F. Henry Edwards, *The History of the Reorganized Church of Jesus Christ of Latter Day Saints* (Independence, MO: Herald House, 1967–), 1:152–53 (hereafter cited as *Reorganized History*). Smith prepared a manuscript history of the Wight colony from the Lyman Wight journal, Spencer Smith journal, and William Leyland journal, the only primary sources contemporary with the community's existence in Texas. All were later destroyed in a fire.
3. Lyman Wight journal, in *Reorganized History*, 1:154; Heman C. Smith, "Newell K. Whitney," *Journal of History* 2, no. 2 (January 1909): 70–77; B. H. Roberts, *A Comprehensive History of the Church of Jesus Christ of Latter-Day Saints* (Salt Lake City: Deseret News, 1930), 1:231, 243. See D. Michael Quinn, *The Mormon Hierarchy: Origins of Power* (Salt Lake City: Signature Books/Smith Research Associates, 1994), 576–77, 602–3, for a biographical description of the two men's professional, public, and personal histories.
4. Kenneth H. Winn, *Exiles in a Land of Liberty: Mormons in America, 1830–1846* (Chapel Hill: University of North Carolina Press, 1989), 132.
5. *Times and Seasons* (Nauvoo, IL) 1 February 1844, 416; *History of the Church*, 1:175–76; Donald Q. Cannon and Lyndon W. Cook, eds., *Far West Record: Minutes of the Church of Jesus Christ of Latter-Day Saints, 1830–1840* (Salt Lake City: Deseret Book, 1983), 6–7.

Lyman Wight matured as a charismatic champion during the initial ten years' growth of organized Mormonism. A visionary, he claimed to have seen the Savior when he was ordained a high priest.[6] Ordered to go to Missouri and provide a gathering place for other Mormons, he settled in Jackson County in November 1831. During a missionary trip to Cincinnati, Wight preached repeatedly in the courthouse, evangelizing "after the order of Melchisedek," and baptized more than one hundred during his stay.[7]

Lyman Wight's first experience with anti-LDS persecutions occurred in Missouri. The Missouri "old settlers," Southerners and defenders of slavery, drove Wight and his co-religionists from Jackson County into Clay County. Enraged at an article titled "The Free People of Color" in the LDS *Evening and Morning Star*, a mob destroyed the press and the editor's home. The earlier settlers, according to Kenneth H. Winn, feared the Mormons' growing numbers as a threat to their way of life, clashing in origin, sentiments, social behavior, politics, and religion. The Mormons originated mostly in New England, the upper Mid-Atlantic states, and the Western Reserve. The older inhabitants were outraged that the newcomers seemed to be encouraging free African Americans from the eastern states to immigrate to Missouri. Although the assumption was false, they were aware that the Mormons' antislavery attitudes could create a majority culture change of rigid sectarianism antithetical to the Southern way.

Little doubt exists that Mormon cultural attitudes influenced the conflict between the groups. Orange Lysander Wight (a son of Lyman Wight) later recalled that Mormons' "fanatical" attitudes were partially responsible for the expulsion. Some believed "they were the Lord's favored people," and that all of the land "would all eventually belong to them." According to the younger Wight, these feelings "exasperated the [non-Mormons] and they were ready to add to what they heard, and all the efforts of those of the saints—

---

6. Journal History of the Church, 183:11; Brigham Young, *Journal of Discourses, delivered by Brigham Young, his two counsellors, the twelve apostles, and others, reported by G[eorge] D. Watt*, (Salt Lake City: Deseret Book, 1966; originally published 1854–86), 11:4, 15 November 1864.

7. Andrew Jenson, *Latter-Day Saint Biographical Encyclopedia: A Compilation of Biographical Sketches of Prominent Men and Women in the Church of Jesus Christ of Latter-Day Saints* (Salt Lake City: A Jenson History Co., 1901–36): 93–94.

who could see the evil effects of the fanaticism—to reconcile the people of Jackson County proved in vain, thus, it went on from one thing to another until it ended in real persecution." He concluded the Mormons were not strong enough to arbitrate the issue "by force of arms," and "were conquered and driven from the county."[8] Lyman Wight was one of the few to resist; one LDS church newspaper many years later described him as "a dread to his enemies and a terror to evil doers, and his life was often sought after."[9]

Lyman Wight, with Parley Pratt, carried messages from Missouri to Joseph Smith in Kirtland, Ohio. They next aided in providing men and provisions for Zion's Camp by recruiting among the LDS in the northern sections of Illinois and into Michigan. In May and June, Pratt and Wight guided fourteen members from the Pontiac branch in St. Clair, Michigan, to Zion's Camp on the Salt River in Missouri. The Pontiac group's gear was barely sufficient (two light wagons, two span of horses, and a tent) for the trip. Besides Wight, several individuals in the party, including Samuel Bent, Meacham Curtis, Sophronia Curtis, and Lyman Curtis, participated in the Wightite trek from Wisconsin to Texas (1845–1846).

Although Zion's Camp was a failure, foundering in a welter of dispiritedness and disease, Wight's rise continued. He was appointed by Smith as general of the camp and second in command, and he also joined the Zion Stake High Council. As the members of Zion's Camp were losing a battle to cholera, the war for Jackson County ended before it began. A new sanctuary had to be found, and political compromise with reality was the answer. Alexander Doniphan, a non-Mormon legislator and lawyer who had earlier befriended the religionists and deplored their removal from Jackson County, pushed through a measure in the Missouri legislature organizing Caldwell County as a home for the Mormons.[10]

---

8. *Reorganized History*, 3:788; Orange Lysander Wight, "Recollections of Orange L. Wight, Son of Lyman Wight" (photocopy of typescript copy of manuscript, 1966), 7, LDS archives.
9. Nathan Tanner Porter, "Reminiscences" (unpublished manuscript, ca. 1879), 69, LDS archives; *Latter-Day Saints' Millennial Star*, 22 July 1865, 455.
10. *Reorganized History*, 3:786; journal of the branch of the Church of Christ in Pontiac, Michigan, Huron branch, 1834 (handwritten manuscript), LDS archives; Quinn, *The Mormon Hierarchy*, 100–101; see subject name listings in

Wight, commensurate with his growing leadership roles, returned to Ohio at Joseph Smith's direction to receive a religious endowment in the Kirtland Temple. He later would receive new temple rites at Nauvoo, and be initiated into the doctrine of polygamy. Thomas G. Alexander has clarified major differences between the temple ceremonies of Kirtland in the 1830s and Nauvoo in the 1840s. The first was individual and charismatic, the second communal and dealt with salvation. The Kirtland ceremony centered on the gifts and influences of the Holy Ghost, relying on "the visitation of angelic beings" and "the infusion of Pentecostal gifts." Thus the Kirtland ritual emphasized the recipient's charismatic and spiritual regeneration. On the other hand, the Nauvoo ritual involved the salvation of the participant and his familial dead. The Nauvoo participants "gained a more thorough understanding of the purpose of life and of Christ's mission. They made further covenants committing themselves more fully to the work of God and Christ on earth and to the eternity of the family." Participants stood proxy for deceased family members, being baptized and receiving the endowment for the dead in hope the family generations would be joined together after Judgment Day.[11]

Along with temple ritual, Joseph Smith also indoctrinated the Twelve in Mormonism's ultimate secret, plural marriage or polygamy, at Nauvoo. They began marrying "plural wives and began solemnizing such marriages for others."[12] Wight continued both polygamy and temple ritualism in Texas. There he fused the endowments of Kirtland and Nauvoo and developed his own ritual of the endowment, washings, anointings, sealings, and baptism for time and eternity.

Wight attempted to influence LDS doctrine. Evil spirits, Wight thought, caused illness. Consequently, he believed strongly in faith

---

Toni R. Turk, "Mormons in Texas" (photocopy of typescript manuscript, 1987), LDS archives.

11. Thomas G. Alexander, "A New and Everlasting Covenant: An Approach to the Theology of Joseph Smith," *New Views of Mormon History: A Collection of Essays in Honor of Leonard J. Arrington*, ed. Davis Bitton and Maureen Ursenbach Beecher (Salt Lake City: University of Utah Press, 1987), 47.

12. *Latter-Day Saints' Millennial Star*, 22 July 1865, 456; blessing given by Joseph Smith Jr. to Lyman Wight, Kirtland, Ohio, 29 December 1835, recorded 1 January 1836, with Oliver Cowdery, recorder, and Frederick G. Williams, clerk, Patriarchal Blessings, 2:56 (transcript 53), RLDS Archives; Quinn, *The Mormon Hierarchy*, 66; B. Young, *Journal of Discourses*, 2:6 April 1853, 31.

healing. In 1834, John Corrill charged Wight in a church council with teaching that "disease in this Church is of the devil, and that medicine administered to the sick is of the devil; for the sick in the Church ought to live by faith." The church record notes Wight rather smugly "acknowledged that he had taught the doctrine, and rather believed it to be correct." Joseph Smith decided "that it was not lawful to teach the Church that all disease is of the devil," but "all who had faith to follow the doctrine were welcome to do so."[13]

Christian primitivism remained always a strong part of Wight's beliefs. He supported religious communitarianism, considering church members' private property to be economic assets for church use and never to be used for the needs or profit of the individual. When a church council tried certain leading Mormons, Wight remarked that all other offenses were minor in stature compared to the one that charged them with selling their lands in Jackson County for private profit. Their behavior, Wight stated, "was a hellish principle . . . and that they flatly denied the faith in so doing."[14]

Wight also believed the 1833 *Book of Commandments*, the first printed body of Joseph Smith Jr.'s revelations, was a higher law (or divine law) than the later work, the *Doctrine and Covenants*, which he believed to be a lower law (or human law). Church authorities advised him to repent of teaching such doctrine. This may be the same case in which D. W. Patten leveled a charge of false doctrine against Wight, of which the High Council found him guilty in 1837. If Patten's charge related to Wight's stated belief concerning the *Book of Commandments*, it was a serious one. Quinn notes that Wight was nearly excommunicated, the avoidance of which required his confession of repentance.[15]

The Mormons' removal from Jackson County did not resolve their religious differences with the old settlers. In June 1836, certain non-Mormons in Clay County repeated the old differences between

13. *History of the Church*, 2:147.

14. *History of the Church*, 3:4; "Minutes of the Proceedings of the Committee of the Whole Church in Zion," *Elders' Journal of the Church of Latter Day Saints* (Kirtland, OH), July 1838, 44; *Latter-Day Saints' Millennial Star*, 22 July 1865, 456.

15. *History of the Church*, 2:481–82; *Latter-Day Saints' Millennial Star*, 22 July 1865, 456; Quinn, *The Mormon Hierarchy*, 38.

the two groups. They claimed too many Mormons were immigrating to the area, they were obtaining much of the local property, and they were stating that it was to be their heaven. Additionally, most Mormons were Easterners, "whose manners, habits, customs, and even dialect" separated the newcomers from the old settlers. Also, they did not own slaves and opposed slavery. And, finally, the Mormons supported the Indians, even to declaring "from the pulpit, that the Indians are a part of God's chosen people, and are destined by heaven to inherit this land, in common with themselves."[16]

The leadership, including Lyman Wight, had begun to plan as early as 1834 to forcefully resist if their enemies came against them again. An irregular, paramilitary force, with as many as one thousand males, ages fourteen and over, was organized. Joseph Smith in his secret rank of "Barak Ale," commanded the church's armed forces. He confirmed Wight, supposedly in the presence of an angel, to the office of "Baneemy," a senior leader of the holy army. These Danites included several of Wight's future Texas followers, including Truman Brace and Joel S. Miles.[17]

Wight's religious and civic duties to church and state became confused. While he commanded the Mormon forces at Adam-ondi-Ahman and served as President John Smith's counselor in the Stake Presidency there, he was also the colonel commanding the organized 56th Regiment of Missouri militia. Muddling further his ecclesiastical and secular duties, Wight ordained Joseph Smith into the Danites.[18] Thus Wight commanded both the Missouri and Mormon armed forces of his region.

---

16. Quinn, *The Mormon Hierarchy*, 90, 625, 628, 641, 642, 659.
17. *History of the Church*, 3:280, 404, 432–33, 449, and *Document Showing the Testimony Given Before the Judge of the Fifth Judicial District of the State of Missouri, on the Trial of Joseph Smith, Jr., and Others, for High Treason and Other Crimes Against That State* (Washington, DC: U.S. Government Printing Office, 1841), 4.
18. Lyman Wight, Medina River, to Cooper and Chidester, July 1855, Lyman Wight letterbook, RLDS archives; sworn statement of Gideon Carter to Brigham H. Roberts, 27 February 1894, LDS archives, 1; *Reorganized History*, 3:788; Quinn, *The Mormon Hierarchy*, 337; also see Appendix A, "A Partial List," 479–90 in *The Mormon Hierarchy*, for membership in the Danites. William G. Hartley, *My Best for the Kingdom: History and Autobiography of John Lowe Butler, a Mormon Frontiersman* (Salt Lake City: Aspen Books, 1993), 37, records that the Mormon militia was organized in 1837, with Lyman Wight as its colonel.

Lyman Wight did not separate his roles as a commander of both church and state troops, and had no difficulty in making his decision. Winn has written, "Wight positively itched for combat," and his fighting attitude continued to improve Smith's opinion of him. In June 1838, William Swartznell wrote that Wight's sermons at Adam-ondi-Ahman in Daviess County called for military action against church enemies. He reportedly told some that Saint Peter's cutting Caiphus' servant's ear "was a strong argument for war," and because the laws of Missouri had not protected him, he "owed nothing to the laws." He suffered "the rack" of persecution for seven years and now "God did not require him to endure more. . . . He would not yield to the laws of Missouri—he would sooner die and be buried." Wight had chosen his religion over his country. Although Wight's war speeches created unrealistic hopes among the Mormons, John Corrill thought local Mormons began to believe, and boast that their military arms could defeat Missouri's militia and even the federal army.[19]

Danite John D. Lee wrote that Wight's "war speech" made Lee believe, with others, that they would be indomitable against their enemies. Lee described a warlike Wight, standing by his horse and wearing a red bandana "wrapped around his neck, regular Indian fashion," with open blouse and cutlass in hand, whose "address struck terror to his enemies, while it charged his brethren with enthusiastic zeal and forced them to believe they were invincible and bullet proof." Corrill noted a year later that Wight often had boasted "in his discourses of what they would do if the mob did not let them alone,—they would fight, and they would die upon the ground, and they would not give up their rights, etc.; when, as yet, there was no mob. But this preaching inspired the Mormons with a fighting spirit, and some of the other citizens began to be stirred up to anger." However, the killing of Daniel W. Patten, senior apostle of the Twelve and known to church members

---

19. Ibid. Hartley, *My Best for the Kingdom,* 132. Wight's remarks can be found in William Swartzell, *Mormonism Exposed, Being a Journal of Residence in Missouri from the 28th of May to the 20th of August, 1838* (Pekin, IL: privately printed, 1840), 13, 17, 32. Winn, *Exiles in a Land of Liberty,* 252n10, notes that Swartzell became opposed to Mormonism; Winn also reports that Swartzell's statements concerning Wight's temper are reflected in other writings of the period. Also see John Corrill, *A Brief History of the Church of Christ of Jesus Latter-Day Saints (Commonly Called Mormons)* ([St. Louis?]: privately printed, 1839), 29.

as "Captain Fear Not," at Crooked River returned many Mormons to their senses.[20]

Patten's death, however, only enraged Lyman Wight. He deliberately chose his duty to his religious faith and paramilitary rank in the church's armed forces over his militia commission and sworn duty to Missouri. Waging offensive warfare against his church's enemy, and, thus, against the People and State of Missouri, Wight chose the path of sedition. He called out the Mormon militia and fell on his fellow Missourians.

Official LDS histories defend LDS militia operations as necessary for restoring order and suppressing mob violence. Other histories argue Mormon savagery incited the Missourians. Wight has been celebrated among the folk as a defender of helpless women and children who were being driven into the cold and ice; "he was no coward" for protecting the helpless. One story recalls an incident when several Missourians led by a preacher confronted him, wanting the return of land he had sold to the Mormons. Wight "jumped over the fence and caught hold of his bridle . . . and the man wilted which was no surprise for Lyman looked like he would tear him to pieces. [The preacher] agreed to be rather" quiet in his requests. There was no doubt Wight would use violence to protect his own.[21]

Stephen C. LeSueur, the historian of balance about the civil war and particularly the Danite organization, believes both that the Mormons share culpability for their troubles and that the Danites contributed to the blame. Further confusing the issue is the fact that Mormon militia units, including Wight and his troops, were acting subject to the state's military authority when they marched into Daviess County, a stronghold of their foes. General H. G. Parks of the Missouri militia joined them the next day. Several Mormon homes had been burned, and the refugees, after traveling all night through the snow and over icy streams, struggled into the militia camp. The Mormon troops were inflamed. General Parks ordered Colonel Wight and others, on 18 October 1838, to act. The fighting, which caused

---

20. John Doyle Lee, *Confessions of John D. Lee* (Salt Lake City: Modern Microfilm, 1970; reprint of 1877 edition titled *Mormonism Unveiled; or, The Life and Confessions of the Late Mormon Bishop, John D. Lee*); Corrill, *A Brief History*, 27–28.
21. Marguerite H. Allen, Henry Hendricks genealogy, 1963, 16–18, LDS Archives.

casualties on both sides, resulted in early Mormon victories, and the looting and burning of non-Mormon towns. According to LeSueur, Joseph Smith knew the offensive intent and acquisitive nature of his commanders' military expeditions against the old settlers. The plunder from the various non-Mormon communities "were brought and distributed among the Saints" with Smith's knowledge.[22]

The fight between Danite forces and state militia troops at Crooked River on 25 October 1838 escalated the struggle into outright civil war. D. Michael Quinn notes that the Mormons showed no reluctance in employing deadly force, but they did not match the Missourians' inhumanity toward noncombatants, which included driving women and children before them. On the 28th, Lilburn W. Boggs, governor of Missouri, ordered that either the Mormons be "exterminated" or driven from the state. Two days later, a state militia unit attacked the Mormon settlement at Haun's Mill. More than a dozen women and children were wounded as they fled from the mill. The militia then systematically slaughtered eighteen men and boys, two of whom were no older than ten. Some of the dead were mutilated.

Alexander Doniphan, lawyer and legislator, and friend of the Mormons during the Jackson County troubles, again came to their aid. After Joseph Smith Jr. and other Mormon leaders had surrendered, Doniphan, serving as a general officer with the state militia, received an order from General Samuel D. Lucas to summarily execute Smith and six others, including Lyman Wight. Wight, although later excommunicated from the church, still figures in Mormon folk

---

22. For an objective, full-length description of the civil war in Missouri, see Stephen C. LeSueur, *The 1838 Mormon War in Missouri* (Columbia: University of Missouri Press, 1987); also see John Portineus Greene, *Facts Relative to the Expulsion of the Mormons from the State of Missouri, Under the "Extermination Order"* (Cincinnati: R. P. Brooks, 1839), 20–21; Linda King Newell and Valeen Tippets Avery, *Mormon Enigma: Emma Hale Smith*, 2nd ed. (Urbana: University of Illinois Press, 1994), 73; Testimony of Samson, Avard, Cause 91, State of Missouri vs. Jos. Smith et al. 12 and 13 November 1838, folder 2, Eugene Morrow Violette Collection, 1806–1921, Western Historical Manuscript Collections, University of Missouri, Columbia, Missouri (hereafter cited as WHMC); Stephen C. LeSueur, "The Danites Reconsidered: Were They Vigilantes or Just the Mormons' Version of the Elks Club?," *John Whitmer Historical Association Journal* 14 (1994): 48, 50; Dean C. Jesse and David J. Whittaker, "The Last Months of Mormonism in Missouri: The Albert Perry Rockwood Journal," *Brigham Young University Studies* 29, no. 2 (Winter 1988): 5–41.

literature as a hero and defender of the faith because of his defense of Joseph Smith and the helpless among the church. Given the opportunity by General Moses Wilson to escape the firing squad if he would testify against Smith, Wight is supposed to have said, "Shoot and be damned." General Doniphan refused to carry out the execution, risking punishment himself for disobeying orders. He wished "Colonel Wight" well before he marched his troops away. General Lucas, in light of General Doniphan's courageous stand, backed down and the prisoners survived.[23]

Joseph Smith, Lyman Wight, and others remained in jail for several months, suffering hardships at the hands of the captors. The quality of food was rank, and its origin at times suspect. One guard at dinnertime supposedly asked Wight how he liked "Mormon beef," the implication that the prisoners were eating human flesh.[24] This suggestion reflects the hatred that continued to burn for several generations between Mormons and Missourians. Wight later wrote that while in jail, he assisted Joseph Smith Jr. to ordain one of his sons as his successor. According to Wight, Smith and he laid their hands on the young boy's head, and Smith blessed the boy as his "successor when I depart." Rebecca J. Ballantyne, in a sworn affidavit in 1908, testified that Wight had told her he had assisted Smith in ordaining Joseph Smith III. Joseph Smith III remembered that he had been ordained when his father was still in the Liberty, Missouri, jail. The question of apostolic versus patriarchal succession to Joseph Smith Jr.'s mantle of leadership has been one of the issues that divided the LDS and RLDS churches after 1860.[25]

Smith, Wight, and the others escaped from custody in 1839 and sought their fellow religionists in Illinois, where the church membership had moved. The Wild Ram emerged from the Missouri troubles

---

23. Johnson, quoted in Quinn, *The Mormon Hierarchy*, 99; *History of the Church*, 3:162–64; Jenson, *LDS Biographical Encyclopedia*, 95; Roger D. Launius, *Alexander William Doniphan: Portrait of a Missouri Moderate* (Columbia: University of Missouri Press, 1997), 63–64.
24. *Latter-Day Saints' Millennial Star*, 29 July 1865, 471; Journal History of the Church, 22:18; Joseph Smith III, *Saints' Herald (True Latter Day Saints' Herald)* (Lamoni, IA), 15 July 1879, also in Joseph Smith III, "Statements of Joseph Smith," *Journal of History* 12, no. 4 (October 1919): 414.
25. *Reorganized History*, 2:789, 3:506; Heman C. Smith, "Succession in the Presidency," *Journal of History* 2, no. 1 (January 1909): 8.

as a renowned and stalwart defender of the Mormon people. Joseph Smith Jr. esteemed him, and gave him increasing responsibility and position in church affairs. Wight again became a counselor to John Smith, this time in the High Council of Iowa. In 1841, Joseph Smith selected and ordained Wight a member of the Twelve. Smith, shortly before his death, made him a member of the select Council of Fifty, a secret organization of Smith's trusted advisers who were organized in late winter of 1844 to find a secure location for the Mormons beyond American jurisdiction. Because age determined ranking in the Fifty, Wight, although the junior member of the Twelve, was senior to his fellow apostles in the Fifty, including Brigham Young. He also became a member of the Quorum of Anointed in 1844, another secret organization of the church's elect.

These appointments brought Wight prominence, if not great power. The Twelve, according to Quinn, were evolving from a supervisory group responsible for missionary work into the second most powerful administrative body in the church. It was subordinate only to the Quorum of the First Presidency, which, from 1837–44, consisted of Joseph Smith Jr., his brother Hyrum Smith, and Sydney Rigdon. Well connected through his close friendships and shared struggles with the Smiths and Rigdon, and by his appointments in the Twelve, the Fifty, and the Anointed, Wight was well positioned for future challenges in the causes of the church.[26]

---

26. *History of the Church,* 1:176n; 3:289–90, 315, 420, 445–49; 4:341; 6:260–61, 356, 377; Willard Richards diary, 14 May 1844, LDS archives; D. Michael Quinn, "The Council of Fifty and Its Members, 1844–1945," *Brigham Young University Studies* 20, no. 2 (Fall 1979): 196; Cannon and Cook, *Far West Record,* 295; Lyman Wight to Cooper and Chidester, July 1855; Lyman Wight to William Smith, 26 July 1849, *Melchizedek and Aaronic Herald* (Covington, KY), 1 (September 1849): 2 (photocopy), LDS archives; Lyman Wight, *An Address by Way of an Abridged Account and Journal of My Life from February 1844 up to April 1848, with an Appeal to the Latter Day Saints,* 3, 4, Iowa State Historical Society archives, Des Moines, IA. *An Address* is Wight's defense of his Texas leadership, and defies the attempts of Brigham Young and the Twelve to control him. The document is annotated with the symbol "No. 183 A8" and inscribed with the notation "Read to the Branch at Zodiac on April 30, 1848. Endorsed on May 1, 1848 and G. Miller, J. Young, W. P. Eldridge, O. L. Wight, and S. Curtis appointed by committee to have it published." Quinn, *The Mormon Hierarchy,* 416n58, states that no sources are available to conclude that Wight used age as a basis for opposing Brigham Young, but this is contradicted in "Preston Thomas: His Life

Lyman Wight had scaled uncommon heights from common beginnings. Now almost forty-five, he had become an apostle in the Mormon church. The charismatic junior member of the Twelve had led hundreds into the new frontier faith of America. A close friend of Joseph Smith and Sydney Rigdon, the two most powerful leaders of the church, he was positioned close to the LDS center in part because of his devotion to, and willingness to suffer for, the Mormon gospel. Friends and foes alike were aware that he was literally willing to wage war for his faith. The years to come would reveal that Wight was not only ready to combat enemies outside the church, but also those inside it, as well, if he perceived them to be inimical to Mormonism and the posterity of Joseph Smith.

Wight's apostolic duties brought both Mormonism and him to the Wisconsin wilds in 1841, and became the seed for the Texas colony. Lumber brought Mormons and Lyman Wight to Wisconsin. The Wightites' journey to Texas by way of the northern frontier came about for two reasons. First, Nauvoo's rapid growth demanded building materials for its material culture; second, Joseph Smith wanted a safe place for his people and his theocratic rule. A severe housing shortage had been the result of the dramatic increase in population. Along with the need for more private, public, and church buildings, problems also had been mounting with the area's non-Mormons. Outside civil authority threatened Smith's primacy. The citizens of Illinois earlier had welcomed the refugees as they fled across the Mississippi River, but soon changed their minds. Mormon theocracy, which both suborned civil authority to religious leadership and suppressed legal dissent, alienated growing numbers in and out of the church. The rumors of polygamy also fueled the flames of discord. Smith knew that he would have to move his people again. The question remained, where? Texas was a possible destination.[27]

---

and Travels," folder 1:45, LDS archives. Quinn does remark, "Wight emphasized ordinations, particularly the last one he received for the Texas mission."

27. Among the works about Smith during this era, see Samuel Woolley Taylor, *The Kingdom or Nothing: The Life of John Taylor, Militant Mormon* (New York: Macmillan, 1976), 85–88; Roberts, *Comprehensive History*, 2:221–23; Fawn McKay Brodie, *No Man Knows My History: The Life of Joseph Smith, the Mormon Prophet*, 2nd ed. (New York: Alfred A. Knopf, 1971), 367–79. Two full-length works that explore in detail the themes of Mormon nationalism and

Douglas Wayne Larche and Michael Van Wagenen have studied Smith's interest in Texas. Larche noted that if the election bid of Joseph Smith and Sydney Rigdon for the presidency and vice-presidency in 1844 failed, then the church would negotiate with the Republic of Texas to purchase some of its borderlands. There Smith could create a new nation and seek an alliance with the Republic against Mexico.[28] Van Wagenen has significantly expanded Larche's premise: "With his power weakening in Illinois and armed mobs at his gates, Smith looked outside the borders of the United States for both refuge and empire." The Mormon prophet had been following the troubles of the Republic in Nauvoo's "secular and religious newspapers." Texas provided three possible alternatives to Smith's problems. Smith's presidential campaign platform in 1844 called for Texas annexation. He also requested authority from Congress "to raise a volunteer army to guard the Texas and Oregon frontiers." Finally, Smith sent an emissary to "negotiate with Sam Houston to purchase the sparsely populated and highly contested southern and western regions of the Republic. In the borderlands," Van Wagenen argued, "Smith planned to establish a theocratic nation that would serve as a buffer between Texas and Mexico. In this new Kingdom of God, Smith and his followers would be free to practice their peculiar religious beliefs from the interference of the United States."[29] But while Smith had been studying the Texas alternative, he had church, city, and citizens to manage.

In 1841, the church's need for milled lumber in Nauvoo, the timber community in Wisconsin, and Apostle Lyman Wight and Bishop George Miller's responsibility for it all became the genesis

---

theo-democracy are Winn, *Exiles in a Land of Liberty*, and Klaus J. Hansen, *Quest for Empire: The Political Kingdom of God and the Council of Fifty in Mormon History* (East Lansing: Michigan State University Press, 1967). For the development of the LDS theo-democratic nation in Utah Territory, see David L. Bigler, *Forgotten Kingdom: The Mormon Theocracy in the American West, 1847–1896* (Logan: Utah State University Press,1998)

28. Douglas Wayne Larche, "The Mantle of the Prophet: A Rhetorical Analysis of the Quest for Mormon Post-Martyrdom Leadership, 1844–1860" (PhD diss., Indiana University, 1977), 175.

29. Michael Van Wagenen, "The Texas Republic and the Mormon Kingdom of God: The Attempt to Establish a Theocratic Nation in the Texas-Mexico Borderlands in 1844" (Master's thesis, University of Texas at Brownsville and Texas Southmost College, 2000), ix–x.

of the Texas colony. A construction and building boom, according to LDS archivist Dennis Rowley, had exploded in Nauvoo due to church immigration, many converts coming from the British mission alone. Within a three-year period, Nauvoo had become one of Illinois's largest cities, if not the largest. The need for housing, however, competed with the growing necessity for more church buildings. Smith and others, entranced at the idea of securing sufficient lumber for Nauvoo House, the Temple, and providing public works employment for new immigrants, decided to go into the sawmill business in the wilds of Wisconsin. Shared responsibility was delegated to Wight, Miller, Peter Haws, and Alpheus Cutler, members of the Nauvoo House Association and the Temple Committee.[30]

Along with the logging, getting the timber to the mill, turning it into lumber, then having to float it as huge log rafts several hundred miles down the Mississippi River to Nauvoo, Wight and Miller would have to recruit workers for the sawmill village, and transform the several frontier lumber fronts and the mill town into orthodox LDS communities. They successfully met the challenge. It would be difficult to understate the importance of the Wisconsin frontier experience in preparing Wight's colonists for their future in the Texas borderlands. The truly terrible tribulations and difficulties of the Black River Pine Company developed a cadre of settlers ready for any challenge on the western frontier. The majority of Wightite colonists came from the Pine Company, which spent two distinct periods in Wisconsin—from late fall 1841 to June 1844, and from the fall of 1844 to the spring of 1845. The latter period completed the transformation of Wight's followers into a distinctive faction opposed to Brigham Young and Utah Mormonism. They later would be described as "the Texas Epidemic" in LDS letters.

In September 1841, Peter Haws and Alpheus Cutler were sent to the Black River camps with supplies for nine months. Although the Pine Company became a thriving community with four sawmills along the Black River and a dozen logging camps in the pineries, the initial efforts were minimal and unsatisfactory. The results of the following summer and fall of 1842 were not much better: $3,000 in debt and a mill that was

30. Dennis Rowley, "The Mormon Experience in the Wisconsin Pineries, 1841–1845," *Brigham Young University Studies* 32, nos. 1–2 (1991): 119–21, 125, 126.

not operating. Henry W. Miller, who had earlier owned an Illinois sawmill with his family and two other families, was directed to go to Black River and take charge of the lumber and milling operations. Bishop George Miller would also go, with court documents to transfer the mills from Jacob Spaulding to church control, and to handle other business matters. Wight and Haws had other duties in the eastern states at that time, but were given instructions to go to Black River the following spring (1843) and supervise logging, milling, and rafting operations.

Bishop Miller, despite the squabbling, brought desperately needed business skills to the operation. He finished negotiations for the Spaulding mills by 22 December 1842. Affairs apparently went smoothly, although a later Wisconsin history suggests that the Mormon loggers began cutting timber on Spaulding's land without permission, and he supposedly sent for assistance from Fort Crawford, located at Prairie de Chien. Miller realized Spaulding was going to fight, so the story goes, and offered to buy his outfit. For $20,000, the Mormons received the two sawmills on Town Creek, which empties into the Black River at the falls. Other buildings included two log cabins, a blacksmith shop, and a boarding house. Four satellite logging camps were soon established along the Black River: at the confluence of Wedges Creek with Mormon Riffles; at Ross's Eddy, a mile south of Neillsville; at Weston Rapids, three miles farther north; and a final site near what is now Greenwood.[31]

The situation was difficult in the winters of 1842–43 and 1843–44. The Mormons were more than 120 miles from their base of supplies and provisions, and the work animals were on half-rations.

---

31. Rowley, "The Mormon Experience," 121, 126; H. W. Mills, "De Tal Palo Astillo," *Annual Publications of the Southern Historical Society* (1917): 93, 95, 119, 120, 125, an edited version of "The Life of George Miller, Written By Himself." Compare the above with George Miller, *Correspondence of Bishop George Miller with the Northern Islander: From His First Acquaintance with Mormonism up to Near the Close of His Life; Written by Himself in the Year 1855*, comp. by Wingfield Watson from his file of the *Northern Islander* (Burlington, WI: [Wingfield Watson], 1916), 8–10. See Consul Willshire Butterfield, *History of La Crosse County, Wisconsin* (Chicago: Western Historical Co., 1881), 188, for the version of Spaulding and the grasping LDS lumbermen. See also Jess W. Scott, "History of the Mormons in Clark County, Wisconsin" (typescript manuscript, n.d.), LDS archives. Scott, a local historian of Jackson County, Wisconsin, cribbed some of his story from the *History of La Crosse County, Wisconsin.*

Disaster lurked—without the animals, the logging could not be done. George Miller wrote later that the men were "almost worn out with the incredible toil that" they "had just passed through, indeed they performed labors that are almost incredible to relate. . . . We were in the midst of a howling wilderness and the aspect of our affairs to some might seem forbidding." Hunger stalked the loggers and their families that winter. The following winter brought a real threat of starvation to the men and their families. Miller remembered, "it was all we could do to keep our families from perishing for want of food."[32]

Successful operations began when Lyman Wight arrived in May 1843. An effective logging project was developed, and the sawmill and mill town grew into solid Wightite common-stock operations. Wight and Miller recruited more workers. Some came for the adventure of breaking in a new frontier, others for the honor of working on making lumber for the temple. Miller, however, was dissatisfied with and jealous of Wight. The bishop boasted in his memoirs that he made the mills profitable and had, that year of 1843, "sent to Nauvoo a large amount of hewed timber, and two hundred thousand feet of sawed timber." Miller ignored Wight's solid contribution to the community's success. Allen Stout wrote in 1843, "[Lyman Wight] works like a slave as fat as he is." Miller later alleged Wight suffered from "his indulgence in a habit that he was occasionally addicted to, his face and body very much bloated or swollen," a reference to Wight's lifelong fondness for alcohol. Miller's accusation was nothing new; Wight had been facing accusations of public intoxication since 1838. A drinking spree of his in 1842 had canceled a deal for the purchase of a steamboat to bring the Mormons from Kirtland to Nauvoo. However, if he had been drinking heavily in Wisconsin, it apparently did not affect his work ethic.[33] Wight was a functioning alcoholic. This was compounded later in Texas with opium use,

---

32. Miller, *Correspondence of Bishop George Miller*, 10, 11.
33. Will Bagley, ed., *Scoundrel's Tale: The Samuel Brannan Papers* (Logan: Utah State University Press, 1999), 47; George Montague, "Reminiscences," *Autumn Leaves* 9, no. 9 (September 1896): 387, 388, 389; Levi Lamoni Wight, "Autobiography of L. L. Wight," *Journal of History* 9, no. 3 (July 1916): 261; Miller, *Correspondence of Bishop George Miller*, 14, 15; Allen Stout letter, quoted in Rowley, "The Mormon Experience," 139; Cannon and Cook, *Far West Record*, 196.

which he used for illness, a not uncommon habit on the frontier. Both contributed to his death in 1858.

The social and material culture of the colony began to stabilize during the winter of 1843–44. The nucleus of Wight's colony in Texas began here. Several young men and women married and started families, including those of Allen and Elizabeth Stout, Spencer and Anna C. Wight Smith, John F. and Rosina Minerva Wight Miller, and Orange L. and Matilda Carter Wight. Only the Stouts did not go to Texas. Pierce Hawley and a "Brother Bird" (probably Phineas Bird, the family patriarch) were counselors to Bishop George Miller, and they comprised the local leadership for the sawmill community and logging camps. All three would become members of Wight's Texas community. Other family names that appear in Wight's Texas villages, as well as in Wisconsin, include Gaylord, Curtis, Jenkins, and Monseer (Moncur).[34]

Wight and Miller organized a common-stock economic order much like the earlier Rigdonite and Mormon communities in Ohio. Allen Stout described these affairs in a letter to family members. The bishopric (Miller, Hawley, and Bird) had "taken a schedule of every mans property to make a general distrabution." Provisions were kept in a storehouse where individuals could draw necessities.

> We have gon in to the whole law of God on Black River that is every man has given a scedule of his property to the bishop and we have all things common according to the law in the book of covenants. . . . Every man his own goods to do what he pleases with. . . . The thing is we are all on an equality eve man fars alike labours alike eats drinks ware alike but at the same time he lives to himself and what he has he has to himself and at his own controll. . . . I have bin thus perticular because of the man falce reports gon out.

Stout invited his readers to come to Black River "if Benj Hoseas or uncle Jim Pace thinks they can go the caper of concecration and

34. Susan Easton Black, comp., *Early Members of the Reorganized Church of Jesus Christ of Latter Day Saints* (Provo, UT: Religious Studies Center, Department of Church History and Doctrine, Brigham Young University, 1993), 6:235 (hereafter cited as Black, *ERLDS*); Turk, "Mormons in Texas," 28, 29, 76, 81; Rowley, "The Mormon Experience," 138.

equality we wish you to come by all means . . . the law of black river is that he will not work shal not eat."[35]

The material culture of the Black River community, by necessity, grew from its environment. Furniture was crafted from milled lumber rather than felled logs. Allen Stout, the community carpenter, described his home as "a frame house one story and a half high sixteen feet square with two loos floors and a petition [partition] and a most half sealed." Before Stout and the others finished sealing the cracks in their walls, floors, and ceilings, the winter winds made the buildings drafty and chillingly uncomfortable, leading to influenza, colds, and pneumonia.[36]

The settlement continued to grow in permanence, as men and boys drove herds of sheep, oxen, cattle, and milk cows to Black River in the fall of 1843 and the spring of 1844. The families prepared for the winter of 1843–44, growing potatoes, turnips, tomatoes, pumpkins, squash, and cabbages in the community gardens, as well as wheat in the larger fields. They took and preserved the bigger game animals (bear, deer, elk, and buffalo), and fished and netted the abundant resources of the nearby lakes and streams. With all that, the winter was still terrible. The snow was heavy, the cold intense, and because the church office, according to the younger Montague, had failed in delivering all of the necessary supplies to Black River, the families and crews had to ration food carefully. George Miller remembered a group of starving Menominee Indians who came to the camp. The Mormons voted unanimously to feed the Indians with their own limited supplies, and gave them flour and an ox.[37]

The hunger caused terrible times. Men, women, and children suffered. Elmira Pond Miller, the wife of Henry W. Miller, wrote: "Before spring opened our provisions gave out and we had only potatoes and salt for several weeks. . . . The baby was only fourteen months old, but when the flour came he could not wait for it to be baked, but wanted a piece of dough." Half-rations were issued. Levi

---

35. Allen Stout letters, 10 and 13 September 1843, quoted in Rowley, "The Mormon Experience," 133, 134, 139.

36. Rowley, "The Mormon Experience," 138; Allen Stout letter, quoted in Rowley, 139.

37. Montague, "Reminiscences," 388, 389; Mills, "De Tal Palo Astillo," 125, 126, 129–30.

Lamoni Wight remembered eating what he called a "miserable article of bread." One little boy was elated when, after several days without bread, he found a biscuit in a rat's nest. The small child ran to tell his mother the wonderful news. She at first would not let him eat it, then, when the child broke into a torrent of hunger-induced tears, relented. Allen Stout recalled that in March, just as he was preparing to eat a cut from an ox that "had been dead three weeks," a shipment of flour arrived, saving him from tainted meat. No one starved, yet no one ever forgot that terrible winter.[38]

Despite the terrible winter, the northern mill operations continued to do well until a federal Indian agent interfered late in 1843, preventing the Mormons from contracting for timber stands on local Indian tribal lands. Cyrus Daniels and George Miller made a sixty-mile journey in snow and cold weather to treat with the Indians and the federal agent; discussions ended in hard feelings. Daniels was seriously frostbitten during the return journey to Black River. The Daniels-Miller troubles made the timber men realize that it was time to pursue other alternatives. Accordingly, on 18 February 1844, a committee at Black River, consisting of Lyman Wight, George Miller, Phineas R. Bird, Pierce Hawley, and John Young, wrote to Joseph Smith Jr. The letter first informed Smith that the lumber to be cut, between 1,500,000 and 2,000,000 feet by the end of the following July, would be "sufficient to finish the two houses [the Temple and Nauvoo House], which will accomplish the Mission on which we started to this country." The second part complained that the federal Indian agent had been meddling with their attempts to secure tribal timberlands, and Wight et al. asked that Smith grant them and several local Indians permission to travel to the Republic of Texas and establish a gathering place for their people, free of interference from the United States government.[39]

The Wight letter from Wisconsin requesting permission to go to Texas encouraged Joseph Smith to initiate a private plan he had

38. L. L. Wight, "Autobiography," 262; Elmira Pond and Allen Stout, quoted in Rowley, "The Mormon Experience," 132, 133, 139.

39. L. Wight, *An Address*, 2; Mills, "De Tal Palo Astillo," 125, 126, 129–30; *History of the Church*, 6:255–60. The order of signatures would indicate that Miller was bishop, Bird and Hawley served as his counselors, John Young was the clerk to the bishopric, and Wight's signature gave his imprimatur to the letter, thus making sure that Joseph Smith would give it his close attention.

been considering, to find a safe gathering place for his people. He created a handpicked Council of Fifty consisting of Mormons and a few friendly non-Mormons. They were charged with finding a gathering place outside the jurisdiction of the United States, where Smith could fuse the functions of government and church into a "theodemocracy." Federal and state jurisdictions were severely hampering his attempts to do this at Nauvoo.

Growing issues not only existed between church members and outsiders, but also within the religion. First, LDS anti-democratic, anti-secular behavior was no secret in Illinois. One church newspaper trumpeted in March 1844 that it would not only "triumph over the state, but actually swallow it up."[40] Second, rumors of plural wives were causing vicious quarrels in and out of the church, turning members and quorums against one another, tearing religious unity to shreds, and opening the community of the faithful to assault by its enemies. Joseph Smith Jr. knew early in 1844 that his followers had to find a new location where he, the church, and its doctrines could be safe from outside interference. By March 1844, he had considered settling large church colonies in various locations outside of the United States, including the Republic of Texas, the Mexican possession of California, or the disputed territory of Oregon. On 14 March 1844, the Council of Fifty instructed Lucien Woodworth to go to Sam Houston and negotiate with the Republic of Texas for lands on which church members could settle. The Wisconsin lumber mission was designated the first group to go. Woodworth had returned to Nauvoo on 2 May 1844, and the next day he reported that President Sam Houston, with whom he had talked personally, was favorable but had to wait for approval by the Republic's congress

---

40. Quinn, *The Mormon Hierarchy*, 121–22; *Times and Seasons* (Nauvoo, IL), 15 March 1844. Quinn noted the following sources—John Taylor revelation, 27 June 1882, Annie Taylor Hyde notebook, 64, LDS archives; and Fred C. Collier, comp., *Unpublished Revelations of the Prophets and Presidents of The Church of Jesus Christ of Latter Day Saints*, 2nd ed. (Salt Lake City: Collier's, 1981): 133. Apostles Lyman Wight and John Taylor, two weeks before Smith's death, informed him in writing that he was "already President pro tem of the world" (Lyman Wight et al. to Joseph Smith, 19 June 1844, LDS archives). Quinn, in *The Mormon Hierarchy*, 321–22n106, notes that the official *History of the Church*, 7:139, dropped the passage by Wight et al. from the statement in which it was originally included.

later that fall. Three days later, the Council ordered Woodworth to return to Texas and complete the negotiations.[41]

Wight and Miller had been unaware of the Fifty's existence, much less its plans, until April 1844, when they came from Wisconsin to attend the General Conference at Nauvoo. Shortly after their arrival, they were appointed to the Fifty. Several weeks before his death, Joseph Smith Jr. coached Wight on his duties concerning the Texas mission. He would lead it as soon as he finished the lumber season in Wisconsin, and Woodworth returned from Texas with a signed treaty between the Republic and the church. George Miller, in the meantime, would go to Henry Clay in Kentucky to intercede on the church's behalf, while Wight went on a brief mission to the Atlantic states. Smith, according to Wight, then ordained him to be like Moses, leading "the armys of Israel to Zion . . . [to] lead the children of Israel out of Egypt." Smith gave him "a white seer stone" to help him. The role and use of paranormal aids (such as a seer stone or peep stone) abound in early Mormonism. Smith's giving the seer

41. Miller, *Correspondence of Bishop George Miller*, 20; Meacham Curtis to Joseph [Smith] III, 15 September 1884, RLDS archives; *Reorganized History*, 4:463; Quinn, *The Mormon Hierarchy*, 132–34; Journal History of the Church, 40:2 May 1844, 1. *History of the Church*, 6:255–57, 261–62, records that on 11 March 1844, Joseph Smith Jr. met with Hyrum Smith, Brigham Young, Heber C. Kimball, Willard Richards, Parley P. Pratt, Orson Pratt, John Taylor, George A. Smith, William W. Phelps, John M. Bernhisel, Lucien Woodworth, George Miller, Alexander Badlam, Peter Hawes, Erastus Snow, Reynolds Cahoon, Amos Fielding, Alpheus Cutler, Levi Richards, Newel K. Whitney, Lorenzo D. Wasson, and William Clayton at Nauvoo to consider the Wight-Miller letter. He organized a "special council," the establishment of the Council of Fifty, to ponder whether or not the Mormons could "secure a resting place in the mountains, or some uninhabited region, where we can enjoy the liberty of conscience guaranteed us by the Constitution . . . [and] denied to us by the present authorities. . . ." This special council met "in the lodge room over Henry Miller's house," indicating the intimate and intricate relationships of the members in the ruling circles of the church (Journal History of the Church, 39:4 May 1844, 1). Joseph Fielding wrote, "I have attended the Grand Council, as I will call it. Elder Woodworth has returned from Texas. The prospect of our obtaining room to form a colony there is fair"; see the Joseph Fielding diary, 1843–46, as transcribed and edited by Andrew F. Ehat, "'They might have known he was not a fallen prophet'—the Nauvoo Journal of Joseph Fielding," *Brigham Young University Studies* 19, no. 2 (winter 1979): 141–66.

stone to Wight reflects the value the prophet placed on the apostle. Following another meeting of the Fifty, Joseph Smith, in the presence of Heber C. Kimball, further "instructed" Wight. The Wild Ram later wrote that this was "the last time I ever saw [Joseph Smith's] face in the flesh. . . . I shook hands with him and bid him good bye." The commitment to carry out his mission to Texas would drive Wight for the rest of his life.[42]

42. Taylor, *The Kingdom or Nothing,* 89; George Montague, "Reminiscences No. 2," *Autumn Leaves* 10, no. 1 (January 1897): 73; *History of the Church,* 1:176n; 3:289–90, 315, 420, 445–49; 4:341; 6:260–61, 356, 377; Willard Richards diary, 14 May 1844; Lyman Wight to Cooper and Chidester, July 1855; L. Wight, *An Address,* 3–4, 5–6; Lyman Wight to William Smith, 26 July 1849, *Melchizedek and Aaronic Herald* (Covington, KY) 1 (September 1849): 2.

2

The Wild Ram Strays from the Fold

Wight, [that] gray-haired sinner, gave us distinctly to understand that none of his flock could marry a Gentile.

—Lafayette Houghton Bunnell

In a prayer meeting on 14 May 1844, Lyman Wight joined the Anointed Quorum, a secret group of members and spouses who had received the Second Anointing,[1] a mark of significance, favor, and power within the elite ranks of the church's leading members. This gave Wight an almost-independent authority as a "king" and "priest" in church and personal affairs. On 8 August 1844, Brigham Young spoke about the Second Anointing at a special general meeting in which the Twelve were chosen to lead the church. Although Young insisted on the primacy of the Twelve in church affairs, he certainly acknowledged the power of those endowed with the anointing, stating that a specially anointed individual, "if he is a king and priest, [then] let him go and build up a kingdom unto himself; that is his right and it is the right of many here." He reminded the audience, however, that the Twelve,—and not these "kings" and "priests"—were the leading authority in the church.[2]

1. "Members of the Anointed Quorum, Nauvoo, Illinois—1842–1845," compiled by Lisle G. Brown from a list of members of the Anointed Quorum contained in the Newel K. Whitney diary and account book (1833–48), Special Collections and Manuscripts Department, Harold B. Lee Library, Brigham Young University, Provo, UT. Wight, Miller, and Woodworth are listed, but not Peter Haws.
2. Andrew F. Ehat, "'It seems like heaven began on earth': Joseph Smith and the Constitution of the Kingdom of God," *Brigham Young University Studies* 20,

On 3 June 1844, John Walton, a Galveston land speculator, wrote a letter to Joseph Smith Jr. The contents must have brought to the surface some thoughts probably contemplated by the prophet. The Texan informed Smith of certain advantages which would accrue to the Mormons should they move en masse to the Republic. Not least would be that once Smith acquired "the controlling vote of Texas," he "might . . . aspire to and obtain any office in the Republic." He could free Texas from dependence on Great Britain and France. The Texas armies could then crush Mexico "at a blow," making "the richest country in the world our tributary, its people our servants, its city's markets for our manufactures and products." Political dominance, the possibilities inherent in colonialism and imperialism, the fusing of civil and religious authority subject to a theocratic government headed by Smith—all this must have whirled in his mind.[3]

Whatever dreams Joseph Smith Jr. had for empire, secular or religious, died with him in gunfire and bloodshed at Carthage Jail. On the warm, muggy evening of 27 June 1844, militia members of the Carthage Grays murdered Joseph and his brother Hyrum. A struggle ensued for church leadership, involving leading personalities and quorums. Lyman Wight and other apostles returned from their missions by early August. The crisis was so serious, Wight wrote in 1848, that it "called for the immediate action of the Twelve Apostles. The Church, with the different branches around it, were immediately called together by the Twelve; whereupon it was unanimously agreed that the Twelve stand as the head of the Church, with the exception of some few who fell victims to those aspirants and have gone to destruction." Several years later, he had changed his mind about the fitness of the Twelve to lead Mormonism. Wight told his following in Texas that the Council of Fifty should have offered up "young Joseph," the prophet's son, "before the congregation of Israel to take his father's place in the flesh!"

---

no. 3 (Spring 1980): 262; "Members of the Anointed Quorum, Nauvoo, Illinois"; William Clayton journal, 3 September 1844, LDS archives; Heber C. Kimball journal, 7 December 1845, LDS archives.

3. John Walton to Joseph Smith, Journal History of the Church, 41:4 June 1844, 1–2. A Dr. Southwick, a Texas land speculator from Louisiana, had also caught Smith's attention about Texas lands during the final week of his life (see *History of the Church* 6:507, 554).

Some of the Fifty apparently tried to influence the reorganization of the church administration. On 30 July 1844, council members George Miller and Alexander Badham attempted to convince apostles John Taylor, Willard Richards, and George A. Smith to use the Fifty to reorganize the leadership. The apostles refused, noting, because the Fifty was not a religious body, that only the priesthood quorums could exercise this duty. Surprisingly, neither the diaries of George A. Smith and Willard Richards nor the writings of George Miller mention any Fifty request to assist in reorganizing the church leadership.[4]

Tempers were running high among the leadership. Wight and Miller came to blows in the late summer of 1844. The *Hancock (County, IL) Chronology* carried a headline on 4 August 1844 reporting a "Fisticuff Fight in Nauvoo Between Bishop Geo. Miller and Elder Lyman Wight." Wight had cause to be upset with Miller. Not only had Miller backed the Fifty rather than the Twelve, the bishop had also backed Joseph Smith in selling a steamship that Wight believed was to be given to his Black Pine Colony in return for the timber and milled lumber they had floated down the Mississippi River to Nauvoo. Any further news about the altercation was suppressed.[5]

The Twelve's succession to church leadership did not end contention, as several members of the Fifty attempted to continue its prestige and status, rivaling the Twelve. It is interesting that only the three members of the Twelve (John E. Page, William Smith, and Lyman Wight) who later separated from the Church and denied their quorum had the authority to choose the proper successor to Joseph Smith Jr. were appointed to the Council of Fifty, after Smith's direction to the Twelve early in 1844—in the presence of the Fifty—that the Twelve should govern the church if he were to die. This may have been because these newer members of the Twelve had more influence in the Fifty than they did in the Twelve. Since Joseph used

---

4. L. Wight, *An Address*, 9; Lyman Wight, quoted in *Reorganized History*, 2:791 (Quinn, *The Mormon Hierarchy*, 193n32, believes that the original source for this statement was removed from the Lyman Wight letterbook, at pages 15 and 16); manuscript history of the church, book A-1, (microfilm), addenda, 9, Harold B. Lee Library; *History of the Church*, 7:213.
5. *Hancock (County, IL) Chronology*, 4 August 1844, quoted in Larche, "The Mantle of the Prophet," 182.

age to determine ranking in the Fifty, certain dissenters, including "Alpheus Cutler, George Miller, Peter Haws, Lucien Woodworth, and Lyman Wight, all ranked ahead of Young and the other apostles." Wight used this argument with Preston Thomas in January 1849, stating because he was older than Young he was at least his equal, if not his senior.

After the Twelve became the leading body of the church, friction developed among quorum members, as well as among the general church body. By 1848, a slight majority of the Mormons had settled either in Utah Territory or were under the direction of the Twelve in Winter Quarters, Iowa. Almost one-half of the membership, along with apostles John Page, William Smith, and Lyman Wight, had rejected the leadership of the Twelve. By then Wight's colony had journeyed to the Texas frontier, John E. Page was editorializing for James J. Strang in Michigan, and William Smith, Joseph Smith Jr.'s brother, was trying to set up his own church along the Ohio River.[6] In August 1844, however, Brigham Young assumed Wight had accepted the former's leadership and would follow the counsel and advice of the other apostles. Young failed to understand Wight's signals that he intended to stay independent. After "his return to Nauvoo," Wight was quoted as saying, "I would not turn my hand over to be one of the Twelve;

6. Quinn, "Council of Fifty," 195–96; William Clayton diary, 1 March 1845, in George D. Smith, ed., *An Intimate Chronicle: The Journals of William Clayton* (Salt Lake City: Signature Books / Smith Research Associates, 1991), 158; Quinn, *The Mormon Hierarchy*, 196; "Preston Thomas: His Life and Travels," folder 1, 45. In the Helen Vilate Bourne Fleming Collection 1836–1963, folder 8, LDS archives, however, there is an undated, unsigned, penciled list of what appears to be the fifty-two members of the Council of Fifty, listed by age, with two exceptions. Joseph Smith is listed as No. 1, because he was the church leader and chairman of the Council. Others, such as Samuel Bent, No. 2, John Young, No. 3, George Miller, No. 13, Brigham Young, No. 23, etc., are in order by age. Yet the list concludes with Lyman Wight, the oldest of the Apostles, as No. 52, coming only before William Clayton, Clerk, No. 53, and Willard Richards, Recorder, No. 54. See the *Gospel Herald* (Voree, WI), 31 August 1848, 106, 107, for Page's attack on Brigham Young and Lyman Wight as alternatives to James Strang; and Lyman Wight to William Smith, 22 August 1848, in Heman C. Smith, "Lyman Wight on Succession" (typescript manuscript of archive notes, n.d.), 1, RLDS archives. This is a typescript of private notes written in the hand of Heman C. Smith for an article. Smith, an RLDS historian and grandson of Lyman Wight, had pieced it together from a letter recorded in the missing Lyman Wight journal.

the day was, when there was somebody to control me, but that day is past."[7]

This remark makes clear Wight's devotion to Joseph Smith Jr. and his resentment of Brigham Young. Joseph Smith was dead, and Wight believed that, first, as a "priest" and "king" of the Anointed Quorum, and, second, as a senior member of the Fifty, he possessed the right to make decisions independently from the Twelve. He believed that he had made such an agreement with Young in return for his agreement to support the Twelve in the succession crisis. On 7 August 1844, Sydney Rigdon met with the Twelve about the succession. Wight remarked that only Joseph Smith could teach him, denying his old friend and original mentor any pretensions to succeeding Smith. The unspoken implication of another comment by Wight, that only at church headquarters could he find enemies, went unnoticed. Brigham Young never understood the depth of Wight's commitment to the Texas mission, nor did he comprehend Wight's literal interpretation of Smith's instructions, that is, to prepare a gathering place for the church membership in Texas. Young may also have discounted too lightly how Wight felt about the primacy of the Fifty, or the patrilineal privileges of Joseph's sons for the future.[8]

Smith's death must have seemed not only to Wight, but to every other Mormon also, as if the world were shifting under them, as if all truths had become subject to question. At this time, Wight had not yet developed his final beliefs concerning the Twelve, the Fifty, and the patrilineal rights of the Smith family. The immediate era in Nauvoo after Joseph Smith's death was one of flux and confusion. As had all the Twelve, as had all of the church—Wight relied on the prophet for direction and counsel. At the time of his death Joseph Smith Jr. was a vital, dynamic man in the prime of health, not yet forty. It seemed as if he might live forever. A Mormon of 1844 might well believe the millennium would commence during a normal man's lifetime.[9] It seems possible that Young, Wight, the other members of the Twelve, and the church membership felt they would be

7. *Latter-Day Saints' Millennial Star*, 29 July 1865.
8. Quinn, *The Mormon Hierarchy*, 199.
9. Alexander, "A New and Everlasting Covenant," 36, notes that Joseph Smith Jr.'s revelation (*Doctrine and Covenants* 130:15–17) in 1843 deferred the coming of Christ to 1890 or later.

waiting with Joseph when the Second Coming began. Thus those high days of summer in Nauvoo were not for theological debate but for action, for protection of the church, for carrying forward the legacy of Joseph Smith.

Young himself appeared confused about whether or not the Texas mission should continue. Despite Bishop George Miller's later assertion that Young would have nothing to do with Texas,[10] the head of the Twelve acted initially as if he intended to use Wight in the larger scheme of moving the church to the West. On 12 August 1844, the Twelve authorized Wight, along with George Miller and Lucien Woodworth, to "carry out the instructions he has received from Joseph"—to take a colony to Texas. Wight, speaking later that day, encouraged the church membership to join his Texas journey. Young modified Wight's recruitment of members the next day, instructing that only Nauvoo was the gathering place for the church. Young further limited those who could go with Wight to the membership of the Black Pine Lumber Company. The Twelve directed Wight to take his followers back to the Black River Falls area and prepare to depart for Texas the following spring.[11]

---

10. Miller, *Correspondence of George Miller*, 24. Miller recalled that he "was really cast down and dejected" with the rejection by Brigham Young of his and Lucien Woodworth's request for authority to treat with the Texas Congress. Young had said he lacked faith in the project and would not support it.

11. Ibid.; Willard Richards diary, 12 August 1844; *History of the Church*, 7:250–52, 254–55, 261; Marvin S. Hill, *Quest For Refuge: The Mormon Flight from American Pluralism* (Salt Lake City: Signature Books, 1989), 140; Asher and Effelinda [Essilinda] Gressman to Levi Moffet, 6 November 1844, in Albert Hart Sanford, "The Mormons of Mormon Coulee," *Wisconsin Magazine of History* 24 (December 1940): 135. The Journal History of the Church, 42:12 August 1844, records "That Lyman Wight go to Texas, if he chooses, with his company, also George Miller and Lucien Woodworth, if they desire to go." See Quinn, *The Mormon Hierarchy*, 199, for an example of the general misunderstanding, repeated in Mormon historiography, that Wight departed Nauvoo directly for Texas. For the belief that the Texas mission had not been abandoned by LDS officials in the summer of 1844, see Journal History of the Church, 42:14 July 1844, for the note Woodworth wrote to Sam Houston explaining his previous lack of communication because of the turmoil surrounding the murders of Joseph and Hyrum Smith. Woodworth encouraged Houston that if he still considered "the plan practicable, communicate, and a reply would be forthcoming. Of the particular views of the Mormons, I have not time now to write." The last comment may be interpreted as meaning that the succession crisis delayed new church policy regarding a Mormon colony in Texas.

Wight continued to follow apostolic counsel and returned to Wisconsin. An Iowa newspaper published an item dated 12 September 1844: "About 150 Mormons passed up the river this week, on the *Gen. Brooks*, for Black River, where a new settlement is to be formed about Prairie la Cross in the Pine County. One of the Twelve accompanied them."[12] Although seemingly in accord with the Twelve, Lyman Wight had been pondering the will of the Council of Fifty and his private instructions from Joseph Smith concerning Texas.

The Twelve had changed its mind by the end of 1844 about Lyman Wight and Texas. The fact that Wight was not a member of the quorum's inner circle made the situation more difficult. Research by Davis Bitton and the work of Allen, Esplin, and Whittaker clarify the religio-social dynamics of the Twelve.[13] Cultural barriers had blocked Wight's full integration into the dynamics of his apostolic brethren. First, in 1838 and 1839, he did not participate in the quorum's limited participation in the resettlement of the Mormons. Second, Wight did not share in the Twelve's British missionary activities, which had welded many of them into a close working group. Third, unlike others among the apostles, Wight's plural marriages did not create binds to its inner circle. Fourth, Wight was absent from Nauvoo from most of 1842 to 1844 because of the Wisconsin Pine Mission and other duties assigned by Joseph Smith. Fifth, Wight's Texas mission did not support the Twelve's vision of church resettlement in the Rocky Mountains.

Bitton has examined a Venn diagram designed by Andrew Ehat for his thesis, "Joseph Smith's Introduction of Temple Ordinances and the 1844 Succession Question." This diagram indicates (1) who was in the "inner Quorum" and (2) reveals Wight's exclusion from the privy circle. Because Wight was in Wisconsin for most of

12. *Dubuque (IA) Transcript*, 6 September 1844, quoted in "Mormon Movement," *Iowa Standard* (Cedar Rapids), 12 September 1844.

13. Davis Bitton, in "The Ram and the Lion: Lyman Wight and Brigham Young" (unpublished manuscript, 1996), develops ideas independently that are also found in James B. Allen, Ronald K. Esplin, and David J. Whittaker, *Men With a Mission, 1837–1841: The Quorum of the Twelve Apostles in the British Isles* (Salt Lake City: Deseret Book, 1992). Bitton's major work in the field is Levi Lamoni Wight, *The Reminiscences and Civil War Letters of Levi Lamoni Wight: Life in a Mormon Splinter Colony on the Texas Frontier*, ed. Davis Bitton (Salt Lake City: University of Utah Press, 1970).

1843 and early 1844, he missed the almost daily sessions with Joseph Smith and the Twelve at Nauvoo. He missed the tough incidents that bound together Mormonism's elite echelon of leaders. He missed the evolution of the First Presidency and the Twelve into an integrated hierarchy with a centralized purpose and common policy-making procedures. The "inner" Twelve's psychological and sociological relationships can be defined as an evolution of masculine intent and purpose within the informal and formal dynamics of this body. Purposely or not, the result was the exclusion of those, such as Wight, who did not share in the select events that fashioned this homogenous inner group.[14]

Wight's polygamous marriages also did not help in developing close social relationships with the other apostles. His first plural marriage was no earlier than 1844, but whom Wight married was more important than when he married. The plural marriages linking the members of the future First Presidency of Brigham Young, in 1847, had been concluded by 1844 and 1845. The Presidency included Brigham Young, President; Heber C. Kimball, First Counselor; and Willard Richards, Second Counselor. Young's marriages linked him also to the families of Joseph Smith Jr. and apostles Amasa M. Lyman, Parley P. Pratt, Daniel Wells (a future counselor in the First Presidency), and Lorenzo Snow. Kimball's plural relations included Joseph Smith Jr., Brigham Young, Willard Richards, Parley P. Pratt, John Taylor (the third church president), and Newell K. Whitney (a leading bishop of the church). The plural relations of Willard Richards linked him to Joseph Smith Jr., Brigham Young, and Heber C. Kimball.[15]

Wight's marriages, and those of his children, did not have the broad, church-wide dynamics of Young, Kimball, or Richards. Marriages among the Wightites were local and insular, forming an axis of plural kinfolk relationships throughout the Wisconsin and Texas colonies. These bonds created a welter of links: economic, cultural, religious, and familial. Wight's marriages to Mary Hawley and Jane

---

14. Quinn, *The Mormon Hierarchy*, 64–65; Bitton, "The Ram and the Lion," 2–3; Allen et al., *Men With a Mission*, 319; Andrew F. Ehat, "Joseph Smith's Introduction of Temple Ordinances and the 1844 Mormon Succession Question" (master's thesis, Brigham Young University, 1982), 194.
15. Quinn, *The Mormon Hierarchy*, 542, 556–57, 575, 608–9.

Margaret Ballantyne connected him to the leading families in his group, the American Hawleys and the Ballantynes of Scotland,[16] thus mitigating ethnic differences as a possible source for intra-colony irritation. Other plural marriages within and without Wight's family joined individuals and families in his colony into more cohesive social units than monogamous marriages could produce. The doctrine and its practice knotted together the village at Mormon Coulee, Wisconsin, before its journey to Texas. During this critical period, from the fall of 1844 through the first months of the trek the next spring, these associations and geography socially excluded the Pine Colony members from their fellow Mormons at Nauvoo.

A final reason for excluding Wight from the Twelve's inner core was the quorum's collective attitude toward his Texas mission. Partly because of the murders of Joseph and Hyrum Smith, they had concerns about the Twelve's physical security and that of the church membership. A gathering place safe from mayhem and murder was necessary. The Twelve believed with Wight that Texas was a possible place of refuge, but others existed as well: California, Oregon, and the Rocky Mountains. All were outside the boundaries of the federal and state jurisdictions of the United States. The Twelve, however, wanted first to preserve a continued unity of leadership before making decisions about where to move the church.[17]

If the above premises are reasonable, another follows logically: that Wight would trade his support for the Twelve to succeed Joseph Smith Jr. in return for its approval of Wight's mission to Texas. If Brigham Young was, in Wight's estimation, indeed overusing "I" in place of "we" in terms of the Twelve's policy-making procedures, it would not be surprising that Wight was harboring a growing indignation toward the Twelve and a personal dislike for Young. Wight indisputably supported the Twelve with his prestige among the rank-and-file membership during the succession contest; in protecting the Twelve, he also protected his own prestige and furthered his plan for the Texas colony.

Wight's suspicions of Brigham Young's motives must have contributed to his brethren's general wariness about him. A letter from

16. Subject name listings in Turk, "Mormons in Texas."
17. See Bitton, "The Ram and the Lion," 5–8, for his discussion of the degeneration of communication among Young, the Twelve, and Wight.

Wight to his old friend Sydney Rigdon in 1850 offers a possible reason for Wight's skepticism. The copy of the letter is found in an annotated commentary in the hand of Wight's grandson, Heman C. Smith, an RLDS historian who had a personal stake in a patrilineal rather than apostolic succession. Smith wrote,

> Speaking of the time just after the death of Joseph he [Wight] says: "They (the Twelve) then proposed to have a meeting one week from the Thursday following Bro. Rigdon's appointment, and we accordingly sent out to all the branches for a hundred miles around. Bro. Rigdon having previously given his word for his meeting they were by this time coming from various quarters. Now for some reason, or other, to me unknown brother Brigham took the alarm, and on the morning of brother Sydneys appointment I was solicited by four different persons to attend meeting on that day; stating that Brigham had altered [one word gone—hole in paper] appointment, and brought it to Bro. Rigdon's appointment. I enquired for his authority for so doing, but received no satisfactory ~~reply~~ answer, and believing it to be absolutely wrong I did not attend. It certainly gave the brethren who were abroad, and who were waiting to come to the meeting of the Twelve no chance to vote."[18]

Wight's sympathetic reply to Rigdon that he, Wight, had done nothing underhandedly (implying Young had) about the hastiness in changing the meeting's time is not surprising. Rigdon and Wight had worked together for fifteen years, and they both mistrusted the senior apostle. Wight believed that Young was manipulating the succession issue to his own ends, without the entire Twelve's advice and consent.

Brigham Young's reservations about Texas hardened during the first half of August. The "permission" given by the Twelve ("counsel" in the mind of Wight—a distinct difference to him) signaled to him that he "may go if you desire," with the admonition that the group could consist only of Wight, Miller, their families, and those of the lumber company. In a letter to Young in 1857, Wight asserted that they had some kind of agreement for Young's public approval of the

18. H. C. Smith, "Lyman Wight on Succession," 19n94.

Texas mission: "I ask, did not the Twelve unanimously give me the right hand of fellowship just previous to my start for this place? And I again ask, did they ever notify me that they thought it would be better to relinquish it since that day? And did you not state to me it would turn out? I gave you that privilege without reluctance believing you to be an honest man."[19] Wight, selective as always in memory and argument, ignored the fact that two groups of messengers, in 1848 and the beginning of 1849, had done just that—told Wight that it was time to end the mission and come to Utah Territory.

The letter indicates the existence of some dissension among the Twelve about the Texas mission. It appears that Young brought Wight to his side in return for limiting his opposition to Wight's call to a restricted few. The only purpose would be to avoid discussion among the Mormons about whether they could freely choose to stay with the Twelve or go to Texas with Wight. Accepting the reasonable assumption that Wight in 1857 had little if any use for Brigham Young, his letter suggests the issue of Texas had become a cause of disagreement within the Twelve's private meetings. Most of the surviving Twelve probably remembered the events differently. Young apparently thought Wight's siphoning off a few followers was acceptable if he could not make the Wild Ram herd with the rest of the flock.

George Miller remembered Brigham Young's emphatic dislike of the Texas Mission. The Fifty had authorized four negotiators to confer with the Republic on behalf of the church, but Joseph Smith's murder changed everything. Young, acting on Wight's application, not only refused to approve the original mission, but also "dissolved the appointment" of the emissaries, and the Twelve, on its own behalf, refused to approve church letters of introduction and credentials to the Republic. This curbed the Fifty's authority and dealt a death blow to Woodworth's earlier successful negotiations with President Houston. Young and the Twelve, instead, directed Wight to return to Wisconsin and prepare the Pine Company for Texas the following spring.[20]

---

19. Lyman Wight to Brigham Young, 2 March 1857, LDS archives and photocopy, RLDS archives.
20. George Miller to James J. Strang, 12 June 1849, quoted in Heman Hale Smith, "George Miller," *Journal of History* 2, no. 2 (April 1909): 230–31; Meacham Curtis to Joseph [Smith] III, 15 September 1884.

Wight led 160 persons, many former members of the Black River community, onto the riverboat the *General Brooks*, and then to Black River. Disease struck the passengers, and one adult and one child died. The family removed the body of Lavinia Hawley, confused in some genealogy histories with her mother, and buried her at Potosi, Wisconsin, with Masonic rites. The company, plus sixty tons of hay, were off-loaded at the mouth of Black River and moved up the valley in clear weather. On excellent agricultural terrain near what later became Oeler's sawmill, the colonists built a comfortable village of twenty to thirty log cabins, centered on a main street. Construction began for a lime kiln and a mill. The good weather continued, without cold or snow, which prompted Wight to write in November that they were not suffering from "the chills and fevers" of Nauvoo. The colony spent that winter "upon a beautiful stream of clear water, where we have all gained our health." In order to make some money, the Mormon men split rails, cut cordwood, and made shingles for the firm of Myrick & Miller. The Wightites worked for the common welfare of the whole community, pay being drawn by their elders for community provisions as a whole.[21]

As Wight sang praises about Wisconsin, the journal entries of Joseph Fielding, church elder in Nauvoo, reveal the difficulties Wight and his followers were having with the much larger LDS community at Nauvoo. Wight allegedly had cursed the temple because he believed it had become an obstacle to his Texas goals. One of Wight's people supposedly had made a snide remark that those who remained in Nauvoo "were too corrupt for them to keep the commandments of God amongst us." The feeling in Nauvoo was mutual. Fielding finished his comments by stating that the departure of

21. Asher and Effelinda [Essilinda] Gressman to Levi Moffet, 6 November 1844, in Sanford, "The Mormons of Mormon Coulee," 135; Elsie Hawley Platt and Robert Hawley, *House of Hawley* (Port Huron, MI: privately printed, 1909), 46; Mills, "De Tal Palo Astillo," 135, 136; Montague, "Reminiscences No. 2," 73; L. H. Pammel, *Reminiscences of Early La Crosse, Wisconsin* (n.p.: Liesenfeld Press, 1928; reprinted from Lacrosse, WI *Tribune and Leader Press*), 19; L. Wight, *An Address*, 10; (La Crosse) *Liberal Democrat*, 24 February 1878, in Sanford, "The Mormons of Mormon Coulee," 138; Albert Hart Sanford and J. H. Hirshheimer, *A History of La Crosse, Wisconsin 1841–1900*, assisted by Robert F. Fries (La Crosse, WI: La Crosse County Historical Society, 1951), 27.

Wight, Rigdon, and others "has caused some to say that Nauvoo has had a mighty puke and it is the bad stuff that is thrown up."[22]

Wight's patriarchal communitarianism socialized Mormon Coulee. Otis Hobart, the local branch clerk, recorded the important moments of a conference held there on 6 November 1844. First, Wight addressed the people on the principles of baptism, then sixty-nine individuals were rebaptized at Town Creek for the remission of sins. The assembly then met "in front of the buildings on the prairie" and sustained the Twelve and other LDS authorities in their offices. Hobart wrote that the evening meeting was held in the home of Pierce Hawley, a former counselor to Bishop George Miller. The area around Mormon Coulee was named the "Valley of Loami," and Town Creek became "the waters of Helaman," places from the *Book of Mormon.* Lyman Wight delivered "many interesting remarks on the subject of the Word of Wisdom." The company then voted to not use tobacco or "spirituous liquours," after which Wight blessed nine children. Perhaps Wight was feeling a temperance moment at Mormon Coulee, but one local anti-LDS writer noted that Wight was "the hardest swearer and freest drinker in the vicinity."[23]

Hobart's sense of permanence about Mormon Coulee in the church minutes is reinforced in a private letter written that evening by Asher and Esselinda Gressman to Levi Moffet. They give more details about the conference and strengthen an impression of a growing community stability in the village. They told Moffet that:

> We have come to a complete organization. . . . All the brothers and sisters assembled on the bank of the waters of Helaman and entered into the Kingdom anew by the door and after they repaired to the place that had been prepared to partake of the passover. . . . Then a Patriarch and Bishop were ordained; then the confirmation of all took place and then Bro. Wight, after exhorting the brethren and sisters to receive all the authorities of the Church that now is

22. Ehat, "The Nauvoo Journal of Joseph Fielding," 149–50.
23. Hawley, "Autobiography of John Hawley," 6; conference minutes, Black River, Wisconsin, recorded by Otis Hobart, 6 November 1844, in Sanford, "The Mormons of Mormon Coulee," 134, 135; Allen Stout, quoted in Rowley, "The Mormon Experience," 139; *Liberal Democrat* (Lacrosse, WI), 29 May 1881.

> and has been a vote was taken and there was a unanimous vote to sustain the Twelve and those above them. . . . The oldest male took his seat at the head of the table and his wife facing him on the opposite of the table and so on until the table was full.

The Gressmans invited Moffet to join them. The writers fervently described the great mining country surrounding them, waxing enthusiastic that the village was located on the best mill site with the best water supported by the best springs.[24]

Tension existed between community aspirations and Wight's plans for the future. Hobart's minutes and Gressman's letter indicate that Mormon Coulee was a semi-permanent community. The village had been snugly built, with mills for lumber and grist production, and a communalistic, patriarchal religious and social order had been organized. Phineas Bird and Pierce Hawley filled the offices of local bishop and patriarch, respectively. This continuity of religious leadership connected the settlers to the earlier days at Black River. Many members were rebaptized, and all had committed themselves to sustaining the Twelve as successor to Joseph Smith Jr.[25] Nothing indicated the settlers of Mormon Coulee, despite Wight's preaching about Texas the previous August, harbored any serious plans about a thousand-mile trip across the borderlands of the United States to the Texas frontier.

Wight had several reasons to leave Mormon Coulee. The unfulfilled Texas mission was one. Another was his growing dissatisfaction with Young and the Twelve. A third was the unrest the local non-Mormons felt about the villagers of Mormon Coulee. They certainly resented the social aloofness the Mormons directed toward outsiders. Lafayette Houghton Bunnell, in 1881, recalled Wight's treatment of several local suitors for the young women from the Mormon community. Some "were very beautiful Welsh and English lassies . . . , good singers and quite entertaining." The Mormon girls, however, "were in closer communion than Baptists. . . . Wight, [that]

---

24. Asher and Effelinda [Essilinda] Gressman to Levi Moffet, 6 November 1844, in Sanford, "The Mormons of Mormon Coulee," 135, 136.
25. Allen Stout, quoted in Rowley, "The Mormon Experience," 139; Hawley, "Autobiography of John Hawley," 6, 7.

gray-haired sinner, gave us distinctly to understand that none of his flock could marry a Gentile,"[26] a Mormon designation for non-members and a word that Bunnell did not like.

Bunnell disliked Wight and patronized his followers. He insisted he treated them well (as he did the local Indians) out of the goodness of his nature, so they, in return, out of gratitude, would never steal from him. Bunnell once traded some fat oxen to keep the village from starving. He employed the Mormon men on the recommendation of his friend, Scoots Miller, whom he used as paymaster for the Mormons. The men did a good job by improving ten acres he owned with a tight-knit fence to keep out Indian ponies.[27]

Plural marriage was another problem. Once again the practice was causing talk among the neighbors. The marriage practice at Mormon Coulee had its origins in Nauvoo, where Wight's eldest son learned about the doctrine. Orange Lysander Wight discovered that it "was taught in secret. The first I knew about it was in John Higbee's family. He lived close to us. . . . I discovered he had two wives. The next I noticed, when in company with the young folks, the girls were calling one another spirituals," a term referring to secret, plural wives of certain church leaders. After serving a church mission to the eastern states, young Wight, not yet twenty, returned to Nauvoo and "concluded to look around and try to pick up one or more of the young ladies before they were all gone." He fixed his attentions on Flora Woodworth, only to be told by her mother that Flora was a plural spouse of Joseph Smith Jr. Orange had believed "that Eliza R. Snow and the two Partridge girls were [also] his wives, but [had not been earlier] informed about Flora." "After giving Flora a wild lecture," Orange remembered, he "left her and looked for a companion in other places and where I could be more sure."[28]

At Black River, young Wight married Matilda Carter and Sarah Hadfield. Orange had first squired Sarah, but the two had a lovers'

26. Lafayette Houghton Bunnell, *Morning Chronicle* (La Crosse, WI), 29 May 1881, in Sanford, "The Mormons of Mormon Coulee," 139.
27. Lafayette Houghton Bunnell, *Winona (We-no-nah) and Its Environs on the Mississippi in Ancient and Modern Days* (Winona, MN: Jones and Kroeger, 1897), 236.
28. O. L. Wight, "Recollections," 5.

quarrel, and Orange married Matilda on 6 February 1844. However, after the colony returned to Wisconsin, Orange and Sarah reconciled. Sarah became the colony's first known plural wife on 7 February 1845. Orange simply wrote, "it would be uninteresting to relate all the ups and downs I had in my courtship, so I will merely say I succeeded in marrying both of them."[29]

In 1893, John Hawley testified in the Temple Lot Case that he had first heard about plural marriage only after the colony had returned to Wisconsin. During the journey to Texas, he learned that members were practicing it. Hawley had been courting a secret plural wife, the fact unknown to him, whom Lyman Wight married shortly before Hawley began his suit of true love. His testimony, nearly fifty years after the fact, strikes a chord of surprised chagrin similar to that felt by Orange Wight. Their feelings of being fooled by the young "plurals" were not unusual in the secretive Mormon society. Hawley's and Wight's confusion was echoed by John D. Lee in his *Confessions.* The need to keep plural marriages secret created situations when "a young man did not know when he was talking to a single female."[30] Apparently such marriages could be kept secret for a short time, even in such a small group as the Wight community.

Lyman Wight's attitude toward women was patriarchal and patronizing. In his journal in June 1844, Joseph Fielding noted the dismay he and his wife felt about Wight's comments about women, particularly women who were bothered by plural marriage. Fielding's wife had "been troubled at . . . the subject of spiritual wives, so much talked about at this time." Mrs. Fielding took offense at Wight's public statement in their presence, "that if a woman complained of

---

29. Sworn statement of Gideon H. Carter to Brigham H. Roberts, 27 February 1894, in which Carter affirmed that he had never joined the church; O. L. Wight, "Recollections," 6; subject name listings in Turk, "Mormons in Texas."

30. O. L. Wight, "Recollections," 5, 6; "John Hawley, in the Circuit Court of the United States, Western District of Missouri, Western Division, at Kansas City," *The Reorganized Church of Jesus Christ of Latter Day Saints, Complainant, vs. The Church of Christ at Independence, Missouri; Richard Hill, Trustee; Richard Hill, Mrs. E. Hill, C.A. Hall . . .* [et al.] . . . *as Members of and Doing Business Under the Name of the Church of Christ, at Independence, Missouri, Respondents* (Lamoni, IA: Herald House, 1893), 451–62 (hereafter referred to as Hawley, *Temple Lot Case*); Lee, *Confessions*, 167.

being insulted by any man, she ought to be set down as a strumpet, on the ground that no man would do it unless she gave him some liberty." She believed it to be "hard if a female is to be insulted as she has been and to have no redress." The LDS leaders, Fielding believed, were wrong to wink at Wight's beliefs, that in his case it was an "instance of man's weakness to hold forth such . . . and for the elders to smile at it is no proof of their approval of it." Fielding thought Wight's chauvinism was not inherently part of polygamy itself. The practice itself gave Fielding no qualms: "I see nothing [with the issue of spiritual wives] . . . that troubles me at all."[31] Nonetheless, his tone and subject matter reveal that even if the "brethren" gave no overt approval of a woman's subordinate role to a man, Wight's gender patronization, and her consequent inability to dissent without having her character slurred, were shared by some Mormon leaders.

The Wisconsin neighbors certainly disapproved of polygamy. J. T. Miller's emendation of a local history, although definitely anti-Mormon in tone, authentically voices local resentment toward Black River polygamy. A theology "laid in superstition and morality" was odious. He stated (wrongly) that only a simple revelation from Lyman Wight was necessary for a couple to set up housekeeping. A revelation probably was required, but Wight loved a ceremony (witness that of 6 November 1844 described above), and Wight or Hawley would have performed the rites. Bunnell's *La Crosse (WI) Liberal Democrat* article reinforces the local bias felt toward the Mormons. Bunnell was outspoken in his personal dislike, noting that "Wight is said to have been a Mormon and a sinner of the most pronounced type: the hardest swearer and freest drinker in the vicinity."[32]

Wightite marriage relationships did operate within an organized system. John Hawley, no defender of polygamy later in his life, noted twice in different venues that Wightite ceremony and ritual were involved in their marriages, in monogamy as well as polygamy. Pierce Hawley and Lyman Wight, for example, selected a young bride for Hawley and conducted the young man's first marriage ceremony. Gideon Carter stated that Lyman Wight performed the

---

31. Ehat, "The Nauvoo Journal of Joseph Fielding," 149–50.
32. Butterfield, *History of La Crosse County, Wisconsin,* 346; *Liberal Democrat* (La Crosse, WI), 29 May 1881.

first plural marriage of Orange Lysander Wight in Wisconsin. Carter also affirmed that Wight had performed other plural ceremonies, stating the apostle had believed he had the priesthood authority from Joseph Smith to do so.[33]

Plural relations on the Black River soon bore fruit; one of the twelve babies born in 1844 and 1845 was to a plural couple. Amos Wight, the eldest son of Lyman Wight and plural wife Jane Margaret Ballantyne, was conceived during the fall or winter of 1844–45 and born most likely during the trek of 1845.[34] These plural marriages and births strengthened a series of in-kin relations that linked the community members and families together in tight bonds. The in-kin marriages also had the effect of separating the religionists from their non-Mormon neighbors.

Tension increased between the Twelve and Wight's colony. Within weeks of the Pine Colony's return to Wisconsin, the apostles knew that Wight intended to make the trek to Texas. Some members at Mormon Coulee were opposed to Wight. David Clayton wrote to Brigham Young on 24 September 1844, revealing his desire and that of another person, probably Jacob Morris, to be in harmony with the Twelve. Clayton proceeded to tell tales about Wight. He and Morris had heard rumors that Wight's desire to go to Texas was recognized by the Nauvoo leadership. Some of the older members at Mormon Coulee, at Wight's suggestion, were keeping watch on the newer members. This would make sense, in that any newcomers were more likely to follow direction of the Twelve at Nauvoo rather than Wight. The Wild Ram, according to Clayton, "did not care a God dam for the Twelve." Wight supposedly had berated fellow apostle Orson Hyde in a sermon, and argued that the time for completing the Nauvoo Temple had expired. God would not accept it when finished, Wight had told his group. Clayton also accused Wight of attempting "to part husband and wife as he has tried repeatedly in my case."[35]

---

33. Hawley, *Temple Lot Case*, 452; Hawley, "Autobiography of John Hawley," 6, 7; J. T. Miller manuscript, LDS archives; sworn statement of Gideon Carter to Brigham H. Roberts, 27 February 1894, 2, 3.
34. Subject name listings in Turk, "Mormons in Texas."
35. David Clayton to President Brigham Young, Journal History of the Church, 42:24 September 1844, 1, 2.

How much personal ire motivated Clayton's letter, and how much it actually represented the actual state of affairs in Wight's colony, are difficult to assess. Nonetheless, such a letter, arriving just a few short weeks after the tumult of the succession fight, must have been unsettling to the Twelve. On 31 December 1844, William Clayton noted that both Ira S. Miles and Jacob Morris from Wight's company had arrived at Nauvoo about 25 September 1844. Morris told church leaders that Miles had been sent to burn the lumber for the Nauvoo Temple construction, in order that "the building might be hindered, as Lyman Wight said the Temple could never be built." William Clayton admitted that it was impossible to substantiate the truth of the matter; a police guard, however, was set about the lumber pile.[36] Another wedge had been hammered between the Nauvoo leaders and Wight.

Resentment at Mormon Coulee was not limited to Wight. In July 1844, some Black River members had floated a final raft of lumber to Nauvoo. They believed that they would exchange the lumber for a river schooner, the *Maid of Iowa.* Brigham Young, however, kept both the lumber and the ship. Yet Joseph Smith Jr., who was sole trustee-in-trust for the church, had earlier leased the steamboat to Arthur Morrison and Pulaski Cahoon for $100 per month. Young was stuck with the contract, and the Wightites returned to Mormon Coulee. John Hawley wrote that they believed they had been "robbed of all we had by the church under Brigham's rule."[37]

Lyman Wight used community bitterness to further his own agenda. He must have felt slighted in the limitations of his Black River assignment—a small community and less than 200 followers. Other apostles, for instance, had supervised entire missions and sub-missions, with dozens of church buildings and thousands of converts, in the United Kingdom. Additionally, he may have felt that his apostolic office was poorly used, in that Young did not wholeheartedly support the Texas mission. The Twelve's enthusiasm seemed to be granted grudgingly, despite the enthusiastic support by Joseph Smith and the

---

36. William Clayton, recorded in Journal History of the Church, 43:31 December 1844.
37. Lease warranty, 15 June 1844, folder 7, Helen Vilate Bourne Fleming Papers 1836–1963; Hawley, "Autobiography of John Hawley," 6, 12–13.

Council of Fifty. The cold winter of Wisconsin weighed heavily on Wight's spirit. His imagination bounded off to Texas as a promised land of unique opportunity and warmth. There, thousands of Mormons could gather, whom Wight would supervise and lead, to his own credit and that of the dead prophet. His enemy in Wisconsin, Lafayette Houghton Bunnell, supposed that simpler cares motivated Wight, in that "he told me that he himself was going to Texas; that the country about La Crosse was too—cold for his constitution."[38]

Lyman Wight decided to follow his own counsel, and he wrote a letter in November 1844 to family members. He called on them and other Mormons to gather to Black River Falls for a great exodus to Texas. He linked "the principles of salvation and the advancement of the cause of Christ" to the journey to "a land which the Lord will bless to us and our posterity; where we can build a city in peace." Wight noted the chance to bring Mormonism to the Native Americans (supposedly the remnants of Israel in North America), "to the light and truth as it is in Jesus Christ." Wight claimed his gospel understanding had expanded tremendously. He would teach his family "things pertaining to the Kingdom of God, and your salvation, and the salvation of your dead friends, that would exceed those principles of charity which I then taught you [earlier]." These comments are coded references to the ordinances of baptism for the dead, marriage for time and eternity, and polygamy. As Moses led the Children of Israel in search of the promised land of Canaan, so Wight would lead his followers to Texas. Wight concluded with the note that he and his colonists were "making every preparation for an early start in the spring."[39]

Wight's letter was a warning that he no longer followed the Twelve's counsel. It certainly indicated that he did not consider his authority subordinate to the Twelve. He may have known Brigham Young had not completely made up his mind where to move the church. For instance, Young told the Nauvoo city council on 30

38. Toni R. Turk, "The Kingdom of God As a Buffer State: The Mormon Decision for Texas" (photocopy of unpublished graduate manuscript, University of Texas, 1974), 11, 12, LDS archives; Bunnell, *Morning Chronicle* (La Crosse, WI), 29 May 1881.

39. L. Wight, *An Address*, 10–12.

January 1845 that the United States should give "the north part of Texas" to the church. Although such remarks were arrogant—in light of the fact that Texas was still an independent republic—the comments reflected uncertainty as to the Mormons' ultimate destination.[40]

Wight had given up on the completion of the Nauvoo Temple. If Morris's report to the Nauvoo leadership in September was true, then Wight may actually have conspired to burn the temple lumber. It would have served a two-fold purpose. The contemplated arson would be revenge for not receiving the lumber's worth from Young, and an opportunity to prevent construction of the temple. The Twelve's commitment to the temple irritated Wight, who no longer had the same desire. The possible idea that Young even could be considering Texas as a possible gathering place, but without Wight as the leader for the move, would further embitter the older man. He was senior to Young in the Fifty, the Texas project had been ordered by Joseph Smith Jr., the Fifty had developed it, and it had been given to him to fulfill it. Wight must have felt that both he and his mission from Joseph were being slighted.

Nauvoo-Mormon Coulee relations continued to deteriorate. During the General Conference of October 1844, Young called Wight a coward for leaving Nauvoo; the conference sustained Wight as a member of the Twelve only after deliberating the matter. On 4 February 1845, the Council of Fifty met for the first time since the death of Joseph Smith. Young, consolidating the strength of the Twelve, dropped several from the Fifty, including Lyman Wight, as well as all non-members. Young then instructed the Fifty to prepare for the movement of church to the Rocky Mountains or beyond.

Young still hoped Wight would bring the Wisconsin Mormons into harmony and immigrate with the remainder of the church. William Clayton, a confidant of the Twelve and Fifty, reflected such hope, recording in his journal that Wight would soon return to Nauvoo and be joined with his apostolic brethren. Such a wish for harmony may have caused Young, after the General Conference of April 1845,

40. Nauvoo city council minutes, 30 January 1845, LDS archives.

to again refuse to drop Wight from the Twelve. Speaking on Wight's behalf, Young stated there was hope for reconciliation because of Wight's character, that "there may be a time that he will hearken to counsel . . . for he is a noble-hearted man." The Conference reversed its vote and sustained Wight to the Twelve.[41]

---

41. For Young's statement, see *Times and Seasons* (Nauvoo, IL), 1 November 1844, 694; *History of the Church* 7:250–52, 254–55, 261, 295, 301–2, 392, 460; William Clayton diary, 4 February 1845, in G. Smith, *An Intimate Chronicle*, 157; Quinn, *The Mormon Hierarchy*, 176; William Clayton journal, Journal History of the Church, 7 April 1845.

3

Gone to Texas

those days was days of order to do as we was told and in this we was well schooled.

—John Hawley

As the Latter Day Saints gathered in Nauvoo during the first week of April 1845 for their semi-annual General Conference, only a few knew the Wightites had begun their journey to Texas the previous month. John Hawley later wrote that when leaving Wisconsin, the group "entered into [a covenant] and that was we would have to take as Lyman said 'the orders of God' and those days was days of order to do as we was told and in this we was well schooled."[1] The covenants taken that day were serious affirmations of a true believers' community. These covenants held the Wightites together for almost thirteen years.

Flatboats were built in the lengthening daylight. One Wisconsin history records that the boats were stolen. In fact, the Wightites settled their debts with the logging firm of Myrick & Miller, giving up some horses and oxen to extinguish any liabilities. Then the colonists fired their log cabins and left. On the night of 27 March 1845, while singing "Let Zion in Her Beauty Rise," the immigrants boarded the homemade water craft and sailed the next morning. Selling their clothing along the way for food and supplies, after three hundred miles, they stopped at Duck Creek, some miles north of Davenport,

1. Hawley, "Autobiography of John Hawley," 6.

Iowa, on 13 April 1845. William P. Eldridge, a prosperous local settler and a member of the local Baptist congregation, was converted there by Lyman Wight and joined the group in its journey. Eldridge became instrumental in re-outfitting the colony so that each group of twenty-one settlers had a small wagon and a small team. The outfits were much like those used by the Pontiac Branch that Wight had shepherded into Zion's Camp in 1834.[2]

Soon after the end of General Conference, Brigham Young knew the Wightites were but a little more than a hundred miles distant and heading for Texas. Samuel Bent left Nauvoo on 17 April 1845, carrying a conciliatory but patronizing letter from the Twelve. Bent, senior to Lyman Wight in the Fifty, had been instructed to read the communiqué to the entire company. The assembled company heard from Bent that spiritual concerns in Nauvoo were going well. Counseled against going west, the Wightites, instead, were instructed to return to Nauvoo and receive the blessings associated with finishing the Temple.[3]

The Wightites demonstrated a literary ability to patronize equally as well as what they received. Samuel Bent reported his failure to Brigham Young on 29 April 1845, and delivered a letter signed by Otis Hobart, the Pine Company clerk, which informed the Twelve that the immigrants were doing well. Having decided to proceed by land, they had sold the boats and had purchased wagons and teams. Hobart carefully continued that the colonists had received "our much esteemed friend Bro. Bent," who had read the letter to the company. The clerk noted that Ira S. Miles had been dispatched earlier to Nauvoo to apprise the Twelve "of our present situation and our future prospects." "A unanimous vote thanks was then taken," Hobart continued, "in behalf of the Twelve for their kindness. . . . We now bring our letter to a close by saying to you that we shall ever sustain and consider you as our friends. More anon." The message was clear—the Wightites used a clerk's letter to answer the Twelve's missive.

---

2. H. H. Smith, "The Lyman Wight Colony in Texas," 2, 3; journal of the branch of the Church of Christ in Pontiac, Michigan, Huron branch, 1834. See Heman C. Smith, "Pioneer Trails Across Iowa," *Journal of History* 10, no. 1 (January 1917): 47–59, for a fuller description of the trek.
3. Letter from Brigham Young & 12 to Lyman Wight, Journal History of the Church, 44:17 April 1845; *History of the Church*, 7:395, 400–401.

The Wightites were going on to Texas. More than two years would pass before Brigham Young again contacted Wight.[4]

Wight and his followers did not recognize the authority of Young and the Twelve to direct their movements. If the Wightites had known the events of a church financial conference held two weeks earlier at Nauvoo, Brigham Young may not have received even the courtesy of a reply. Present at the meeting were church officials, including the Twelve and the local bishops, who, among other matters, decided the bishops would sell the *Maid of Iowa*, the steamboat the Wisconsin lumbermen thought that they were to receive in return for the lumber rafted to Nauvoo the previous summer. Forty years later John Hawley reported a conversation he had with Brigham Young about 1860, the gist being that Young told Hawley Bishop George Miller had sold the *Maid of Iowa* out from under the Wightites. Young implied that he had no or little responsibility in the matter. The Wightites began distrusting Young's administration of economic affairs, and it would rankle them for decades. Both John Hawley and George Montague mentioned the *Maid of Iowa* matter more than forty years later, and Pierce Hawley, living in the Cherokee Nation, refused rebaptism into the LDS Church in 1856, unlike other family members, because he still could not forgive Brigham Young for evidently stealing Wightite property. The elder Hawley affirmed his belief he would be better off waiting for Joseph's sons to assume their roles as successors to their father than follow the lead of Brigham Young.[5]

Singing praises to God and "to Joseph the Prophet and Seer, the Angel of the Seventh and Last Dispensation of God on earth," wrote Lyman Wight, his followers moved on 12 May 1845 with eighty-two oxen, eight wagons, a cart, and several tents. Stopping occasionally to work for provisions, the following six months found Wight's little group journeying through Iowa, Missouri, Kansas, and Indian Territory. In the first part of November, they crossed into Texas. Lyman

---

4. *History of the Church*, 7:405; Otis Hobart to the Twelve at Nauvoo, Journal History of the Church, 44:21 Aug 1844, 2.

5. Hawley, "Autobiography of John Hawley," 6, 18; Montague, "Reminiscences No. 2," 73; Journal of Henry W. Miller and Elmira Pond Miller, Cherokee Indian Mission, April 1855–October 1862 (typescript manuscript, 1948), 8, 10, 13, 14, LDS archives; Pierce Hawley to Jacob Croft, 6 June 1856, George Wise Cropper Collection 1823–98, LDS archives.

Wight and David Monroe scouted for a location where the group could spend the winter. On 19 November 1845, the trekkers stopped at the site of abandoned Fort Johnston, near Georgetown in Grayson County. They wintered near present-day Dorchester, an area still called Mormon Grove.[6] They were the first sizeable group of Mormons to enter the Republic. Two years earlier, Elder William Steffey, ordained by Willard Richards to preach the Mormon gospel in the Republic while on a business trip, was the first Mormon recorded to enter Texas.[7]

About 150 persons had been organized into twenty-one households at the beginning of the trek. The deaths of four heads-of-household resulted in the dissolution of those family organizations: they were Donald Sutherland, William Ballantyne, John Hinckson, and Truman Brace. At least four new households were formed during the journey: William Eldridge, the Baptist elder who joined the colony in Iowa, as well as three more family units near Mound City, Kansas. On 27 September 1845, Bernice Monroe was married to Charles Bird, Eliza Curtis to George W. Bird, and Marion Sutherland to William Curtis.

Others married during the journey. Lyman Wight took Mary Hawley as his fourth wife, having earlier that year, if not in 1844 at Mormon Coulee, wed Mary Ann Hobart. These two marriages linked the families of Pierce Hawley (the patriarch) and Otis Hobart (the company clerk) to the Wight group. His third wife, Jane Margaret Ballantyne, had brought the extensive Scots in-kin family group of John Ballantyne into Wight's circle of relations. Sometime during the trek, Joel Simonds Miles married Patience F. Curtis as a plural wife, who joined her husband and his wife Delilia in their household. Patience may have been the young plural wife with whom John Hawley had been enamored.[8]

---

6. L. L. Wight, *Reminiscences,* 1, 3; Hawley, "Autobiography of John Hawley," 6; Sanford and Hirshheimer, *A History of La Crosse, Wisconsin,* 27; L. Wight, *An Address,* 13, 14; H. H. Smith, "The Lyman Wight Colony in Texas," 8–11; C. Stanley Banks, "The Mormon Migration into Texas," *Southwestern Historical Quarterly* 49, no. 2 (October 1945): 235, 236; Mattie Davis Lucas and Mita Holsapple Hall, *A History of Grayson County, Texas* (Sherman, TX: Scruggs, 1936), 11.
7. *History of the Church,* 6:61–62.
8. Subject name listings in Turk, "Mormons in Texas"; Hawley, *Temple Lot Case,* 452; sworn statement of Gideon H. Carter to Brigham H. Roberts, 27 February 1894.

Death and hardships struck the Wightites. Levi Lamoni Wight remembered the trek's privations for the rest of his life. Many years later he described the expedition as one of "hunger, thirst, and fatigue, accompanied with a few snake bites and quite a number of deaths." He remembered two small boys, stricken by pangs of hunger, fighting over a gar's head. At least eight colonists, and possibly more, died. Death destroyed the Hinckson family. John Hinckson lost an infant, then his ten-year-old daughter, and finally his wife during a ten-week ordeal. He then simply disappears from Wightite history. The Sutherland orphans had to be distributed among various households. Truman "Father" Brace and William Ballantyne lost their wives. Ballantyne's newborn child died the day following its mother's death. Ballantyne lost his father-in-law the following month.

Heman C. Smith, an RLDS historian, gave a different account of the Sutherland and Ballantyne deaths. Smith, a grandson of Lyman Wight and born at Zodiac, Texas, in 1850, recorded that at least four people died during the trek in 1845. Two babies, the grandmother of one of the dead infants, and David Sutherland all died between 12 July 1845 and 30 October 1845. At Thompson's Fork, four miles to the east of Grande River, an infant born to the Hinckson family died. In the last week of September, an infant born to the Ballantynes died, and so did its grandmother, Jane Menzies Sutherland. The baby was buried in her arms. On 30 October 1845, David Sutherland, the infant's grandfather and husband of Jane Menzies Sutherland, died near the Verdigris and Arkansas rivers.[9]

A little more than a week after the burials of Jane Menzies Sutherland and her unnamed granddaughter, General Conference was held at Nauvoo. The Wightites were far out of touch with the church in Illinois. The names of the Twelve were offered to the membership, and the motion to sustain Lyman Wight once again was opposed. A. W. Babbitt said, "I cannot conscientiously give my vote in his favor. My reason is this: If there is a council in this church that

9. L. L. Wight, "Autobiography," 263; population schedule, census of 1850, Zodiac, Gillespie County, Texas, East Texas Research Center; H. C. Smith, "Pioneer Trails Across Iowa," 47–56. See also subject name listings in Turk, "Mormons in Texas."

ought to be united, and act in unison as one man, it is the Council of the Twelve." Wight, he continued, "has not acted in unison with the Twelve, nor according to their counsel," and his "teachings have been contrary to the counsel of the church, and his conduct calculated to destroy it." However, Heber C. Kimball, first counselor to Brigham Young, advised moderation, suggesting, "the case of Brother Lyman Wight lay over for the present." The conference supported Kimball's resolution. Kimball, however, did tell the assembled conference that he did not favor the "Common Stock Business Religion." Kimball believed each man was responsible for his own affairs.[10]

The Wightites wintered in the new state of Texas, which had just joined the Union.[11] The final move to winter quarters was made about 24 November 1845, with them staying at Fort Johnston until the following April. John Hawley recalled they worked for the local Texans and Native Americans, while repairing their own equipment for the trek in the spring. James Tyson, a prosperous Choctaw, had the millers build a beautiful two-story home that stood for many decades. Life continued on the frontier as it had in Wisconsin; the colony was graced in February 1846 with the birth of John Ammon Taylor, son of Eleanor and John Taylor.[12]

By the end of April 1846, the colonists were again on the move. They crossed the Trinity River near Dallas on 30 April, and swam their animals over the Brazos River near Marlin in Falls County several days later. On 6 June 1846, they settled four miles north of

---

10. *History of the Church*, 7:459, 460, 466.

11. Fort Johnston (or Johnson), located in northern Grayson County, was built in 1840 as a small outpost of the Republic of Texas. It has been identified in historical sources by both names. The site has been located west of Fink. Abandoned and reoccupied several times, Lyman Wight's party wintered there in 1845–46. See Gerald S. Pierce, "The Military Road Expedition of 1840–41," *Texas Military History* 6 (Summer 1967), and Gerald S. Pierce, *Texas Under Arms: The Camps, Posts, Forts, and Military Towns of the Republic of Texas, 1836–1846* (Austin: Encino Press, 1969).

12. Grayson County Frontier Village, *The History of Grayson County, Texas* (Winston-Salem, NC: Grayson Frontier Village / Hunter, 1979), 18; Banks, "The Mormon Migration into Texas," 236; Lucas and Hall, *A History of Grayson County, Texas*, 61; Hawley, "Autobiography of John Hawley," 6; L. L. Wight, *Reminiscences*, 5, 6; H. H. Smith, "The Lyman Wight Colony in Texas," 11; subject name listings in Turk, "Mormons in Texas," 73.

Austin, at the foot of Mt. Bonnel near the falls of the Colorado River. They immediately set about building a water-powered mill.[13] Viktor Bracht noted that the name of the mill site near Austin was Sycamore Springs. The falls and the rapids provided an adequate supply for the mill, while the millers dammed the mouth of a deep ravine through which ran water from a large spring. In seven weeks, the mill was up and turning a large water wheel made of cypress and oak timbers.[14]

Brigham Young, meanwhile, knew little more than that the Wight party had left Duck Creek, Iowa, a year earlier. He believed they were somewhere in Indian Territory. By the end of 1846, several of Brigham Young's associates received false information that Wight's colony was causing trouble in the Indian territories. According to Colonel Thomas D. Kane, a friend of the Mormons, a large body of their people was enjoying a "comfortable existence" somewhere on the upper waters of the Arkansas River. "No doubt," concluded Kane, it must have been the Wightites. Orson Spencer confidently informed Brigham Young that Wight's group had been living with the Creeks but "had been driven away by them." The Nauvoo Municipal High Council, a week later in January 1847, wrote to apostles Orson Hyde, Orson Pratt, and John Taylor that Wight was located near the "land of the Big Blue."[15]

Wight's followers, in the meantime, besides milling and building their community, had been engaged in getting along with their neighbors in Austin. Ferdinand Roemer, a traveler from Germany,

---

13. L. L. Wight, *Reminiscences*, 6
14. Viktor Bracht, quoted in Ernest G. Fischer, *Marxists and Utopias in Texas: The Lone Star State's Pioneer Flirtation with Socialism-Communism* (Burnet, TX: Eakin Press, 1980), 97, 98, 103; A. T. Jackson, *Mills of Yesteryear* (El Paso: Texas Western Press, 1971), 13.
15. Thomas L. Kane to Brigham Young, 2 December 1846, and Orson Spencer to Brigham Young, 26 November 1846, Brigham Young Papers, LDS archives; Col. T. L. Kane to Dr. Richards, Journal History of the Church, 55:5 December 1846; [Orson Spencer] to President Brigham Young, Journal History of the Church, 55:31 December 1846; [Municipal High Council] to Elders Hyde, Pratt and Taylor, Journal History of the Church, 56:7 January 1847, 5. Winn, *Exiles in a Land of Liberty*, 108, has documented that in December 1846, Colonel Thomas Kane informed Young that Wight and his group were interfering with the Cry [Cree] Indians and the interests of the federal government in Texas. Wight's behavior was supposedly a "reason" for "prejudice to the body of Saints."

reported the local concern about the newcomers. He wrote, "this peculiar, communistic, religious sect had been driven away by an enraged populace of Illinois from their former home in Nauvoo on the Mississippi," supposedly for "repeated robberies and murders committed by individual members." Although the Texans, a people somewhat familiar with violence, felt uneasiness about the reported bloodthirsty nature of their new neighbors, Governor James Henderson and others, like frontiersman and businessman Noah Smithwick, felt differently. The water-powered gristmill at Sycamore Springs was the first industrial operation in the Austin area, and it started grinding corn on 30 July 1846. It is difficult to overstate how much mechanically ground cornmeal improved local attitudes among the Austinites about these peculiar outsiders. Not only was the mechanized mill at Sycamore Springs the first on the frontier, but its rigging also powered woodworking machinery for milling chairs, tables, wooden dishes, and other items. The Mormon operation benefited the entire community, for the people had been handmaking furniture and laboriously grinding corn with steel hand mills. The Wightites became involved in the local construction trade as well, building the new jail and some new houses in the capitol.[16]

The Mormons' limited contact with the larger community went well. Wight did not neglect his religious duties, as he preached twice at Noah Smithwick's, as well as elsewhere in Austin. Smithwick, who came to know the Mormons as well as any Texan, wrote in his memoirs that "they were a novelty in the religious world. . . . The neighbors all gathered in and listened with respectful attention while the Elder expounded the doctrine of the Latter Day Saints, being careful to leave out its more objectionable features." Some, believed Smithwick, may have been concerned about their reputation as "a lawless band." A faction developed with the intent to drive Wight and his followers from Texas. Smithwick, however, argued the newcomers had the strength "to stand off the Indians, and, it being their policy to isolate

16. Ferdinand Roemer, *Texas, with Particular Reference to German Immigration and the Physical Appearance of the Country*, trans. Oswald Mueller (San Antonio: Standard, 1935; reprint of 1846–47 edition), 213; Turk, "Mormons in Texas", 64; L. L. Wight, *Reminiscences*, 9, 10, 11; H. H. Smith, "The Lyman Wight Colony in Texas," 11, 12.

their communities which relegated them to the outskirts of civilization, I was willing to utilize anything that formed a barrier against the savages. I therefore counseled [against] hostilities till some overt act called for their expulsion."[17] Others agreed with him.

The *Houston Telegraph* reported that summer that Lyman Wight's people "have lately settled near Austin, are erecting a large flouring mill . . . about three miles above that city." The newspaper suggested that the Mormons could "confer lasting . . . benefit," although it had been "feared their presence would be but a precursor of evil." The paper's conflicted hopes echoed the feelings of Smithwick and others. The Mormons might have had a bad reputation in the West, but Wight's colony also had a mechanical mill and had done nothing wrong, as yet. Machinery trumped morality among the Austinites.[18] The clamor soon stilled for their expulsion.

The *Austin Texas Democrat* reported on 17 June 1846, under the headline "Mormons," that Elder Lyman Wight preached on the *Book of Mormon* and the role of the Native Americans in the new land. Having been told that the gospel of Jesus Christ was the inheritance of the Indians, the reporter asked Wight to "read Buffalo Hump [a Comanche chief leading raids on Texan farms and villages] and his party a few lectures." The newspaper recorded later that fall that the Wightites seemed to be "honest hardworking people." Polygamous relations at Sycamore Springs must have been well hidden from Texan notice, for Richard Lamb Isom, quoting from Frank Brown's "Annals of Travis County," wrote that it was "not remembered that [the Mormons] practiced polygamy." Brown noted also that the citizens' initial prejudice vanished, and the newcomers were considered a good addition to the frontier community. Wight could brag rightfully in 1848 that the governor and other leading citizens had become pleased to have the Mormon millers as part of the community.[19]

---

17. Noah Smithwick, *Evolution of a State; or, Recollections of Old Texas Days* (Austin: University of Texas Press, 1983; reprint of 1900 edition), 172.
18. Larche, "The Mantle of the Prophet," 176.
19. *Texas Democrat* (Austin), 17 June 1846 and 7 October 1846; Frank Brown's "Annals of Travis County," quoted in Richard Lamb Isom, "What Became of Joseph Smith's Early Associate Lyman Wight" (photocopy of typescript manuscript, n.d.), 16, LDS archives (Isom's work purports to be a "creative history" of the Lyman Wight colony); L. Wight, *An Address*, 13.

Levi Lamoni Wight recalled playing as a boy of ten on the "little hill," the site of the new state capitol. He and other children from the Springs attended school in Austin with the children of the Metz household, where some of the men boarded while working on the jail. Two colonists, both family heads, are known to have died at Austin. On 27 September 1846, Jeremiah Curtis Sr., age fifty-one, passed away, and John Ballantyne, a father-in-law to Lyman Wight, died the following month. The family units continued with Ruth Stratton Curtis, the wife of Jeremiah, and Andrew Ballantyne, the eldest son of John, becoming household heads. Ruth Stratton Curtis is the only woman known in the colony to have functioned in such a capacity. Three babies (Lyman Spencer Smith, Rollondo H. Wight, and Amelia Minerva Wight) were born to the colony that year. Rollondo H. was Lyman Wight's daughter by Mary Ann Hobart, while Amelia Minerva (John F. and Rosina Wight Miller) and Lyman Spencer (Spencer and Anna Christina Wight) were his grandchildren.[20]

Three arranged weddings were celebrated on 4 July 1846—John Hawley (age 22) and Harriet Hobart (age unknown), George Hawley (21) and Ann Hadfield (16), and John Young (about 31) and Priscilla Hawley (14). Hawley's "Autobiography" offers insight into the unusual pattern of Wightite marriage, including monogamous unions, which these were. The intended mates had little if any voice in the choice of their partners. The younger Hawley recalled "father and Lyman made a selection of girls for George and myself and a man for my sister Priscilla. This being the order of the Patriarchs, the girl selected for me was a daughter of Oates Hobart and her name was Harriet. . . . When July the 4th came, I with George and Priscilla was married by Lyman Wight. Here we began a life of Patriarchal orders." Lyman Wight was very concerned in creating eternal family units through marriages and adoptions that would last beyond the grave.

The patriarch, Pierce Hawley, gave the candidates a blessing of family lineage before they were married. John's father, supposedly having the power to determine ancestral heritage through the authority of his office, blessed him with the knowledge that he was

---

20. L. L. Wight, *Reminiscences,* 11; Turk, "Mormons in Texas", 22, 35; subject name listings in Turk, "Mormons in Texas."

a descendent of the Hebrew tribe of Ephraim and descended from the royal blood and lineage of Joseph of Egypt. Many special requirements, reminiscent of Old Testament *dicta*, surrounded Wightite marriage and family practices. Described as "the law of Moses corrected and revised," the decree included self-restraint in sexual habits. One feature of the "law of impurity" required men to forego intercourse with their wives for eight days during her menstruation. Childbirth required an absence of relations between spouses: thirty-three days if a male child, and sixty-six days if a female child.[21]

If the Mormons in Texas were practicing restraint in matters temporal, Lyman Wight, nonetheless, cut quite a figure in frontier fashion. The leading Mormon of Austin had become a local personage of regard, having made giant strides in appearance as well as have coming hundreds of miles from Wisconsin. A Methodist minister described Wight as a dark-bearded and black-headed man, standing over six feet, weighing more than 200 pounds. His attire included polished black boots, black broadcloth, a black hat, and holsters for two revolvers strapped across his middle. Several bodyguards escorted Colonel Wight whenever he was in public. Black mules pulled the French-style carriage, which always carried a rifle in an attached boot.[22]

Even though accepted by the larger community, Wight was considering relocating his colony farther west. Several reasons prompted the move. Although high water had washed out the mill, the colony was not forced to move because it was quickly rebuilt and soon operating again. Viktor Bracht noted in 1847 that both the Mormon mills, the

21. Sworn statement of Gideon H. Carter to Brigham H. Roberts, 27 February 1894, 3, 4; Hawley, "Autobiography of John Hawley," 6, 7, 10.

22. Josiah Clifton, quoted in C. C. Booth, "Lyman Wight—in Early Texas," *Improvement Era* 62 (January 1954): 27. This article was based, in part, on a letter from C. C. Booth to Rufus Hardy in 1930. Josiah Clifton, Booth's grandfather, told him that "Lyman Wight was often asked to address the senate when he came to Austin, and was always well received by the governor and senators." The Wild Ram was of "very commanding appearance, over six feet, about 200 pounds, and very handsome; wore a beard that he kept in perfect condition." He kept his hair long, groomed himself well—a Prince Albert coat, fresh-polished boots—and armed himself with two six-guns and a knife. Sprightly mules pulled a carriage dressed "with glittering harness, trimmed with brass and silver."

older, rebuilt one at Sycamore Springs and the newer one at Zodiac, Gillespie County, were assisting the German immigrant communities, providing "our colonists in the upper county with cornmeal." The publicly stated need to move, Lyman Wight later wrote, was that the location of Sycamore Springs was "to[o] limited for our society, (having had frequent accessions)," and "we concluded to sell it, and move seventy-five miles up in the Valley of the Pedernales." Unstated needs, including a private setting hospitable to the village's family system, apparently influenced Wight's decision, echoing the Smithwickian assertion that Wight's people sought after isolation for their communities.[23]

Two parties from Sycamore Springs searched to the west for a permanent place. The first party, which left 19 October 1846, consisted of John Taylor, Spencer Smith, Meacham Curtis, and William Curtis. They returned to Sycamore Springs on 14 November 1846, reporting a location on the Pedernales River "with plenty of good water and timber and abounding with game and honey." Roemer recorded, while the first party was still exploring, that "three elders of a Mormon colony, who had settled near Austin, came to Herr von Meusebach [the German leader of Fredericksburg]" and "asked for permission to settle a company of forty-six families on the grant of the Verein colony." Some of Roemer's acquaintances had been impressed with "the industry, order and frugal mode of living of these people. As a matter of fact I did not hear one word of complaint against them during my stay, on the contrary, their behavior was exemplary, although they were at first watched with suspicion." Roemer believed a few black sheep were responsible for the terrible reputation of the entire Mormon body. He continued that the Mormon "elders were not given an unqualified promise to their petition; however, a contract was signed with them whereby they agreed to build a mill at Fredericksburg similar to the one they had built at Austin."[24]

Roemer's account agrees generally with the records in the Solms-Braunfels Archiv, located at New Braunfels, Texas. A Tr. Bromme

23. L. L. Wight, *Reminiscences*, 6; Isom, "What Became of Joseph Smith's Early Associate," 15; Bracht, quoted in Fischer, *Marxists and Utopias in Texas*, 103; L. Wight, *An Address*, 14; Smithwick, *Evolution of a State*, 172.
24. H. H. Smith, "The Lyman Wight Colony in Texas," 11–12, 15; Roemer, *Texas*, 213, 214.

reported to Herrin Carl, Grafen zu Castell, that a party of Mormons arrived in October 1846 in the Fredericksburg area. The director of Fredericksburg, an F. Schubbert, recorded in his official record that he was reviewing a Mormon petition to settle near Fredericksburg and build a mill.[25] Schubbert wrote, "Korn is necessary without it this place cannot exist. There is nothing of it in the ground yet, and I have no seed." A Mr. Wurzbach earlier had contracted to build a mill in the Fredericksburg region, but in Schubbert's opinion "Wurzbach will not set up a mill in three years. If I take care of the matter, I have the Mormons set up a saw mill within six weeks. We are not able to mill corn or wheat yet because we have no grain." Schubbert later recorded that he had "accepted" the Saints "as immigrants of the association." In order to receive lands of the German Emigration Company, the Mormons would have to have their debts recorded at the county court house.[26]

The Mormons planned to move in the early part of 1847. An advance party of John Taylor, Lyman Wight, Orange Wight, John Miller, William Curtis, John Curtis, John Hawley, and David Monroe moved out first. The site recommended by the earlier exploring party was ignored, for the group initially selected a small creek about twelve miles east of Fredericksburg. A one-hundred acre farm was cultivated near Grape Creek, probably under the direction of George Bird, and construction of a mill site was begun, then, surprisingly, abandoned. The reason for abandoment, although farm operations continued on Grape Creek, probably had to do with the logical fact that the German leadership wanted the mill much closer to Fredericksburg. They succeeded, for records from the

25. Solms-Braunfels Archiv, 3:29 and 146–51 (transcription by Rudolph Leopold Biesele, 1934–35), original at Bienecke Library, Yale University, and typescript copy at Sophienburg Archives, New Braunfels, TX. These extensive journals, of which very little has been translated into English, consist of documents, letters, business accounts, newspaper cuttings, and other materials pertaining to the experiences of the German Emigration Company, and are a rich documentary source for the German settlements in Texas during the Republic and after. The Department of Archives and Collections, Church of Jesus Christ of Latter-day Saints, Salt Lake City, Utah, has provided the translations from the Solms-Braunfels Archiv for this work.

26. Solms-Braunfels Archiv, 31:67, 68; 43:96/146, 99/149, 101/151.

Solms-Braunfels Archiv note, "The Mormons have delivered their first flour shipment and are now installing their mill in Piedernales. It should be ready in six weeks, a grist and saw mill. They said that the corn will be sold for at least" four cents a pound. The Germans hoped the mill eventually would be moved to Fredericksburg. Director Schubbert informed his superior, "Col. Whight [*sic*] from the Mormons was here yesterday to receive here by the city 10 city lots and wheat ready for milling, and then they will set up the mill right here. I told him that I would inform you about it and so I asked for detailed instructions about it." The German hope remained unfulfilled, as the Wightites built on the banks of the Pedernales River, about three miles east of Fredericksburg.[27]

On 1 May 1847, the new mill site on the banks of the Pedernales, seven miles west of Bird's farm, was established. The milling and farming community of Zodiac (as the new community was named) rested on an intermittent flat-to-rolling terrain of stony clay soils. Stands of juniper, mesquite, and live oak grew among the undergrowth of brushes and grasses. The advantages of the location were notable. Foliage grew close and thick at times along the streams and creeks, offering shade, water, timber, and fertile soil. Another 200 acres were cultivated in land that Levi Lamoni Wight thought fruitful and full of game.[28]

The issue of slavery also may have influenced Wight's decision to move. Although his writings reflect little interest in the slavery issue, other than its economic advantages to the church, some of his followers felt differently. RLDS historian Heman Hale Smith echoes the comments of Levi Lamoni Wight that settling near Fredericksburg offered the Mormons not only security, but also neighbors who were thought to be freesoilers in sentiment. The mill property at Sycamore Springs was sold for $1,500 and the move to the Pedernales River was completed. The journey of two years appeared to be at

---

27. Ibid., 41:192, 205.
28. H. H. Smith, "The Lyman Wight Colony in Texas," 11; L. L. Wight, *Reminiscences*, 12; Ronnie C. Tyler, Douglas E. Barnett, and Roy R. Berkeley, eds., *The New Handbook of Texas* (Austin: Texas State Historical Association, 1996), 4:840.

an end. The Wightites worked quickly. By the middle of June, they had added a gristmill, some rude homes and shops, and planted more crops.[29]

John Schmidtzensky, a local German farmer and politician, passed an oral tradition about Zodiac on to his family. A political opponent of Wight and a keen observer and participant in the affairs of Gillespie County, he served it as a commissioner during the period of the Zodiac community. The Mormons, according to this tradition, built Zodiac on the north bank of the Pedernales River next to the original Austin-Fredericksburg road. They drew water from a well eighty-one feet deep. About twenty-five houses, corrals, and other buildings, as well as the mill, were built in the first year at Zodiac. The houses stood about fifty feet apart, constructed of upright poles set into the ground. The settlers then filled cracks in the sides with a plaster made of straw, adobe, and rock. The roofs were finished in the same fashion. Fitted, flat rocks made the flooring.[30]

Noah Smithwick, the Texas frontiersman who knew many of the Hill Country Mormons and later led several families of them to California, found them much like other Texans, who all shared a wide range of human foibles and frailties. He described their society as one sharing communally in

> the perfect equality of all members. . . . All titles of respect were disgarded, men and women being universally called by their first names. And these first names, by the way, were perhaps the most striking peculiarity about the Mormons. The proselytes were permitted to retain their Gentile names, but those born in the fold

---

29. L. L. Wight, *Reminiscences*, 13; L. L. Wight, "Autobiography," 264; Isom, "What Became of Joseph Smith's Early Associate," 15; Bracht, in Fischer, *Marxists and Utopias in Texas*, 103; H. H. Smith, "The Lyman Wight Colony in Texas," 12; Darrell Debo, *Burnet County History*, for the Burnet County Historical Commission (Burnet, TX: Eakin Press, 1979), 23. See L. Wight, *An Address*, 4, for his assertion that the conversion of the slave owner could result in "turning over his yearly proceeds into the hands of the trustee in trust for the whole Church." Implicit in this statement is Lyman Wight's common-stock philosophy of a communal economy directed by the presiding elder.
30. "The Mormon Colony (Zodiac) Near Fredericksburg, Texas" (unpublished manuscripts, 1969), compiled by John Cotter and Dorothea (Weinehiemer) Cotter, Pioneer Heritage Memorial Library, Fredericksburg, TX.

> received their baptismal names from the Book of Mormon; and have no counterpart elsewhere. There were Abinadi, Maroni, Luami, Lamoni, Romali, Cornoman and many others equally original.

He noted some gender disparity in name giving, possibly because "women cut no figure in the Book of Mormon; at any rate, there was nothing distinctive in the names of the girls."[31]

The great trek was over. Ironically, the attempt to escape the jurisdiction of the United States came to naught, for Texas had joined the Union about the time the Mormons arrived in Grayson County in November 1845. A diffident welcome by the Texans improved as the Wightites gained favor for their mechanical abilities and quiet ways. In their new village in the buffer zone between white settlements and native tribes, only time would tell if they would survive.

31. Smithwick, *Evolution of a State*, 228.

4

Frontier Mormonism in the Texas Hill Country

in the days of Peter and John; and also in the days of Lyman
—Lyman Wight

Wightite separatism informed its interactions with other Texans before the Civil War. Two reasons explain this exclusion. First is the sacred-and-profane socialized daily life that subordinated individual life to the larger community. The religious system discouraged members from general interaction with outsiders beyond village attachments. Second, polygamy, despised—if not feared—by non-Mormons, created a barrier between the societies.

Wightite economic and cultural successes directly sprang from separatism. Zodiac, from 1847 to 1851, became important economically to the Texas Hill Country. The later Wightite villages of Hamilton Mills (1851–53) and Mountain Valley (1854–58) also distinctly influenced the economic and political development of Burnet and Bandera counties. That the villages were small made little difference, for only five communities enumerated during the Texas census of 1850 had populations exceeding 1,000. The German communities of New Braunfels (almost 1,300) and Fredericksburg (about 750) were, respectively, the fourth- and seventh-largest towns in Texas. While Wight and others claimed that Zodiac had a population of about 250, a survey of the census of 1850, family records, and genealogical indexes reveals that the normal population fluctuated between 135 and 170 individuals, living in about thirty residences. As many as another fifty at any time had religious and familial ties to Zodiac, but lived outside of its boundaries.

Zodiac milling clout and communal industriousness created an economic dominance in the Hill Country. The community's mechanical and agricultural cooperatives, which included approximately sixteen percent of the county's population, directed regional commerce by 1850 and owned more than sixty percent of the real and personal wealth in Gillespie County alone.[1] The communal dynamics of religious/secular organization, plus the Wightites' ownership and control of the mill, distinctly influenced the situation. Religious tenets directed everyday activity, including commercial endeavors as well as those involving individual and families.

Singular community deportment defined the Wightites among their neighbors. Samuel E. Holland, a leading figure of Burnet County, knew the Mormons and found them honest, socially aloof, and religiously devout. Wight, he wrote, possessed "a brilliant intellect, an abundance of energy, fair business ability, a pleasing personality that at the same time impressed me as being somewhat sinister." His followers, Holland believed, were treated "with a lenient hand." Noah Smithwick characterized the Wightites as sharing similar ranges of qualities as other Texans: "some of them were honest and industrious, others were shiftless and unreliable," which, in his opinion, "must ever prove a potent argument against community holdings—the thriftless got just as much as the thrifty." He did not find "anything objectionable in the Mormons as neighbors."[2]

Smithwick, however, believed the faithful to be credulous respecting matters of faith, mockingly describing Wight's behavior, for instance, in locating a set of mill stones that had been lost in a flood:

> Old Lyman Wight, the high priest, set about the task of recovering the lost stones. After wrestling alone with the spirits for some little

---

1. Population schedule, census of 1850, Comal County, Texas; population schedule, census of 1850, Gillespie County; Zodiac database of individuals and families, compiled by Melvin C. Johnson (1996), in the author's possession, compiled in part from subject name listings in Turk, "Mormons in Texas"; products of industry schedule, census of 1850, Gillespie County; agricultural production schedule, census of 1850, Gillespie County; ancestral file index and genealogical family index, LDS archives.
2. Mrs. Alta Holland Gibbs, *Burnet (TX) Bulletin*, quoted in Debo, *Burnet County History*, 28; Smithwick, *Evolution of a State*, 228.

> time he arose one morning with joy in his heart, and summoning his people, announced to them that he had had a revelation, and bidding them to take spades and crowbars and follow him, set out to locate the millstones. Straight ahead he bore as one in a dream, his diving rod in his hand; his awestruck disciples following in silence. . . . In the middle of the sand bar deposited by the flood he stuck his rod down.

Wight commanded the people to dig. After uncovering several feet of sand, the millstones appeared. Another incident of faith among the Wightites excited further Smithwick's skepticism, in this case the credence exhibited by one Mormon who told Smithwick about the miraculous healing of a boy who had broken his leg. Several elders ministered by the laying on of hands and by prayer, which supposedly healed the child. Smithwick assured the man that, "if you had told me that you yourself felt of that boy's leg and found it broken, I should never believe another word you speak." The old Texan mused in his memoirs that although the man who told him the story might be suspect in matters of intellect, nonetheless, "there were some really intelligent men among them, and it was a mystery to me how they could lend themselves to such a course, when there was so little to be gained by it."[3]

The Wightites and Smithwick, as a representative of frontier Protestantism, were closer alike than he realized. Smithwick, despite mocking the Mormon faith, himself accepted the orthodox Christian folkway that came to many on the frontier life through self-conviction, searching faith, and divine intervention. He was instrumental in converting fellow scout and future minister Andrew A. Potter. The Reverend H. A. Graves described the influence the recently converted Smithwick had on Potter. Potter, hearing that Smithwick, formerly "his strongest partner in vice," had joined the faith, "felt the shock, as some great building is shaken when its principal girders give way." Potter sought out Smithwick, who told him that "it was true, and urged him" to at once begin seeking for divine confirmation. The believer who mocked credulous Mormons led the sinner later that day to the altar. Potter joined the Methodist-Episcopal

3. Smithwick, *Evolution of a State*, 223–25, 228.

Church and became a preacher for decades, known as the "Indian Fighting Parson" of West Texas.[4]

Conversion by conviction of one's sinful state, as in the case of Smithwick, and the credulity of the Wightite who believed that the boy's leg truly had been healed by faith and prayer had much in common. They both partook of the miraculous wonder invested in frontier Christianity. Faith-healing, the laying on of hands for blessing and power, the searching spiritual investigation provoked by conviction of sin, and other such practices were part of the folk practices of Hill Country religion. It was not uncommon for numerous frontier Texans to take refuge in prayer and faith-healing against the commonplace accidents and diseases in their lives.

An incident involving George Montague's mother illustrates such practices in Wight's colonies. Mercy Lincoln Montague was a slight woman of frail constitution and often ill. She had been suffering a particularly difficult bout with sickness. The elders laid their hands on her, blessing her to become well. She immediately arose, her son wrote, and went about the household duties as if she had never been ill. Another involved George Miller, which happened shortly before his baptism in 1839. He believed two Mormon elders had healed him of a disease, so deadly that three doctors, according to Miller, had advised him "if I had any matters to arrange in regard to my estate I had better be about it, as I could not possibly live." His healing set the "entire village [in an] uproar." Many of Miller's neighbors exhibited Smithwick's later doubt, thinking the elders and Miller had preyed "upon the credulity of the people."[5]

Because it is not unnatural for one to misjudge the depth and quality of another's religious life, many Texans had trouble in accepting the legitimacy of the Mormon faith experience in Zodiac. The village's covenanted life, particularly when involving practices disapproved of by local secular and sectarian belief, undoubtedly encouraged the Wightites to develop private modes of communication intelligible only among themselves. From the earliest days of

---

4. H. A. Graves, *Andrew Jackson Potter, The Fighting Parson of the Texan Frontier* (Nashville: Southern Methodist Publishing House, 1881), 80–81.

5. *History of the Church,* 1:147; Montague, "Reminiscences," 386; Miller, *Correspondence of Bishop George Miller,* 6–7.

Mormonism, church leadership and plurally married members became masterful in the art of hiding their marriage and family practices. They communicated, in what Lawrence Foster refers to as dialogue full of "ambiguous passages with double entendres," in a manner which only an initiate could properly interpret.

Although selected Mormons had lived in polygamy before 1841, Utah Mormonism did not publicly acknowledge the doctrine until 1852, in an announcement made in the United Kingdom. From the earliest days, then, according to Foster, the Mormons'

> public statements relating to the topic were couched in a special language, the significance of which could be grasped by only those who knew its inner meaning. . . . The casuistry involved in these denials seemed justified to Mormon leaders because they felt that the perversions ascribed by them bore no resemblance to the regulated practices that they were trying to introduce.

He argues that socialization of Mormon community life during the first decades transformed it "into a new organized unity, which, in turn, had its place and meaning in the cosmic order."[6] The result of this socialization resulted naturally in the exclusion of its followers from the larger community.

Finally, the order of plural marriage, according to Foster, juxtaposed against frontier religious mores, separated Mormon from other American communities. A masculine domination of marriage arrangements characterized this development of new familial and in-kin paradigms. This reinforced the patriarchal order and, in the process, discouraged what Foster calls "the careless individualism of romantic love, which seemed to threaten the very roots of family life and social solidarity." The selection by Lyman Wight and Pierce Hawley of mates for the Hawley siblings typifies themes emphasized by Foster: rejection of romantic love, and the enfranchisement of religious domination by male priesthood holders.

Polygamous marriage, antithetical to the overwhelming sentiment of Protestant and Catholic America, helped to reinforce the

---

6. Lawrence Foster, *Religion and Sexuality: Three American Communal Experiments of the Nineteenth Century* (New York: Oxford University Press, 1981), 133.

individual Mormon's subordination to familial and societal interests. Mormon marriage and divorce were ecclesiastical rather than state matters, separating the membership further from the secular society. Foster noted that at times "Mormon arrangements were not fully in harmony with local marriage regulations or mores." Neither Joseph Smith Jr. nor Sydney Rigdon were ordained to celebrate marriages, and both had troubles with secular governments about their unusual activities concerning marriage. Because polygamy never was sanctioned in any American civil jurisdiction, the Mormon leaders' control of marriage and divorce provided them with a powerful key for directing the lives of their communities and people.[7]

Lyman Wight fused the role of church and state in directing his communities in Texas, and he did it better than he had earlier. For instance, the state's military leaders in Missouri nearly executed him because he committed treason, unable to reconcile his roles as a state regimental commander and a Mormon paramilitary chieftain. In Texas, he acted with more sophistication when religious matters had secular consequences. He did not hesitate to use secular authority in such matters; for example, the marriage registers in Gillespie, Burnet, and Bandera counties include many Wightite marriages. However, Wight could ignore local authorities when convenient, particularly in matters involving plural marriage.[8] The Wightites' unique religious practices and the subordination of the individual to the larger community separated them from others in the Hill Country.

The very forces creating continuity and separatism, however, also threatened the stability of Wightite villages. A balance of gender, age, and marriage status and availability among its membership were critical in maintaining village stability. An evaluation of Zodiac's 1850 census, cross-checked with other sources, provides a tool for estimating the village's social order. Thirty-two households, with almost 170

---

7. Foster, *Religion and Sexuality*, 139–40; Hawley, "Autobiography of John Hawley," 7.

8. Foster, *Religion and Sexuality*, 135–36; Hawley, "Autobiography of John Hawley," 7, 9; book A, index to marriage records, Burnet County, Texas 1852–62, Burnet County Courthouse, Burnet, TX; cross index to marriage records, Burnet County, Texas 1852–65; Gillespie County marriage records, vol. 1, Gillsepie County Courthouse, Fredricksburg, TX; Bandera County marriage licenses, vol. 1, Bandera County Courthouse, Bandera, TX.

individuals, made up Zodiac that year. Females constituted forty-one of ninety-one adults, and thirty-three of sixty-five children. The role of wife dominated the lives of the Zodiac women and older teenage girls—only old age, widowhood, or death provided a release from it. Thirty-eight of the forty-one adult females were known to be married, of whom at least twelve—and possibly fourteen—were plural wives (Ellen Bell and Jane Moncur, daughters of the Ballantyne family, may have been concurrent wives of Abram Moncur). Widow Ruth Stratton Curtis remained the only female household head. Widow Janet Turnbull Ballantyne lived with her son Andrew.[9]

When comparing the males and females and their marriage status, a serious shortage of marriage-age females and an excess of marriage-age males emerge. This growing disparity plagued the community throughout its existence. For example, at Zodiac in 1850, only slightly less than sixty percent of the adult males were married heads-of-household, while almost every female over the age of fifteen was a spouse. Polygamy compounded the problem. Only four—and possibly two more—of twenty-nine married males had plural spouses: Lyman Wight, Ezra Chipman, George Montague Sr., and Orange Lysander Wight. Abram Moncur probably had a conjugal relationship with his wife's sister, Ellen Bell (Helen Ballantyne), who lived in their household. John F. Miller may have been another polygamist. On the other hand, a female was two to three times more likely than a male to be a polygamous spouse. In a small village, polygamy then

9. Population schedule, census of 1850, Zodiac, Gillespie County; Zodiac database and Wightite family database. Marriage and family relations were not always obvious. For instance, the plural status of one wife, Margaret Francis Andrews, before the death of Rosina Minerva Wight Miller on 26 March 1850, is problematic. Although Margaret Francis became John Miller's legal wife on 11 July 1850, it is not known if Miller and Andrews had been plurally joined before the death of Rosina Wight Miller. Margaret Francis was the daughter of plural wife Nancy Daniels Richardson Montague, who lived next door to the Millers. In a strange twist of irony, Margaret Francis Andrews Miller divorced John F. Miller before 25 March 1852, the date she married George Montague Jr., making Nancy Daniels Richardson not only the mother but also the mother-in-law of her own daughter, as well as making Margaret Francis the stepsister of her husband, George (see Turk, "Mormons in Texas," 19–20, 65). The marriage of Montague and Andrews is not recorded in the records of Burnet County, although that of John F. Miller to Martha Chatfield can be found in book A, index to marriage records, Burnet County, Texas 1852 62, 7.

was paradoxically both the strength and weakness of the community, for it contributed a socio-economic strength in the present, while robbing the village's future.[10]

The seriousness of this problem relating to gender, age, and marriage becomes evident when examining the vital statistics of Zodiac, found in Table 1, next page. In part because Wightite marriages were arranged, wives were significantly younger than husbands. This was particularly the case with second, third, and fourth wives in the plural-marriage households, a phenomenon common in Mormon relations. Lyman Wight and Ezra Chipman were at least twenty years older than their younger plural wives. Zodiac men were about eight years older than their wives. The age disparity decreases to five and a half years when the two oldest polygamists, Lyman Wight and Ezra Chipman, are removed from the sum. Only Elizabeth Hewitt, of the eleven wives who were twenty-two or younger, was her husband's age. Seven teenage females were wives, the youngest being Henrietta Maria Curtis, then sixteen. This left only six other unmarried teenage girls available: two were just seventeen and the other four thirteen and fourteen. On the other hand, seventeen working males at Zodiac in 1850 were unmarried, with twelve of them in their twenties, a prime age for marriage. Thus, the ratio of eligible females to males was almost one to three. If the thirteen- and fourteen-year-old girls are removed from the figures, the gender eligibility shrinks to almost one to nine.

After 1850, the age of brides continues to grow younger while grooms grow older. Although no Wightite records reveal discord among younger males about the lack of eligible females, nonetheless, a certain level of tension and resentment must have existed. A growing scarcity of marriage-age females created a serious probability that some younger males would begin searching outside the community for wives or, even more disagreeable to village relations, challenge the affections of Zodiac's married women and excite the jealousies of their husbands. When already-married males approached females already married to polygamous males, which did happen and will be discussed below, dissension and schism resulted.

The majority of Wightite marriages, as demonstrated in Table 2, page 80, still were being made within in the colony, although toward

10. See population schedule, census of 1850, Zodiac, Gillespie County.

TABLE 1
MARRIED INDIVIDUALS AT ZODIAC IN 1850

Residence	*Household Heads and Spouses*	*Ages*	*Married Status*
243	Lyman Wight and Henrietta Benton Wight	54, 49	Legal husband and wife
	Jane M. Wight	29	Plural Wife
	Mary Hawley Wight	28	Plural Wife
	Mary Ann Hobart Wight	22	Plural Wife
244	Pierce Hawley and Sarah Schroeder Hawley	61, 52	Legal husband and wife
245	George Hawley and Ann Hadfield Hawley	27, 24	Legal husband and wife
246	John Hawley and Sylvia Goodale Hawley	26, 18	Legal husband and wife
247	Spencer Smith and Anna Christina Wight Smith	32, 24	Legal husband and wife
248	Ruth Stratton Curtis	55	Widow and head-of-house
249	Samuel Heath and Jayne Haynes Heath	62, 65	Legal husband and wife
250	Meacham Curtis and Emeline Curtis	31, 22	Legal husband and wife
251	William Curtis and Henrietta M. Rosig Curtis	28, 16	Legal husband and wife
252	William P. Eldridge and Nancy A. Eldridge	38, 34	Legal husband and wife
253	Truman Brace	63	Widower
254	George Bailey and Barbara Urie Bailey	31, 35	Legal husband and wife
255	Abram Moncur and Jane V. Ballantyne Moncur	30, 28	Legal husband and wife
	Ellen Bell (Hellen Ballantyne)		Possible plural wife
256	James Goudy (wife Isabella Tenuck not listed)	30, (30)	(Legal husband and wife)
257	Orange L. Wight and Matilda Carter Wight	26, 23	Legal husband and wife
	Sarah Hadfield Wight	24	Plural Wife
	Rosilla Carter Wight	25	Plural Wife
258	Irwin Carter and Mary Ann Six Carter	27, 17	Legal husband and wife
259	Andrew Ballantyne	26	Bachelor
260	Ralph Jenkins and Verona Brace Jenkins	35, 34	Legal husband and wife
261	John F. Miller and M. Francis Andrews Miller	27, 18	Legal husband and wife
262	George Montague Sr. and Eliza Segar Montague	48, 37	Legal husband and wife
	Nancy Anderson Daniels Montague	39	Plural Wife
263	Asher John Gressman and Essilinda Gressman	45, 43	Legal husband and wife
264	John Young and Priscilla Hawley Young	39, 18	Legal husband and wife
265	Ezra A. Chipman and Malinda Porter Chipman	45, 43	Legal husband and wife
	Janette Sutherland Chipman	24	Plural Wife
	Marian Curtis Sutherland Chipman	19	Plural Wife
266	Norman and Sarah Chatfield	46, 45	Legal husband and wife
267	James McKeen and Ann McKeen	28, 25	Legal husband and wife
268	Alexander St. Marie and Mary Ann St. Marie	37, 31	Legal husband and wife
269	E. B. Hewitt and Elizabeth Hewitt	22, 22	Legal husband and wife
270	George W. Bird and Eliza Curtis Bird	27, 23	Legal husband and wife
271	Joseph Dwight Goodale and Elvira Kay Goodale	30, 28	Legal husband and wife
272	Phineas Bird and Millicent "Polly" Bird	48, 49	Legal husband and wife
273	Cyrus Isham and Sofia Isham	27, 20	Legal husband and wife
274	Benjamin Bird and Mary Bird	22, 18	Legal husband and wife

the end of its existence, members were more likely to marry mates from outside of the village. Almost forty marriages are documented between 1844 and 1858. Polygamous ties, as always, are more difficult to prove than monogamous relationships. Between nine and twelve of these marriages were plural, including the probable plural relationships of Abram Moncur–Ellen Bell and George Hawley–Ann Hadfield, each woman a sister to the man's legal wife. Some marriages outside the original Wightite families included Rebecca Jane Connyers to Andrew Ballantyne, Rosetta Jane Howard to Silas Porter Chatfield, and Mary Vicero to Joseph Smith Curtis. The Wightite system resulted in some unusual marriages within the community. Two younger sons of Lyman Wight, for instance, each married one of their adopted "sisters," the Leyland girls. This seems a startling consideration until one notes that, unlike the elder brother, William Leyland, who had been adopted as Wight's son, the three Leyland girls had been taken in as members of the family only until they became adults. The Leyland girls apparently fulfilled the roles of Wight's wards more than as sisters to his sons.[11]

In the period from 1860 to 1866, former Wightite marriages in Bandera reveal the colony descendants were likely to marry one another slightly more often than outsiders. Such marriages included Levi L. Wight and Sophia Leyland, Oscar D. Johnson and Malinda M. Chipman, and Richard Bird and Jenemie Moncur. Four of the Minear girls—Amanda, Emma, Marinda, and Virginia—married within their heritage: Emma to Joseph L. Sutherland; Marinda to Robert Ballantyne; and Amanda and, after her death, Virginia, to George Hay. Other Wightites and second-generation descendants married non-LDS partners, including Marion Sutherland (only after divorcing two Wightite husbands, one monogamous and one polygamous), Samuel H. Bird, Andrew Hoffman, Jenette Moncur, Heber N. Chipman, and Loami L. Wight.[12]

---

11. William Leyland journal in H. H. Smith, "The Lyman Wight Colony in Texas," 21–22; Hawley, "Autobiography of John Hawley," 7, 10; Gillespie County marriage records, 1:1, 2; Bandera County marriage licenses, vol. 1; book A, index to marriage records, Burnet County, Texas 1852–62:5 October 1857, 111; cross index to marriage records, Burnet County, Texas 1852–65.
12. Bandera County marriage licenses, 1:1, 2, 10, 13, 14, 20, 23, 24, 30, 31, 32, 33, 34.

TABLE 2

LYMAN WIGHT COLONY MARRIAGES AND PLURAL RELATIONSHIPS 1844 TO 1858

Date	*Names*	*Place*	*Status*
6 Feb 1844	Rosina Minerva Wight to John F. Miller	Black River Falls, WI	Monogamous
6 Feb 1844	Matilda Carter to Orange Lysander Wight	Black River Falls, WI	Monogamous
24 Mar 1844	Verona Brace to Ralph Jenkins	Nauvoo, IL	Monogamous
7 Feb 1845	Sarah Hadfield to Orange Lysander Wight	Prairie La Crosse, WI	Polygamous
Before 1845	Margaret Ballantyne to Lyman Wight	Unknown	Polygamous
1844/1845	Mary Ann Hobart Otis to Lyman Wight	Unknown	Polygamous
Early 1845	Mary Hawley to Lyman Wight	DuPage, IL	Polygamous
Spring 1845	Patience F. Curtis to Joel Simonds Miles	Unknown	Polygamous
27 Sep 1845	Bernice Monroe to Charles Bird	Near Mound City, KS	Monogamous
27 Sep 1845	Eliza Curtis to George W. Bird	Near Mound City, KS	Monogamous
27 Sep 1845	Marian Sutherland to William Curtis	Near Mound City, KS	Monogamous
4 Jul 1846	Priscilla Hawley to John Young	Sycamore Springs, TX	Monogamous
4 Jul 1846	Harriet Hobart to John S. Hawley	Sycamore Springs, TX	Monogamous
4 Jul 1846	Ann Hadfield to George Hawley	Sycamore Springs, TX	Monogamous
16 Apr 1847	Jenette Sutherland to Ezra A. Chipman	Sycamore Springs, TX	Polygamous
—— 1848	Ellen Bell (H. Ballantyne) to Abram Moncur	Zodiac, TX	Possible Polygamous
—— 1849	Sylvia Johnson to John S. Hawley	Zodiac, TX	Monogamous
1849/1850	Margaret Francis Andrews to John F. Miller	Zodiac, TX	Possible Polygamous
1849/1850	Emeline Curtis to Meacham Curtis	Zodiac, TX	Monogamous
1849/1850	Elizabeth Hewitt to E. B. Hewitt	Zodiac, TX	Monogamous
1849/1850	Rosilla Carter to Orange Lysander Wight	Zodiac, TX	Polygamous
1849/1850	Nancy Richardson to George Montague Sr.	Zodiac, TX	Polygamous
1849/1850	Marian Sutherland to Ezra A. Chipman	Zodiac, TX	Polygamous
1849/1850	Mary Bird to Benjamin F. Bird	Zodiac, TX	Monogamous
15 Aug 1850	Maria Henrietta Racig to William Curtis	Zodiac, TX	Monogamous
1 Jan 1852	Jennet Hay to Andrew Hoffman	Mormon Mill, TX	Monogamous
11 Nov 1852	Martha Chatfield to John F. Miller	Mormon Mill, TX	Monogamous
25 Dec 1852	Margaret Andrews to George Montague Jr.	Mormon Mill, TX	Monogamous
ca. 1853	Lydia P. Minear to Meacham Curtis	Mormon Mill, TX	Monogamous
1 Jan 1853	Eliza Leyland to Lyman Lehi Wight	Mormon Mill, TX	Monogamous
24 Jan 1853	Rebecca Jane Connyers to Andrew Ballantyne	Mormon Mill, TX	Monogamous
1854/1855	Sarah Curtis to Rodney Brace	Mormon Mill, TX	Monogamous
1853/1854	Sarah Hadfield Wight to George Hawley	Mormon Mill, TX	Probable Polygamou
24 Jan 1854	Ann Elizabeth Andrews to Aaron Hawley	Bandera County, TX	Monogamous
13 Sep 1855	Abigail Emma Andrews to James A. Ballantyne	Mountain Valley, TX	Monogamous
2 Sep 1856	Rosetta Jane Howard to Silas P. Chatfield	Mountain Valley, TX	Monogamous
6 Sep 1856	Sophia Leyland to Levi Lamoni Wight	Mountain Valley, TX	Monogamous
1856/1857	Mary Vicero to Joseph Smith Curtis	Mountain Valley, TX	Monogamous

Table 3
Divorces in the Lyman Wight Colony, 1844 to 1855

Date	*Spouses*	*Location*	*Status*
1848/1849	William Curtis from Marian Sutherland	Zodiac, TX	Monogamous
1849	John Hawley from Harriet Hobart	Zodiac, TX	Monogamous
By 11 Nov 1852	John F. Miller from Margaret F. Andrews Miller	Mormon Mill, TX	Monogamous
1852/1853	Orange L. Wight from Sarah Hadfield Wight	Mormon Mill, TX	Polygamous
ca. 1855	Ezra A. Chipman from Marian Sutherland	Mountain Valley, TX	Polygamous

Divorce was a common-day fact of the colonies. As disclosed in the table above, five men and four women ended their marriages this way. Wight's subordination of civil and secular process to spiritual and religious authority created interesting situations. For instance, one divorce resulted in his attempt to have a monogamous couple take plural vows. John Hawley's first wife deserted him, and Wight informed him that he was divorced and to prepare for a new wife. Hawley desired Sylvia Johnson, but the apostle preferred her for his monogamous son-in-law Spencer Smith. The Old Ram offered Hawley, instead, one of the Leyland girls living in the Wight household. Hawley (who refused to give Sylvia up) typically did not mention in his "Autobiography" that Spencer Smith already had a wife. Wight, somewhat peeved at the situation, refused to marry Sylvia and John for almost a year.[13]

Marion Sutherland ended two marriages, a monogamous relation with William Curtis and a plural one to Ezra Chipman, about 1848/1849 and 1855/1856, respectively. She married William Harmon, a non-colonist, in 1857. William Curtis married Maria Henrietta Rosig, a German girl of Fredericksburg, in 1850 and remained with the colony. Ezra Chipman remained with his other wives, Malinda Porter and Jenette Sutherland, a sister of Chipman's divorced wife. Margaret Francis Andrews and John Miller were monogamous

13. Hawley, "Autobiography of John Hawley," 7, 10. Heman C. Smith and Heman Hale Smith, the son and grandson of Spencer Smith and both RLDS historians and church authorities, do not discuss the story of Wight attempting to make a polygamist of his daughter and her husband.

TABLE 4
PARTIAL LIST OF DEATHS AT ZODIAC, TEXAS, 1847 TO 1850

Year	*Name*	*Location*	*Age in Years*	*Gender*	*Marital Status*
1847	Lyman Spencer Smith	Austin	Under 1	Male	N/A
1848	William Bell	Zodiac	39	Male	Monogamous
1848	Sophia Wallace Leyland Miller	Zodiac	48	Female	Polygamous
1848	Permelia Young	Zodiac	Under 1	Female	N/A
1849	Sally Goodale Johnson	Zodiac	48	Female	Monogamous
1850	Clarissa Cornelia Smith	Zodiac	Under 1	Female	N/A
1850	Sarah Wight	Zodiac	Under 1	Female	N/A
1850	Mina Wight	Zodiac	Under 1	Female	N/A
1850	Rosina Minerva Wight Miller	Zodiac	22	Female	N/A
1850	Amalona (Amahona) Chipman	Zodiac	3	Male	Male
1850	William Leyland, Jr.	Zodiac	22	Male	Unmarried
1850	William P. Eldridge	Zodiac	38	Male	Monogamous
1850	Otis Hobart	Kentucky	48	Male	Monogamous
1850	Minerva Jenkins	Zodiac	Under 1	Female	N/A
1850	Romilia Carter	Zodiac	Under 1	Female	N/A

at the time of their divorce, although they may have been plurals before the death of John's first wife, Rosina Minerva Wight Miller. Margaret and John both remained in the colony. Miller married Martha Chatfield on 11 November 1852, and on 25 December 1852 Margaret became the wife of George Montague Jr., the son and namesake of the man who had earlier taken Margaret's mother as a plural spouse.

Sarah Hadfield left plural husband Orange Lysander Wight in 1852 or 1853 and married George Hawley, the husband of her sister, Ann Hadfield. In part because of this and other issues, most of the Hawley clan eventually left the colony and moved to Indian Territory. Orange Wight and his two other wives remained with his father until at least 1855. John Hawley, again, typically does not mention his brother's polygamous marriage in any of his writings.[14]

The birth and death statistics, although incomplete in the tables above and opposite, reflect a stable community despite the frontier environment. Of the fifteen individuals documented who died during

14. Subject name listings in Turk, "Mormons in Texas"; Gillespie County marriage records, 1:William Curtis and Mary Rosig, 12 August 1850; book A, index to marriage records, Burnet County, Texas 1852–62:John F. Miller to Martha Chatfield, 11 November 1852; Bandera County marriage licenses, 1:1; "Early Reorganization Minutes, 1852–1871," Book A:418, RLDS archives; Hawley, "Autobiography of John Hawley," 10.

TABLE 5
LIVE BIRTHS IN THE WIGHT COMMUNITIES 1847 TO 1850
** Plural Household ** Possible Plural Household*

Date	*Location*	*Infant's Name*	*Child's Parents*
1847	Austin	Harriet Martnesia Wight*	Orange & Sarah Hadfield Wight
1847	Austin	Aseneth M. Wight*	Orange & Matilda Wight
1847	Unknown	Byron Chatfield	Norman & Sarah Chatfield
1847	Unknown	James O. Hobart	James & Sophronia Hobart
1847	Unknown	James Jenkins	Ralph & Verona Brace Jenkins
1847	Unknown	Sarah McKeen	John J. & Enghradia McKeen
1847	Zodiac	Permelia Young	John & Priscilla Hawley Young
1848	Zodiac	Ameleta Gressman	Asher & Essilinda Gressman
1848	Zodiac	Joshua C. Miller	Jackson L. & Elizabeth Miller
1848	Zodiac	(Infant) Wight*	Lyman & Mary Ann Wight
1848	Zodiac	Sarah Wight*	Orange & Sarah Hadfield Wight
1848	Zodiac	Jenemie Moncur**	Abram & Jane V. Moncur
1848	Zodiac	George G. Miller	John F. & Rosina Wight Miller
1848	Zodiac	Mildred M. Chipman*	Ezra A. & Jenette Chipman
1848	Zodiac	Frances A. Killmer	Jonas & Caroline Miller
1848	Zodiac	Sanford P. Chipman*	Ezra A. & Malinda Chipman
1848	Zodiac	Menamento Wight*	Lyman & Mary Hawley Wight
1848	Zodiac	Hyrum Taylor	John & Eleanor Taylor
1848	Zodiac	Clarissa C. Smith	Spencer & Anna Wight Smith
1849	Zodiac	William N. Eldridge	William & Nancy Eldridge
1849	Zodiac	Martha A. Hawley	George & Ann Hadfield Hawley
1849	Zodiac	Rufana J. Chipman*	Ezra A. & Jenette Chipman
1849	Zodiac	Mina Wight*	Orange & Matilda Wight
1849	Zodiac	Romala L. Young	John & Priscilla Hawley Young
1850	Zodiac	Rosina R. Miller	John F. & Rosina Wight Miller
1850	Zodiac	Morgan Moncur**	Abram & Jane V. Moncur
1850	Zodiac	Ramora Montague*	George Sr. & Nancy Montague
1850	Zodiac	Hiram H. Wight*	Orange & Sarah Hadfield Wight
1850	Bexar	Edward J. Killmer	Jonas & Caroline Killmer
1850	Zodiac	Helen A. Bird	Charles & Bernice Monroe Bird
1850	Zodiac	Heman C. Smith	Spencer & Anna Wight Smith
1850	Zodiac	Romalia Carter	Irwin F. & Mary Ann Six Carter
1850	Zodiac	Minerva Jenkins	Ralph & Verona Brace Jenkins

the Zodiac years (1847–50) only Otis Hobart and Lyman Spencer Smith perished elsewhere. Six were males: four adults and two young boys. Three of the adults were married: William Bell, William P. Eldridge, and Otis Hobart. Six female infants did not reach their first birthday. The deaths among adult females included two older women, Sally Johnson Goodale and Sarah Wallace Leyland Miller, both beyond the age of childbearing, and one young mother of three living children, Rosina Minerva Wight Miller. All three women were married, although Sarah Miller was estranged from her husband, Bishop George Miller, at the time of her death in 1848.

At least thirty-four births occurred in the colony between 1847 and 1850. Children under the age of four maintained a birth-to-death rate of more than four to one, indicating strong natural increase. Almost fifty-six percent of the babies were female, offsetting the higher incidence of their deaths. More significantly, the birth rate greatly exceeded the death rate of infants and small children. Although less than sixteen percent of the families were polygamous in September of 1850, at least thirty-three to thirty-eight percent of births were in plural households, reflecting polygamy's impact on population replacement.[15]

Despite Mormon aloofness, some social interaction, as well as commercial transactions, took place among the populations of Fredericksburg, Fort Martin Scott, and Zodiac. The Mormon mills offered immediate advantage to the struggling German community, not the least being ground meal. New German arrivals at Fredericksburg found help from their neighbors, including work in the mills. Some of the more prosperous Germans built their houses with milled Zodiac lumber. Both civilian communities supplied the military post with goods and services. The soldiers patronized the civilian stores. Even one Wightite, Thomas Ballantyne, served at Fort Martin Scott, with Company K, 8th Infantry. Utah missionary Preston Thomas noted that eight to ten "Dutchmen and women" attended the New Year feast at Zodiac in 1849. The climax of this socialization was the marriage of William Curtis of Zodiac and Maria Henrietta Rosig of Fredericksburg, on 12 August 1850.[16]

The Comanche and Tonkawa bought animals and corn at Zodiac, and relations were peaceful. The Germans were more responsible than the Wightites for this enviable situation. Fierce Comanche tribal bands from the northwest began invading the Hill Country

---

15. Zodiac database; Wightite family database; mortality schedule, affixed to the census of 1850, original at Gillespie County Historical Society, Fredericksburg, TX; other community records; and secondary sources. Phineas Reaves Bird is not included because of the inconsistency of death records in his case.

16. Bracht, in Fischer, *Marxists and Utopias in Texas*, 103; Ted Thompson, "When the Mormons Came To Texas," *San Antonio Express*, March 18, 1928; population schedule, census of 1850, Gillespie County; Gillespie County marriage records 1:11 August 1850 and 12 August 1850; "Preston Thomas: His Life and Travels," folder 1, 43.

as early as the seventeenth century, and drove the Lipan Apache to the west. The Comanche followed their ancient, nomadic ways in the Hill Country and throughout western Texas for more than two centuries, raiding each year into Mexico and the encroaching Anglo-European settlements to the east. Neither conquered nor converted by the Spanish or Mexicans, these were the Native Americans the settlers normally encountered and, with good reason, greatly feared.

All settlers had to cope with the geo-spatial vastness dominating the mid-nineteenth-century Hill Country. Time, space, and the Comanche were real and, at times, deadly facts of life. August Hoffman remembered that, although a modern automobile trip to Indianola on the Texas coast took six or seven hours in the 1920s, almost seventy years earlier when he was fourteen, a freighting trip with four oxen and a wagon from Fredericksburg to the coast and back took twelve weeks. The continuing increase of Anglo-European settlers in the Hill Country rubbed against the native cultures. Conflict was inevitable. Captain Friedrich von Wrede and Lieutenant Oscar Claren became the first German casualties in October 1845; as they were returning to their new home in New Braunfels from Austin, they were killed and scalped.[17]

Although Claren and Wrede were not the last Germans killed—nor were other local settlers spared—the Gillespie County colonists suffered far less from Comanche troubles than other settlements in the Hill Country. John Meusebach, known to the Comanche as *El Sol Colorado*, "The Red Sun," had succeeded Prince Carl von Solms-Braunfels as general director of the German Emigration Company and successfully treated with the Indians. The natives and Germans, as well as the Mormons, honored the treaty until the early 1850s. However, other Americans did not, and bloody warfare eventually and continually stained the Hill Country until after the Civil War.[18] Some of the

---

17. Gilbert J. Jordan, "Excerpts From My 'Hill Country' Talk," *Journal (German-Texan Heritage Society)* 8, no. 3 (Fall 1986): 2; August Hoffman (handwritten memoirs, 6 October 1925), 4, Center for American History archives, University of Texas, Austin, TX; Rudolph Leopold Biesele, *The History of the German Settlements in Texas, 1831–1861* (Austin: Von Boeckmann-Jones, 1930), 182.
18. Francis Edward Abernethy, "*Deutschtum* in Texas: A Look at Texas-German Folklore," in *German Culture in Texas: A Free Earth; Essays from the 1978 Southwest Symposium*, ed. Glen E. Lich and Dona B. Reeves-Marquardt (Boston: Twayne, 1980), 208; Biesele, *German Settlements*, 187.

Wightites, despite the peace, despised the natives. One was Levi Lamoni Wight, who described the Tonkawas as pests who "wanted something all the time and was not slow to make their wants known." Others talked more favorably. William Leyland noted in his journal in 1850 that Comanche chief Buffalo Hump and his followers "have visited us several times this year and gave us the privilege of traveling anywhere through their nation. Lyman talked with them concerning the *Book of Mormon* &c., and they seemed very much pleased."[19]

As noted above, the Wightite common-stock cooperatives were the bedrock of its prosperity at Zodiac. Ernest G. Fischer, in *Marxists and Utopias in Texas*, had obviously read Heman Hale Smith, adopting the latter's definition of LDS stewardship, and then proceeded to describe the Zodiac economy. "Under the common-stock plan," he wrote, "the Mormon community owned everything. They who occupied and worked the property owned shares in the community corporation." Fischer then incorrectly defined the common-stock system as a form of Marxist communism.[20] Although collective in nature, decision- and policy-making were invested in Wight rather than the cooperative membership. The decision-making principles were not communistic, but almost fascistic, dependent on the will of a leader: in other words, always subject to Lyman Wight's desire rather than that of the collective will. The charismatic, autocratic leader brooked little resistance from those who followed him. He believed firmly that the church leadership, meaning himself, should direct the businesses of both individuals and the economy of the community. C. Stanley Banks has estimated correctly Wight's character and the nature of his economy, deciding that the old prophet and not his followers made economic as well as socio-religious decisions. He wrote, "in a literal sense, Wight was their material and spiritual leader" and the colony's "absolute dictator. All business was done and all property was held in his individual name."[21]

The Zodiac closed cooperatives operated differently than church co-ops in Utah Mormonism. Although others at Zodiac, such as Joseph

---

19. L. L. Wight, *Reminiscences*, 14; William Leyland journal, in H. H. Smith, "The Lyman Wight Colony in Texas," 25.
20. Fischer, *Marxists and Utopias in Texas*, 91, 98.
21. Banks, "The Mormon Migration into Texas," 243.

Dwight Goodale, who is listed as the owner of the mill in the census of 1850, might seem to possess title to the property, Wight made the final decisions. John Hawley's memoirs accurately reflect Wight's actual dominion when he recorded that the colonists were meant "to take as Lyman said 'the orders of God' . . . and in this we was well schooled." As early as Mormon Coulee, his followers understood the system. In the late fall of 1844, Wight had written, "no person, embracing the doctrine of the Church of Jesus Christ of Latter Day Saints, should give any part or particle of their property with out a direct counsel, written or oral, from the first Presidency of the Church." Instead of the First Presidency, the Twelve or one of its members was next in authority, which, in Wisconsin and then Texas, was always Wight. His people were indeed well schooled in their leader's doctrine.[22]

The seeds of the Zodiac collective had their origin in the Christian primitivism of "the Family" in Ohio, not the tithing programs of Joseph Smith Jr. and Brigham Young. Heman Hale Smith noted the difference between the economic programs of Wight and those of Smith. Smith's "stewardship plan" required an individual to consecrate all of his properties to the church. In return, the church, normally through the direction and discretion of the bishop, gave the individual stewardship over certain of his properties that he had consecrated. The individual ideally then used part of the increase for his just needs, and turned the surplus over to the church.[23]

Wight defended his common-stock system as God's will. He claimed, in 1848, that the economy of Utah Mormonism needed reform. It should not be supporting a priesthood that, in his opinion, dressed in costly costume and oppressed "the poor, and the hireling in his wages, riding in fine carriages with cushioned seats, bristled carpets, leaving the poor to work out their salvation among those who are their vital enemies." He thought tithing, although its origin was from Joseph Smith, to be a system enabling the prosperous to "increase in opulence by . . . wringing from the hands of the peasant his hard earnings." Citing Mormon and Bible scripture for precedence and authority, Wight linked spiritual salvation with temporal

22. Products of industry schedule, census of 1850, Gillespie County; Hawley, "Autobiography of John Hawley," 6; L. Wight, *An Address*, 5.
23. H. H. Smith, "The Lyman Wight Colony in Texas," 2, 3.

needs. He noted that the *Book of Mormon* city of Enoch, for example, was translated en masse to heaven because its population practiced a common-stock society. Wight linked his own religious authority to that of biblical apostles: "The same example was followed . . . in the days of Peter and John; and also in the days of Lyman, who feels himself abundantly able, through the grace of God." He testified that "no other process of action will save men on the earth." As late as 1855 and 1856, he defended its merits with correspondents of the two other Mormon factions—Salt Lake City, Utah Territory, and Beaver Island, Michigan.[24]

Although the Fredericksburg Germans cared nothing about Wight's religious system, they gladly welcomed its economic benefits. Sarah Curtis has noted in her academic history of Gillespie County that the German immigrants faced tremendous challenges. They staved off starvation, in part, because native tribal charity supplemented the little food stores in the community storehouse. They had, before the Wightite mill at Zodiac, "no adequate knowledge or method of grinding what little corn [they had] into meal." Succor was more than eighty miles away, over poor trails to New Braunfels. Ms. Curtis has written that although the Germans considered the Mormons to be "lawless of religious practices," they accepted the newcomers because they realized the need to learn the American ways of milling, agriculture, and livestock.[25]

Marty and Michelle Mohon have written that the German newcomers "had to adjust to a new climate, new soils, and the unavailability of appropriate tools. Initially the yield of their crops was limited, resulting in a paltry diet of meat and bread. Consequently, a scurvy-type disease claimed many lives." Director Schubbert of Fredericksburg wrote to a Mr. Cappes early in 1847 that his community needed both "korn" and medical supplies, "because I have absolutely no medication left. Half of Friedrichsburg will die if there is no help

24. L. Wight, *An Address*, 26; Lyman and Harriet Wight, Medina River, to Sanford Porter, [Salt Lake City], 7 December 1855, Lyman Wight letterbook; Lyman Wight, Medina River, to the editors, *Northern Islander* (Voree, WI), Beaver Creek, Michigan, July 1855, Lyman Wight letterbook.

25. Sarah Kay Curtis, "A History of Gillespie County, Texas, 1846–1900," (master's thesis, University of Texas, Austin, 1943), 27, 28, 75.

soon." Schubbert discovered in the Mormons of Sycamore Springs an extraordinary answer. Both Don H. Biggers, a popular Hill Country historian, and Rudolph Biesele, an outstanding University of Texas scholar of the German immigrant communities, emphasize the importance of the theme of Mormon assistance to the German settlers. The Wightites furnished them with ground meal and sawn lumber. Mormon sawmilling supplemented as well the material culture of the distinctive German construction pattern of *fachwerk*, or half timber, with its windows, floorboards, and doors, to compliment the stone work of the buildings.[26]

Within a year of the founding of Zodiac, the *Houston Democratic Telegraph and Texas Register* at Houston reported a healthy colony developing large farms expected to raise several thousand bushels of corn, an excess beyond their own needs. The mills provided meal and lumber for the Hill Country inhabitants, and the Germans were receiving instruction in agricultural husbandry from the Mormons. Two military companies that had been stationed at Fort Martin Scott offered new economic markets as well as protection from the natives.

A romanticized description written by Lee C. Harby for the *Magazine of American History* described Zodiac as an idyllic, pastoral community of "thrift, neatness and fertility." The sections fronted "on the river," with "a fine, broad road, well shaded," stretching "along the river bank. Stone fencing divided well-irrigated farms from each other." Harby believed that with "neat stables, barns and dwellings, that . . . a piece of rural Europe [had] dropped down into those wild surroundings."[27] He made it sound as if Eden had come to the banks of the Pedernales.

---

26. Monty Mohon and Michelle Mohon, *Gillespie County: A View of Its Past* (Virginia Beach, VA: Donning, 1996), 67, 68; Solms-Braunfels Archiv (ca. 1847), 43:6–100, 146–50; Don H. Biggers, quoted in J. Marvin Hunter, comp., *The Lyman Wight Colony in Texas, Came to Bandera in 1854* (Bandera, TX: Bandera Bulletin / Frontier Times Museum, 1925), 1; Biesele, *German Settlements,* 148n22.
27. *Democratic Telegraph and Texas Register* (Houston), 17 February 1848, 2, microfilm copy in LDS archives; Hawley, "Autobiography of John Hawley," 6; Lee C. Harby, *Magazine of American History* (November 1888), quoted in *San Antonio Express,* 18 March 1928, microfilm copy in LDS archives.

5

Bishop George Miller and Zodiac: 1848–1849

their was [n]ever a meaner man to profess religion
—Levi Lamoni Wight

Bishop George Miller came to Zodiac early in 1848, left once and returned, then left for good in the fall of 1849. An able bureaucrat, once the second bishop of the LDS Church, and a member of the Council of Fifty and the Anointed Quorum, he was an irritable man who vented his spleen against those whom he disliked. His writings (1855) were not kind to Wight, generally critical of him and his labors in Wisconsin and Texas. Because of this, his generally favorable observations about the prosperity of Zodiac add balance to its evaluation. Additionally, his comings and goings give some insight within the Mormon community as a whole, and to the history of Zodiac and its people during these two years.[1]

Miller had stayed in Nauvoo and followed Brigham Young's leadership after Wight had gone to Texas. Still a bishop and serving as a captain of fifty in the migration from Nauvoo in 1846, Miller's company wintered with that of James Emmett. They combined into a small encampment of fourteen families that fall, some distance from Young and most of the LDS camps. Away from the immediate direction of Young, Miller attempted to create a common-stock economy for his little group. Most of his followers disagreed, and

1. Miller, *Correspondence of Bishop George Miller*, 10, records the bishop's bitter recollection of Henry W. Miller's attempt to circumscribe the other's authority at the Wisconsin sawmill.

many returned to the main body at Winter Quarters. Young was displeased both with the vulnerability of Miller's encampment to attack by unfriendly native tribes, and also with James Emmett's earlier unwillingness to obey counsel. Young, however, did not take action against them. Miller and Emmett, as members of the Fifty, considered themselves the equals of Young and the other apostles. Young was busy organizing the LDS for winter on the Missouri River, and they also may not have obeyed an order to return.[2]

Miller, in character, was unhappy with Young's leadership. Hosea Stout repeated a Miller tirade about Brigham Young to Willard Richards, a cousin and his strong supporter in the leading councils of the Church. When informed of the outburst, Brigham Young stated that Miller and Emmett would leave the Church. He believed that Miller and Emmett were in "the shadow of the deceased Joseph Smith, not the living Quorum of the Twelve."[3]

Andrew Jensen, an assistant historian of the LDS Church, wrote many years later that Young could not manage the fractious bishop, and threatened him with disfellowship "from the camp unless he repented." The historian Juanita Brooks, editor of *On The Mormon Frontier: The Diary of Hosea Stout,* made a note that although Miller had rendered great service as an advance guard—"it was wonderful for the mass who followed to cross streams on bridges that he had built and roads that he had improved"—that tension continued to grow between the bishop and the apostle. Miller believed that Young wanted to succeed Joseph Smith Jr. as church president. Young supposedly had discussed a revelation with Miller, the gist being the necessary reorganization of the First Presidency with Young as the new church head. Miller found such a presumption revolting. Although Miller continued to advise the Saints "to heed to [the] Council" of the Twelve as late as August of 1846, he, nonetheless, was spreading dissension among any who would listen. When Young complained to Miller that such behavior had caused the murder of Joseph Smith, Miller replied that it was effrontery for Young to

2. Winn, *Exiles in a Land of Liberty*, 151–52.
3. Juanita Brooks, ed., *On the Mormon Frontier: The Diary of Hosea Stout* (Salt Lake City: University of Utah Press / Utah State Historical Society, 1964), 1:206–7 (25 and 29 October 1846); Winn, *Exiles in a Land of Liberty*, 153–54.

compare himself with Smith, as similar as a toad comparing itself to an ox.[4]

Young recalled Miller to the main camp in early 1847, and replaced with him Erastus Snow. The bishop argued that Young was interfering with a mission given to him by Joseph Smith. Shades of Wight! This must have grated on Young. Hosea Stout recorded in his diary for 2 April 1847 that he went in the evening to

> Dr. Richard's office on business. Bishop Miller was there. He had met the Twelve there to relate to them his plans in relation to going to the south. He wanted to go and settle between the Rio Grande and the Neuses river and make a treaty with Mexico & have them give us land &c But this was in dispute now between the Untied States & Mexico and [it] was [now] the great thoroughfare for both armies.

Stout himself "thought it a pretty 'dry' job."[5] Nevertheless, Miller oriented his compass to the south and abandoned the western journey under Young. Miller and his followers began an arduous, eight-month journey to find his son's family at Zodiac. Young believed that Miller's "wild and visionary" views risked his group to anti-Mormon mobs. Nonetheless, when Miller and his followers left the camp, no action was taken against their church memberships.[6]

Several who followed Miller, not surprisingly, had ties to Zodiac. Besides the polygamous Miller family, the party included Daniel Newell Drake and wife Cynthia Parker Johnson (a daughter of Zodiac's Heber Johnson and Sally Goodale), her fourteen-year-old sister Sylvia, and two young daughters; it is not known if Sylvia was a plural wife to Daniel Drake. Other families included those of Joseph and Lucy Matilda Johnson Kelting, another sister to Cynthia Drake and Sylvia Johnson; Lewis Anderson; the widow Nancy Daniels and

---

4. Andrew Jenson, quoted in H. H. Smith, "George Miller," 229; Vida E. Smith, "Two Widows of the Brick Row," *Journal of History* 3, no. 2 (April 1910): 208; Mills, "De Tal Palo Astillo," 111; Miller, *Correspondence of Bishop George Miller*, 34–36.
5. Brooks, *The Diary of Hosea Stout*, 1:245n40 (2 April 1847).
6. Roberts, *Comprehensive History*, 2:158–59; manuscript history of Brigham Young (2 April 1847), 79, LDS archives.

her four children; Alexander and Jeanette "Jessie" Ballantyne Hay and their children; and brothers E. B. and Richard Hewitt.[7]

Miller moved his family group and some others to Plattesville, Missouri, where earlier he had been offered a large construction contract. On arrival, however, he discovered that Alpheus Cutler, another member of the Fifty, had taken the contract because Cutler had told the investors Miller was not coming. When Richard Hewitt and Joseph Kelting, whose families had been several days behind Miller's main party, arrived, the wagon train moved on south, then west, to Tahlequah, the capitol of the Indian Territory, where they arrived on 9 July 1847.[8] Many found work. William Leyland, son of Sophia Wallace Leyland, one of Miller's wives, labored as a printer's devil at the *Tahlequah (OK) Cherokee Advocate.* During the Mormons' stay in the capitol, Miller allegedly upset the various ministers with his preaching.

On 16 December 1847, the Miller party started for Texas, $1,200 richer. Crossing the Red River near Warren and passing within four miles of Dallas, the Millerites crossed over the Brazos River. Traveling became more difficult, as the oxen and cattle wasted with a disease causing blood in the urine, which greatly weakened the animals. When the party arrived at Austin, nearly sixty percent of the animals were either dead or dying. After struggling another thirty-five miles west of the capitol, the party could go no further. Miller sent Lewis Anderson and William Leyland to Zodiac for help.[9]

Leyland's journal recalls the general gladness when they reached the farm of George W. Bird on Grape Creek. Bird, who at first mistook them for a couple of "Dutch boys," fed and sent them on to Zodiac. A relief party started back, which included Orange Lysander Wight, John F. Miller (the eldest son of Bishop Miller), and Ezra A. Chipman. Renewed with healthy livestock and provisions, the Miller party was moving again when Lyman Wight and his wife Harriet met the wagon train on the evening of 30 January 1848. The

7. Various subject name listings in Turk, "Mormons in Texas"; 1846 entries in Newell Knight journal and autobiography (1800–1847), LDS archives.
8. Miller, *Correspondence of Bishop George Miller*, 34–35.
9. William Leyland journal, in H. H. Smith, "The Lyman Wight Colony in Texas," 14–15; Miller, *Correspondence of Bishop George Miller*, 38–39.

apostle explained the common-stock principles that ruled the community of Zodiac to Miller's party. Wight insisted these principles were the same as those communal precepts of the New Testament primitive, apostolic church. The newcomers agreed to abide by the village's rules, and were accepted into the Zodiac community.

Zodiac, according to Miller, was verging on prosperity when his party arrived. The "common stock association" of about 150 people "under the control of Lyman Wight" operated a sawmill, a grist mill, a turning lathe, a blacksmith shop, and a wagon-making enterprise. Miller noted the people had "extended every kind of hospitality and aid in helping me build a cabin or cabins suitable for the convenience of my family." He believed, however, that Lyman Wight's lack of business ability contributed to the growing liability of about $2,000 to Austin businesses. Once established in the community, Miller refused to live by the common-stock order. He remembered reaching an agreement with the Wightites to "let them have the use of my wagons, and other property, and money to a small amount, amounting in all to eight hundred and sixty dollars, and putting our labor with theirs until such time as I could make it convenient to leave them and go by myself." Miller later denied agreeing to the Zodiac economic order. This is flatly contradicted by his stepson William Leyland, whose journal carries a statement that Miller earlier had promised to live by the rules of Zodiac's economy.[10]

Again unable to lead yet unwilling to follow, Miller left Zodiac in the summer of 1848.[11] Wight said that Miller and any who left with him would "go out empty." Hard feelings infected the community. Miller's stepson, William Leyland, wrote that some of those who left Zodiac were spreading "false stories." The defections destroyed marriages and split families. John Hawley's wife left him. Some of Miller's own family sided with Wight against their patriarchal head, including his eldest son, John F. Miller, son-in-law to Wight. So did every family member of Miller's plural wife, Sophia Wallace Leyland

---

10. William Leyland journal, in H. H. Smith, "The Lyman Wight Colony in Texas," 15–16; Miller, *Correspondence of Bishop George Miller*, 41–42.

11. This description of Miller's attitude began with Orson Hyde, *To The Saints Scattered Abroad—Greeting: Beloved Brethren And Friends* (photocopy of pamphlet, 1 August 1848), RLDS archives. Compare with the Orson Hyde leaflet, "To The Saints Scattered Abroad," Journal History of the Church 69:1 August 1848.

Miller. William Leyland and his three sisters moved into the Wight household, and their mother sought sanctuary in the home of Pierce Hawley, where she died that November.[12]

Feelings in Zodiac remained bitter toward Miller. William Leyland hated Miller for the poor treatment he and his mother had received since she became Miller's plural wife in Nauvoo. After her death, Wight eventually adopted William and cared for his three sisters. One of the Leylands' adopted brothers, Levi Lamoni Wight, wrote that he did not think "their was ever a meaner man to profess religion" than Miller.[13] Miller, feeling abused, counseled the Wightites about their errors, in his opinion, on adoption, lineage, and marriage. Wight had trouble being counseled by Miller. The bishop wrote in his memoirs that "Lyman would, by innuendoes, allude to the facts that I had in a friendly way advised them to abstain from. I plainly saw the handwriting on the wall, and full discovered that the war was on." A village consensus formed, and Miller was encouraged to leave.[14]

The former bishop did not thrive after moving to Austin. He hired several Germans freighters with a promise to pay them in corn, then he hired out to build a millrace in order to pay those who moved him and his family. Miller's confused writings assert Wight sent assassins to kill him as well as a wagon and some mules to help him finish the millrace. The owner of the millrace, having suffered damages because Miller could not finish the work on time, attached the wagon and mules but not the assassins. Miller next made an unsuccessful attempt to farm several miles north of Austin. In the spring of 1849, Lyman Wight sent Orange Wight and John Miller to Austin to meet with the bishop. They encouraged him to return to Zodiac, with the inducement of a farm some miles from Zodiac (probably the Grape Creek acres) on half-shares, the assistance of teams and provisions,

---

12. William Leyland journal, in H. H. Smith, "The Lyman Wight Colony in Texas," 21, 22; Hawley, "Autobiography of John Hawley," 7, 9; V. Smith, "Two Widows of the Brick Row," 209.
13. Note, however, in the Joseph Fielding journal, Spring 1847, Book 5:126, LDS archives, that Joseph Fielding, a fellow member of the Fifty with Miller and a fervent follower of Young, wrote in his diary that "he was dear to me in the office he held, he was indeed a fine man, and I hope to see him again in our midst."
14. Miller, *Correspondence of Bishop George Miller*, 41–43.

and the direction of the Grape Creek branch of the church. Miller agreed, and returned to Gillespie County in February 1849.[15]

Zodiac's prosperity, despite George Miller and his troubled life, continued throughout 1849. Terry Jordan, in *German Seed in Texas Soil*, mentions briefly the roles of freighting and the military in the economic development of Gillespie County. On land leased from John Twohig, on the west bank of Barron's Creek, about two miles southeast of Fredericksburg and two miles west of Zodiac, the first Army post was constructed. The primary purpose was to enforce treaties with the Comanche and other tribes, and it quickly became an economic windfall for the two villages. Referred to at first as "the Camp near Fredericksburg," then Camp Houston, it was renamed on 10 March 1849 in honor of Major Martin Scott, a battle casualty of the Mexican War. The compliment of troops during the next five years fluctuated from a few squads to two companies. The Census of 1850 enumerated Company K, 8th Infantry, at the post. A military inspection in August 1853 revealed that the fort had twenty-one buildings, including an officer quarters, enlisted barracks, structures for munitions and ordinance supplies, livestock, maintenance, the quartermaster, and medical facilities. The War Department ordered the closure of the fort on 29 December 1853.[16]

Despite the growing commerce of the frontier village, George Miller soon became unhappy again, and started investigating the claims of James Strang to Mormon leadership. Writing to Strang in Michigan on 12 June 1849, Miller informed the Great Lake prophet of his history. He included the Wisconsin lumber company and its mission to Texas, his priesthood callings in the church, and how the murder of Joseph Smith changed matters. Miller concluded that, after arguing with Brigham Young, he had arrived in Texas in search of his son, and there he still resided, "an isolated, frail being."

---

15. William Leyland journal, in H. H. Smith, "The Lyman Wight Colony in Texas," 19, 22; L. L. Wight, *Reminiscences*, 17.
16. Terry G. Jordan, *German Seed in Texas Soil: Immigrant Farmers in Nineteenth-Century Texas* (Austin: University of Texas, 1966), 170, 171; population schedule, census of 1850, Fort Martin Scott, Gillespie County; Joseph H. Labadie, *Archaeological Investigations at Fort Martin Scott (41 GL 52) in Gillespie County, Texas*, Archaeological Survey Report No. 169 (San Antonio: Center for Archaeological Research, University of Texas at San Antonio, 1987), 6–9.

Along with his complaints to Strang, Miller was once again sowing unrest among the Wightites. Richard Hewitt, who had traveled to Texas with Miller, apparently had been receiving instruction from Miller on polygamy. Miller, a polygamist himself and still angry about Wight's interference with his plural family, attacked not the principle itself but rather how Wight and other leaders, such as Brigham Young, were mismanaging it. Miller had told Hewitt that polygamous "whoring would send them all to hell," again indicating his ability to hold a grudge while hypocritically complaining about others' similar marriage practices. Hewitt, confused about the practice, penciled an addendum on Miller's letter inquiring about Strang's mind on the matter. Strang may have indicated some hope to Miller that he could continue his marriage practices, for he took his own first plural wife on 13 July 1849, less than a month after Miller wrote to him. Strang's answer apparently pleased Miller, for he, according to RLDS historian Heman Hale Smith, "went to Strang, on Beaver Island, Lake Michigan." Hewitt, however, did not follow Miller into the Strangite camp.[17]

Strang published Miller's letter of June 1849, but not the Hewitt addendum, in his newspaper, and he wrote that October to invite Miller and his family to Michigan. Miller would later write that prophetic visions from Joseph Smith Jr. confirmed his correspondence with Strang. Having saved about $500, and obtaining animals and wagons, Miller prepared to leave. Never doubting his own anointings

17. Miller, *Correspondence of Bishop George Miller*, 45; George Miller to James J. Strang, 12 June 1849, with addendum by Richard Hewitt, quoted in H. H. Smith, "George Miller," 230, 231, 232. See also John Quist, "Polygamy Among James Strang and His Followers," *John Whitmer Historical Association Journal* 9 (1989): 34. The Quist article, interesting and informative concerning Strangite polygamy, has a couple of flaws and should be handled accordingly. Quist attributes Hewitt's remark on "whoring" to Miller, when it is Hewitt who is quoting Miller; the quote was directed to all Mormon congregations that practiced polygamy rather than just Wight's group. Sarah Wallace Leyland Miller did not leave with her husband in October 1849, not because she refused to do so, but because she had no choice. She died the previous year. See also photocopies of pen-written extracts of the *Voree (WI) Record*, 1, 2 "1 and 2", the Strangite church official record in the hand of Wingfield Watson, president and high priest of the Strangite church (a photocopy of a hand-copied set of notes by Van Dyke Jr., 1909), LDS archives.

and callings, Wight, according to H. H. Smith, encouraged Miller's departure from Zodiac. He even assisted Jarvis G. Miner and his "large family of children who had eaten much more than they had earned" to go with Miller. Miller recalled that Wight told him that Miner and his brood had cost him and the village hundreds of dollars, "and he could not, consistent with the rights of the company, give him anything; . . . but if I would haul him away, that he would add a yoke or two of oxen to my outfit."[18]

Only a few people left Zodiac with Miller. Again, several members of his family did not support him; William Leyland and John F. Miller remained at Zodiac with Wight. Joining Strang in September 1850, Miller soon became a prominent figure in the Strangite church, assisting its reorganization the next spring and summer. He continued in polygamy, sealing others in Strangite-Mormon ceremonies for time and eternity. In August 1855, Miller promised the readership of the *Voree (WI) Northern Islander* that he would complete in the future "my narrative, as subsequent events are fraught with some of the most thrilling incidents of my life." It was another promise he failed to keep. He died the following year while preparing for a trip to California.[19]

Miller's departure did not hinder the growing affluence of the Mormons. The sawmill cooperative had been supplying most, if not all, of the lumber and shingles for construction at Fort Martin Scott. The only other regional mills at the time were the old Wightite site at Sycamore Springs, and one other mill constructed by Wight's people for a third party near Austin. Those two were located more than sixty miles from the fort over poor frontier roads. Brevet Lieutenant Colonel Thomas Staniford, post commander from December 1849 to October 1852, approved an "Estimates of Materials and Labor Requiring to Complete the Post of Fort Martin Scott" for finishing five buildings—an officer's quarters, a guard house, band quarters, a hospital, and a magazine. The estimated cost of construction totaled

18. H. H. Smith, "The Lyman Wight Colony in Texas," 20; Miller, *Correspondence of Bishop George Miller,* 44.

19. V. Smith, "Two Widows of the Brick Row," 209; Miller, *Correspondence of Bishop George Miller,* 48, 50; *Voree (WI) Record,* 1, 2 "1 and 2". For further information on Miller's journey to Michigan, see Miller, *Correspondence of Bishop George Miller,* 44–50.

$5,882.88. The Zodiac mill was the only place where the 32,234 board feet of lumber and the 65,000 shingles, estimated at $2,588.38, forty-four percent of the cost of reconstruction, could be obtained. The Mormons and Germans would have competed in providing labor, which included a master workman and twenty mechanics for two and a half months at a projected labor outlay of $2,437.50, another forty percent of construction expenditures. The mill undoubtedly supplied the post's lumber needs throughout its existence. In 1853, an inspection report recorded that more than 21,000 feet of lumber were still stored at the post. The same report also noted that the "buildings . . . are of a better description than at most of the posts in Texas."[20]

The anticipated arrival of another company of troops in 1851, coupled with the construction of the new post at Fort Mason, promised the best market ever for the agricultural produce of the area. Terry Jordan has noted that the settlers brought "corn, hay, cured meat, vegetables, and butter" to the fort "to sell for cash or to barter for sugar and coffee." The millers at Zodiac cashed in, supplying 2,000 bushels of corn at $1.10 per bushel. The importance of the post's requirements for subsistence, maintenance, and construction cannot be overestimated in evaluating the trade and industry development of antebellum Gillespie County.[21]

The California gold rush of 1849 created other opportunities in the freighting and wagon-building industries for Wightites and Germans alike. Fort Martin Scott was a starting point for many wagon trains, and Orange L. Wight remembered they earned money by outfitting immigrant outfits destined for California. The Upper Emigrant Road, initially routed to Fredericksburg from San Antonio, thus passing Zodiac to the west and permitting travelers to access Fredericksburg for supplies, had been redrawn in 1848 to accommodate the economic growth of the Wightite community. The new route moved on an axis from San Antonio to New Braunfels to Zodiac to Fredericksburg—further spurring the Mormons' freighting

20. Labadie, *Archaeological Investigations*, 7, 49–51, 53, 54.

21. *Zeitung* (Galveston, TX), 27 March 1851; L. L. Wight, *Reminiscences*, 10; Jordan, *German Seed in Texas Soil*, 170. See Thomas T. Smith, "Fort Inge and the Texas Economy," *Military History of the Southwest* 21 (Fall 1991): 135–56, for the importance of the military in the economic development of frontier Texas.

Table 6

The Products of Industry Schedule, Census of 1850, Gillespie County, Texas

Owner	*Type of Operation*	*Capital Value*	*Value of Gross Product*	*Source of Power*
Lyman Wight & Co.	Sawmill	$2,125	$4,250	Flutter-type waterwheel & saw
Joseph Goodale & Co.	Grist mill	$2,000	1,700 bushels	Waterwheel & mill stones
Fredrick Kuhney	Blacksmith	$550	$2,000	Hand power
John Schmidtzensky	Carpenter	$750	$2,000	Hand power
Nick. S. Mosel	Wheelwright	$475	$1,800	Hand power
Fred A. Winkel	Turner and cabinet maker	$300	$1,700	Hand power

Table 7

The Agriculture Production Schedule, Census of 1850, Gillespie County, Texas

Category	*Total in County*	*Wightite Number/Value (%)*
Unimproved acres	2217	1500 (67.6%)
Improved acres	8407	5100 (60.6%)
Cash value of farms	$23,570	$9,800 (41.4%)
Value of farming implements and machinery	$3,978	$495 (13.0%)
Value of livestock	$10,873	$4,176 (38.4%)
Value of animals slaughtered	$1470	$590 (40.7%)

and wagon-construction industry. The census of 1850 noted that Zodiac, besides the three millwrights and a miller, included eight carpenters, five freighters (waggoneers), and two wagon makers.[22]

Mormon communitarianism in Texas reached its zenith during the census year of 1850. The high waters that spring had washed away the dam,[23] but the Mormons rebuilt it. The suggestions by Sarah Curtis that the Germans had developed a vibrant and dominant regional economy by 1850[24] are contradicted by the census of 1850. The inhabitants of Zodiac, with less than twenty percent of the population, overwhelmingly dictated the county's industry, agriculture, and commercial life. Three schedules from the census clearly reveal that the Mormons of Zodiac were not only prosperous but the leading settlers in the Hill Country as well. Table 6, opposite, based on the Products of Industry Schedule for Gillespie County, reveals the common-stock cooperatives possessed the only mechanical means of production west of Austin, and monopolized regional lumber manufacturing and grist milling. The hand-powered activities of the craftsman at Fredericksburg certainly reflect attributes of industriousness and efficiency, but not the substantial German recovery stated by Curtis.[25]

The Social Statistics Schedule is another indicator of Mormon economic dominance in the Texas Hill Country. It includes the number of schools, teachers, and students, and per capita worth in terms of church property. Gillespie County had four schools, two of them

---

22. O. L. Wight, "Recollections," 41; H. H. Smith, "The Lyman Wight Colony in Texas," 12; Debo, *Burnet County History*, 23; L. L. Wight, *Reminiscences*, 10, 13, 18; Caleb Coker and Janet G. Humphrey, "The Texas Frontier in 1850: Dr. Ebenezer Swift and the View from Fort Martin Scott," *Southwestern Historical Quarterly* 96, no. 3 (January 1993): 394, 395; Oscar Haas, *History of New Braunfels and Comal County, Texas 1844–1846*, 1st ed. (Austin: Steck, 1968), 74; population schedule, census of 1850, Zodiac, Gillespie County.
23. L. L. Wight, *Reminiscences*, 18.
24. Curtis, "A History of Gillespie County," 28, 36–37, 42, 71–72; population schedule, census of 1850, Gillespie County. The census of 1850 enumerates only slightly more than 160 Mormons living in the community of Zodiac in September. Some families have not been enumerated, such as those of Jonas Killmer, Levi Kimball, and Joel Simonds Miles; they may have been operating the church's cooperative farm on Grape Creek after George Miller departed for Michigan.
25. Products of industry schedule, census of 1850, Gillespie County.

at the "Latter Day Saints Community." The Wightites employed two of the county's six teachers, and had forty of the 137 pupils. Church property was enumerated as follows: 400 Roman Catholics at $1.25 per capita; 800 Protestant Germans at $0.63 per capita; 150 Methodist Episcopal at $0.67 per capita; and 150 Latter Day Saints at an overwhelming $10.00 per capita worth of church property. The large difference in the proportion of Mormon religious property wealth can be partially accounted for in that much of the Wightite wealth was invested in the large, two-story building at Zodiac. This functioned as a multipurpose center—school, storehouse, church, and temple.[26]

The Agriculture Production Schedule for Gillespie County notes the dominance of the Mormon common-stock companies in farming and livestock. Of the forty-one farms in Gillespie County, Lyman Wight & Co. owned three. Table 7 (page 100) reveals the totals, values, and percentages of the acres, machinery, and animals possessed by the religionists compared to their neighbors. These farms contained more than sixty percent of the improved as well as the unimproved acres in the county. They had almost forty percent of the value of the livestock and more than forty percent of the cash value invested in the farms and the animals slaughtered for food. Only in farming machinery and equipment did the cooperatives dip slightly below the county's percentile average per capita. Additionally, the cooperatives owned almost a fourth of the horses, asses, and mules in the county; more than thirty percent of the swine raised and the Indian corn grown; more than forty percent of the milch cows, working oxen, and other cattle; and more than seventy percent of the sheep, wool production, and bushels of barley. Lyman Wight's folks grew all of the wheat and produced all of the honey and beeswax in the county. Their farms, however, failed to produce any of the county's harvest of 169 bushels of peas and beans, 20 pounds of tobacco, and 260 pounds of cheese. The Mormons did grow 20 of the 111 tons of hay.[27]

Not all observers, however, were impressed with either the Mormons or the Germans. Ebenezer Swift, the fort's assistant surgeon who hailed from Massachusetts, recorded that:

---

26. Social statistics schedule, census of 1850, Gillespie County.
27. Agricultural production schedule, census of 1850, Gillespie County

> About two miles from us on opposite sides are the towns of Fredericksburg and Zodiac. The former contains 1000 the latter 200 inhabitants. . . . The former is Dutch; the latter Mormon; the former the more honest; the other the more thrifty, both poor, very poor. They enjoy none of the luxuries of life save filth and indolence, and have but few of what are called necessaries. They furnish the garrison partially with butter, eggs, and vegetables and get drunk with they [*sic*] soldiers. They chiefly belong to the lowest grade of society and compose the last link of humanity.

Swift's own living and working conditions may have contributed to his feelings about Gillespie County. He lived, according to Coker and Humphrey, "in a tent without a flap," leaving him to the mercy of the elements, and found his operating ward situated under "a tarpaulin-covered log building without proper floors or windows."[28]

John Bartlett's first-hand observations contradict Swift's opinion. Success attended the community that summer, despite another large storm in July that washed out the mill again, flooded the community, and immersed some of the crops. The colonists repaired the mill quickly. Almost 5,000 bushels of corn were ground in 1850, at a gross value of $4,500. The net profit that summer alone came to $600, a goodly sum for frontier Texas at that time. John Bartlett, writing a travelogue on the new Southwest, visited Lyman Wight & Co. in November. He and his companions discovered the colony, "which glories in the name of Zodiac," to be "under the especial care of Elder Wight, as designated by the faithful, though among the more worldly sinners he bore the appellation of 'Colonel.'" The "signs of prosperity," Bartlett thought, were "an example of industry and thrift which" other Texans "might advantageously imitate." Zodiac had "well built houses, perfect fences, and tidy door-yards, [and] gave the place a home-like air, such as we had not before seen in Texas." Bartlett and friends took dinner with Wight and considered the fee of three dollars for dinner and corn for a dozen horses "a modest demand," which, in Bartlett's opinion, placed the prices "between Victoria and Indianola" in poor comparison. He may have been aware that Wight exaggerated when stating that "he was the

28. Coker and Humphrey, "The Texas Frontier in 1850," 395, 401.

first settler in the valley of the Piedernales [*sic*], and for many miles around." Colonel Wight, as always, remained concerned with economic matters. He told Bartlett that "his crop of corn this year would amount to seven thousand bushels, for which he expected to realize one dollar and twenty-five cents per bushel." Lyman Wight & Co. further prospered when Bartlett rented a team and wagon, so that he and his friends could transport the needed corn to Fredericksburg for his horses.[29]

Lyman Wight and his frontier Mormons, by the end of 1850, had created an oasis of prosperity in two and a half years on the western edge of the Texas borderlands. Despite their aloofness, their industriousness helped them become the leading millers and commercial agents of the region. In their community was erected the multipurpose, water-powered mill that, along with the cooperative farms, anchored their prosperity. They served the needs of the locals, the military, and those plying the western immigrant trail. Commentators as different as George Miller and John Bartlett believed that the community was on the verge of being very successful. The members of Zodiac had work, and their children had school. The Wightites survived on the frontier, and they were beginning to prosper.

---

29. Texas Historical Records Survey, *Inventory of the County Archives, No. 86, Gillespie County (Fredricksburg)* (San Antonio: Texas Historical Records Survey, 1941); Jackson, *Mills of Yesteryear,* 44; John Russell Bartlett, *Personal Narrative of Exploration and Incidents in Texas, New Mexico, California, Sonora, and Chihuahua* (Chicago: Rio Grande Press, 1965; reprint of 1854 edition), 58, 59.

Courtesy of Community of Christ Archives, Independence, Missouri

Lyman and Harriett Wight

Courtesy of Lauren A. Langdon

Ezra Alpheus Chipman

Courtesy of Lauren A. Langdon

William Curtis

Courtesy of Community of Christ Archives, Independence, Missouri

Family of George Hay and Minear Hay: *back row, standing, left to right,* Virginia Hay Curry; John Curry holding their child; Mary Hay; John Hay; husband of Georgiana Hay; Georgiana Hay; wife of Willie Hay; *front row, seated, left to right,* George Hay; Virginia Minear Hay; Ora and Ola, twin daughters; Willie Hay standing between them; Lydia Paklehymer Minear Curtis; Willie Hay

Courtesy of Community of Christ Archives, Independence, Missouri

Orange L. Wight Family

Courtesy of Community of Christ Archives, Independence, Missouri

Mill on Hamilton Creek

Courtesy of Robert Hawley

John and Sylvia Hawley (1899) 50th anniversary photo

6

Cutting the Wild Ram from the Flock

He had his bark afloat already rigged with the rudder fixed, and he meant to run it into heaven and would if [the Twelve] did not run their big Steam Boat in his way.

—Lyman Wight

While Zodiac grew in prominence, and Colonel Wight in stature, among the Texans, Brigham Young forged a consensus among the leadership to reorganize the First Presidency, with himself as Joseph Smith Jr.'s successor. This process placed the Wightite flock beyond the fold of Utah Mormonism. Elder Orson Hyde,[1] on 7 October 1860, remembered that it was during February 1848 that "the Twelve" gathered and "the voice of God" proclaimed that Young should lead His church. Anecdotally, the apostle said many people "came running together where we were, and asked us what was the matter. They said that their houses shook, and the ground trembled, and they did not know but that there was

1. Orson Hyde, a longtime LDS apostle, was born in Oxford, New Haven County, Connecticut, the son of Nathan Hyde and Sally Thorpe. Baptized in September 1831 by Sidney Rigdon, he was later ordained an LDS apostle in 1835. Hyde attacked Rigdon later that year, was temporarily disfellowshipped, and, upon repentance, reinstated to the Twelve. Hyde, along with apostles George A. Smith and Ezra Taft Benson, presided at Winter Quarters from 1847 to 1850. Hyde edited the *Frontier Guardian* at nearby Kanesville, Iowa. See Jenson, *LDS Biographical Encyclopedia*, 1:80, and Lyndon W. Cook, *The Revelations of the Prophet Joseph Smith: A Historical and Biographical Commentary of the Doctrine and Covenants*, (Salt Lake City: Deseret Book, 1985), 109.

an earthquake. We told them that there was nothing the matter—not to be alarmed; the Lord was only whispering to us a little, and that he was probably not very far off."[2] Young described the incident as a "power [that] came upon us, a shock that alarmed the neighborhood. . . . Bro. Pratt had the spirit of God like the rest of us all . . . & believed" the divine will for Young to lead the LDS Church.[3]

The underlying theme of Hyde's address and Young's remarks, along with the stressing of God's approval given in voice and thunder, suggests to the believer the unity and subordination of the Twelve to divine will. Neither Hyde nor Young, however, informed their audiences that the decision-making process in achieving apostolic consensus took several months. During his return from the Great Salt Lake Valley, Young believed "the tappings of the Spirit" led him to think the "Church ought to be now organized." He approached his brother, Joseph Young, a presiding president of the Seventy, as well as Wilford Woodruff, a member of the Twelve, about the matter. Joseph Young, startled but receptive, wrote later that his brother "has suggested a new thought to me that the Church has the authority and can make a Presidency." Apostle Woodruff believed that a revelation would be necessary for the Twelve to organize a new First Presidency.[4]

Young could count on Willard Richards, his first cousin; Heber C. Kimball and Amasa M. Lyman, relatives by polygamous relations; and Ezra Taft Benson, the newest apostle and dependent on Young for his promotion. This weakened the core group of five apostles who could have resisted the move: George A. Smith, Wilford Woodruff, John Taylor, Parley P. Pratt, and Orson Pratt. With John Taylor and Parley P. Pratt in charge in Salt Lake Valley, Young set out to win over Smith, Woodruff, and Orson Pratt to the idea that the time for a new First Presidency had arrived. Richard Bennett has succinctly recorded

---

2. Orson Hyde, in B. Young, *Journal of Discourses*, 8:234.
3. Minutes of meetings, 4 April 1860, LDS archives.
4. Leonard J. Arrington and Ronald K. Esplin, *The Role of the Council of the Twelve During Brigham Young's Presidency of the Church of Jesus Christ of Latter-Day Saints*, Task Papers in LDS History No. 31 (Salt Lake City: Historical Department, Church of Jesus Christ of Latter-Day Saints, 1979); Wilford Woodruff diary, 12 October 1847, LDS archives; minutes of a meeting of the Twelve and Seventy, 30 November 1847, LDS archives.

the development of consensus. Wilford Woodruff's diary entries from 15 November to 5 December 1847 have revealed that more than two weeks and several meeting were required to forge an apostolic agreement. Orson Pratt believed that a quorum of the Twelve (at least seven apostles) would be needed. Willard Richards, Young's cousin, tellingly answered that Mormonism was led by a 'theo-democracy,' or rather, that God's will, not popular majority rule, directed the church. Young worked on Pratt. He reminded him that Joseph Smith Jr. and Oliver Cowdery first had become apostles, then Smith became church president as the senior apostle. With Smith dead and Cowdery in apostasy, then he, Young, the senior apostle, should become President. Pratt bowed before the reasoning of Young.[5]

After five hours of fervent discussion on 5 December 1847, the new First Presidency was unanimously approved by the apostles assembled—Young as president of the church, with Kimball and Richards as his counselors. On 27 December 1847, Orson Pratt presented the motion, without prior notice, to the church membership. Quinn writes in *The Mormon Hierarchy* that the leadership ignored the "promise the apostles made in September 1844: 'when any alteration in the presidency shall be required, seasonable notice will be given.'" He also points out that the church members, driven from Nauvoo and creating stable communities at Winter Quarters and Salt Lake City, had more important concerns than unfulfilled promises or internal conflicts. A new First Presidency undoubtedly benefited both individual members and the church body. First, a Young presidency established continuity to Joseph Smith, dead more than three years. Two, an organized First Presidency, autonomous and supreme to the Twelve, legitimized Young's position as leader of the principal sect of Mormons. Third, President Young governed as the singular head of the LDS church and its membership. And, fourth, during this tumultuous era in Mormon history, the majority of believers again had one prophet, a leader in whom they believed, to guide their future in the wild unknowns of the American West.[6]

---

5. Bennett, *Mormons at The Missouri*, 210; Wilford Woodruff diary, 15 November 1847, 16 November 1847, 30 November 1847, and 5 December 1847.
6. Quinn, *The Mormon Hierarchy*, 201, 247–50; Wilford Woodruff diary, 5 December 1847.

In the meantime, George Miller further inflamed the fires at Zodiac against Brigham Young in early 1848. Already antagonistic toward the apostolic presidency generally and Brigham Young particularly, Miller urged Wight to write and publish a pamphlet titled *An Address*, attacking the authority of Young and the Twelve to order him to Salt Lake City. Wight argued for his independence from the Twelve, stating that only Joseph Smith Jr. or the president of the Fifty, John Smith, had religious power over him. Wight believed he had as much right to order the other eleven of his brethren to Texas as they did to call him to the Rocky Mountains. His mission from Joseph Smith, "who holds the keys of the Kingdom of the Almighty God," superseded any instructions from the Twelve or the Fifty. Wight directly criticized Young and his apostolic supporters for wanting "to outstrip their predecessors," and of being "consummately ignorant of all things pertaining to Time and Eternity."

Wight believed the Twelve had not the power to replace him with a "long eared Jack Ass to fill a place which has never been vacated." He then gifted the Twelve with "long ears and slanderous tongues," once again asserting neither the Twelve nor the Fifty could remove him from his position. Wight concluded by condemning the Salt Lake leadership for oppressing "the poor, and the hireling in his wages." The principle of tithing, in Wight's opinion, permitted the rich to "increase in opulence by . . . wringing from the hands of the peasant his hard earnings." Wight argued that Zodiac's common-stock order, not Salt Lake's tithing, was the proper road to salvation. He concluded firmly that economic communalism "was followed in the days of the Nephites, and in the days of Peter and John; and also in the days of Lyman, who feels himself abundantly able, through the grace of God," and "that no other process of action will save men on the earth."[7]

Probably because of Orson Hyde's anger at *An Address*,[8] Peter Haws and Lucien Woodworth set out, at the apostle's command,

7. L. Wight, *An Address*, 16, 18–21, 23, 26. John Hawley, forty years later, noted that he had been "sent out empty" from the Wightite community in 1853.

8. Bennett, *Mormons at The Missouri*, 210, noted that Orson Hyde, "as President of the Church east of the Rocky Mountains" under the direction of Young and the remainder of the Twelve, presided over Winter Quarters and Council Bluffs at this time and for some years to come.

to Winter Quarters in the fall of 1848 to talk to their old friend and former companion. They had shared much history with Wight: membership in the Fifty, the experiences of the Wisconsin mills, the early days of organizing the Texas mission. The fact that they were sent indicated the Iowa church leaders desired to bargain with Wight with some sensitivity. Haws and Woodworth arrived in Zodiac after August 1848, because of their comments that Bishop Miller had left the community for good. They had little success. George A. Smith, on 31 October 1848, wrote to Parley P. Pratt that the messengers had little luck with the recalcitrant Wight, castigating him for being "drunk all the time they had been there."[9]

Orson Hyde, more than a year later, as editor of the *Kanesville (IA) Frontier Guardian,* opined that the Wight colony was doomed to failure because "poor Lyman can't keep sober long enough to get on 'the perfect right track.'" Haws and Woodworth were supposedly "disgusted with Lyman's drunkenness and corruption." His followers were spending nearly $15.00 weekly for liquor of the "choicest quality, costing about a dollar and a half a bottle," to support Wight's drinking. The charges are not substantiated by contemporary sources from Zodiac. One embedded reason for Hyde's ire—patrilineal versus apostolic authority—did surface toward the end of the column, when Pratt fumed that William Smith and Lyman Wight had been exchanging letters.[10]

The publication of *An Address* ended Young's four-year policy of reconciliation toward Wight. The pamphlet resulted in his removal

---

9. George A. Smith to Orson Pratt, Journal History of the Church, 71:20 October 1848, 3; George Albert Smith to Parley P. Pratt, postscript dated 31 October 1848 to letter dated 20 October 1848, *Latter-Day Saints' Millennial Star,* 1 January 1849, 14.

10. "Lyman Wight," *Frontier Guardian* (Kanesville, IA), 14 November 1849, 2. Quinn, *The Mormon Hierarchy*, 417n71. Historians such as Quinn who follow the dating based on Heman Hale Smith's "The Lyman Wight Colony in Texas" err in dating the visit of Haws and Woodworth. William Leyland's journal remarks only that "two men from Brigham Young's head quarters in Council Bluffs arrived in Zodiac" on 31 December 1848. Actually, the visit of Haws and Woodworth took place in the late summer or early August of 1848, as indicated by George A. Smith's letter. Preston Thomas and William Martindale were the two unidentified messengers referred to by William Leyland. Smith's claim for Wight's drunkenness could only have come from Haws and Woodworth, for Thomas was surprised at Wight's sobriety during his visit.

from the Twelve and loss of church membership. His opponents among the Twelve finally had the opportunity to drive him from the fold. Not only was he in communication with avowed enemies (such as William Smith), Wightite and Strangite missionaries were moving among the Mormons along the Missouri River and south. Wight's missionaries in the Winter Quarters area argued that the Twelve could not discipline him, because Joseph Smith Jr. had sanctioned the mission to Texas. The Iowa leaders shuddered at the thought of any Mormons leaving with "Gone To Texas" written in charcoal on the doors of their huts. George A. Smith and Ezra Taft Benson described Wightism to Brigham Young as "the Texas Epidemic."[11]

Orson Hyde, as presiding authority at Council Bluffs, published an answer to Wightite defiance in *To The Saints Scattered Abroad*. George Miller was the inspiration, not the Lord, wrote Hyde, for Wight's writing. *An Address* could not be "received with respect and cordiality" by Mormons. Wight, rather, should have written privately to the Twelve, and he should not, thundered Pratt, have referred to the other apostles as long-eared jackasses. Miller came in for further castigation, as Hyde rebuked Miller for leaving the church body rather than submitting to his ecclesiastical masters. Hyde next attacked Wight's authority and his common-stock economy, letting all Mormons know that he had the same "power and authority that Bro. Wight" had, and warned Wight that he "is not yet so high that the voice of the Council [of the Twelve] cannot reach him and bring him down, and even put another in his place if they deem it necessary." The heart's desire of Lyman Wight, Hyde tellingly hit, was that he wanted a work exclusive of the Twelve, and Hyde predicted Wight's single-mindedness would lead to his downfall. Joseph Smith's mission to Lyman Wight, instead of the glorious purpose for which Wight always lauded it, instead was to reveal Wight's fallibility, comparing him to King Saul, a curse on Israel. Hyde argued: "It is said not to be the nature of 'the wild ram of the mountains' to herd in the domestic fold, and if it does not yet appear that Joseph Smith gave to Lyman Wight his great mission with a similar motive to that with which the Lord gave a soul [meaning king] to Israel, I will confess my

11. George A. Smith to Brigham Young, 7 October 1846, Brigham Young Papers; Bennett, *Mormons at the Missouri*, 226.

mistake." Speaking for his fellow Twelve, Hyde believed that they were "not at war with Bro. Wight's mission, but," instead, "his boasting and defying spirit." He concluded with the ringing affirmation that all authority was invested in the First Presidency and the Twelve, who would inform the members of any authorized changes in church policy pertaining to immigration and gathering.[12]

John E. Page, a former LDS apostle and at that time a prominent member of James Strang's church at Beaver Island, Michigan, found Wight's *An Address* interesting and amusing. Having shared apostolic and evangelical duties at one time or another with most of the Twelve, including Young, Wight, and Hyde, Page knew how Wight's epistle would affect certain apostolic egos. Page denigrated "the idea that is ignorantly held out by" Wight and others "that Joseph, the prophet's son, will yet come up and take his father's original place in the church, as the prophet to the church." Page noted, however, that if he did not already believe that Strang was Joseph Smith Jr.'s successor, he would join Wight's Texas common-stock colony rather than Young's on Utah's salt flats, because "I know that Lyman is neither proud nor lazy, and is content to enjoy an even slice with his friends." Page believed Wight superior to Young, and would "choose Lyman for my captain and leader, for Lyman 'as the saying is' has a pluck as big as an ox, and is willing to live, fare and die on an equal footing with his friends." If "the destiny of our country," concluded Page, was "wielded by such men as Lyman Wight, these United States might become an earthly paradise, instead, as it is now, a region of the most accursed oppression."[13]

Page's letter on "Lymanism" answered not only *An Address*, but also an earlier letter from Orange Lysander Wight to President Strang of 22 August 1848. Writing from Mount Sterling, Illinois, the younger Wight, doing his father's work among the Mormons of the Mississippi and Missouri rivers, had traveled to Illinois by way of New Orleans. He visited various branches of the church, praising Zodiac as a gathering place. The younger Wight informed Strang that

---

12. Hyde, *To The Saints Scattered Abroad.* Compare with the Orson Hyde leaflet, "To The Saints Scattered Abroad," Journal History of the Church 69:1 August 1848.
13. *Gospel Herald* (Voree, WI), 31 August 1848, 106, 107.

he would be leading a group to Texas the following year. Revealing an ironic faculty with words, he described that some were leaning towards Strangism, some toward Wightism, and others "to the salt land spoken of in Jeremiah xvil. 5, 6," an obvious innuendo at Utah Mormonism, an echo of which Page repeated in his own article. The younger Wight preached the doctrine of his father, that is, succession of the church should pass to Joseph Smith Jr.'s posterity, and the common-stock principle should be the church's economic order.[14]

Strang had been interested in Lyman Wight as early as Mormon Coulee. He questioned Wight's religious authority and mission to Texas in his newspaper. He did not disagree with the common-stock economy, but devoted several tightly knit pages of denial that the Smith sons had any right to succeed their father. He, Strang, had been set apart by Joseph Smith Jr. as his successor for Mormonism. Strang's *Voree (WI) Gospel Herald* printed another piece on 9 November 1848 that the Texas Mormons, subservient to Wight's pretended prophecy, were building a "New Jerusalem" on the Pedernales, a land more suitable for grain cultivation and mining adventures.[15]

John Hawley and Joel Simonds Miles had some success along the Missouri River and in Michigan. A few converted and were brought to Zodiac. The fruits of their labor proved tainted, however, for apostasy struck Zodiac, and Hawley's converts "all left with the breakup crowd" of 1849.[16] Lyman Wight continued to send out more missionaries to bring converts to the New Jerusalem on the Pedernales. Miles and Hawley, after their return to the Texas Hill Country, were sent on another mission, this time to the piney woods of East Texas. This distinct regional entity of 22,000,000 acres, ninety percent of it covered by a forest the size of Indiana, had little in community and industrial development but much in isolation and religious parochialism. The people, insular by custom and suspicious by nature, were a mixture of small plantation owners, millers, river men, stockmen,

---

14. Orange L. Wight to Pres. Strang, 22 August 1848, *Gospel Herald*, 21 September 1848, 127.
15. James J. Strang to Moses Smith, Journal History of the Church, 43:25 October 1844; James J. Strang to Dear Brother, 13 September 1848, *Gospel Herald*, 21 September 1848, 127–30; *Gospel Herald*, 9 November 1848, 496.
16. Letter to President Brigham Young, Journal History of the Church, 71:8 October 1848, 2; Hawley, "Autobiography of John Hawley," 7.

trappers, and fishermen.[17] Hawley and Miles wandered into this domain of evangelical, frontier Protestantism, preaching Mormonism's gospel of restoration. They converted a man named Henry Baye, who had been hiding in the canebrake from his pursuers. Detected by his enemies, Baye and Miles escaped, while the pursuers captured Hawley. In apparent need of entertainment, the captors ordered Hawley to preach. He did so, was released, and ordered to leave the country. Hawley believed his Mormonism, not his preaching prowess, was the reason the East Texans cut off his mission. The two Wightites reunited, however, and continued to preach for a while longer before returning to Zodiac.

A spirit of disagreement came between the two missionaries. A female convert named Garberry had been bothered by evil spirits. The two young missionaries decided on a contest of prophecy and prayer to decide the issue. Each man had a vision. Hawley saw "a large tree just 60 feet high and on one side there was a large snake covering half the tree and the other side was covered with small ones. When I saw this I turned to Joel and he turned to me at the same time. I told him what I saw and he said just as he turned from me he saw a bedstead sitting before him with a good bed upon it but no one on it." Neither quite knew what to make of their respective visions, so, deciding it was time to return to the Hill Country, they journeyed home to Zodiac.[18]

Texans were fair game for Mormon missionaries of all stripes. Utahns William Martindale and Homer Duncan faced some difficulties. Martindale, while "hunting and fishing for Israel" in Panola County in 1854 and 1855, was "deluged in protracted camp and revival meetings" railing against the Mormons. He wrote, "it seemed as if the devil well knew and had appraised his emissaries of the approach of the Elders and had forted itself in with the usual material popularity and revivals." In 1856, Duncan wrote that some Texans wanted to

17. See Ruth Alice Allen, *East Texas Lumber Workers: An Economic and Social Picture, 1870–1950* (Austin: University of Texas Press, 1961); Robert S. Maxwell and Robert D. Baker, *Sawdust Empire: The Texas Lumber Industry, 1830–1940* (College Station: Texas A&M University Press, 1983); and Thad Sitton, *Backwoodsmen: Stockmen and Hunters Along a Big Thicket River Valley* (Norman: University of Oklahoma Press, 1995).
18. Hawley, "Autobiography of John Hawley," 8, 9.

mob the missionaries because of polygamy. He believed the outcry hypocritical, for the ministers derided polygamy "while every negro quarter is filled with blue-eyed children." The missionaries had to hotfoot it for the county borders. Martindale was urging his few converts to flee East Texas, even if it was only to Kansas. He feared that "it seems to me this country is ripe for destruction, and it certainly will take fire to purify it from the corruption that is upon it."[19]

In 1848, Wight had other difficulties besides missionary work. Hyde's rebuttal to Wight's *An Address* reached Zodiac, and Wight knew his days as an LDS leader were over. A penultimate note concerning Wight's membership was sounded during the Pottawatamie (Iowa) High Council conference that October. Apostle George A. Smith read certain portions of Wight's pamphlet to local high priests and general authorities, concluding it was "a direct insult to this quorum of the twelve." Robert Campbell read Orson Hyde's rebuttal to Wight's work. Wight's name was submitted to the conference as an apostle, and was opposed by high councilors William Snow and Henry W. Miller, and apostles George A. Smith and Ezra Taft Benson.

George A. Smith believed Wight was not following Joseph Smith's directions about the Texas mission and the role of the Fifty. George Smith said he loved Wight, describing him as "an old Lyon" in defense of Mormonism, but he believed Wight was wrongly relying on George Miller, and should not appeal to the Fifty. The Fifty, Smith believed, was responsible for the temporal affairs of the church, not its spiritual needs. Two other general authorities were harsher than Smith. President of the Seventy Joseph Young equated Wight's actions with those of Sydney Rigdon, William Smith, and James J. Strang, all pretenders to LDS leadership. Apostle Ezra Taft Benson argued that the church had carried Wight long enough, and now "it is our business to bring him to a crisis." The conference concluded that Wight was "directly at variance with the spirit and design of the mission given him by Joseph Smith." *An Address* threatened the

---

19. William Martindale to Geo. A. Smith, 10 September 1856, LDS archives; Homer Duncan, *Deseret News* (Salt Lake City), 2 April 1856, quoted in Journal History of the Church, 119:2 April 1856, 4. Not all missionary labors were hazardous. For instance, Elder John Ostler wrote in May 1856 (Journal History of the Church, 120:12 May 1856) that he and Elders Duncan and Snedaker met by accident near "Waxahatchie, held a meeting and baptized two persons."

harmony and unity of the church, and it attacked the "dignity and honor of the priesthood." The conference stopped only at refusing to sustain Wight as an apostle; it took no action against his membership. The conference, however, did sanction George Miller, not only refusing to sustain him as bishop over the church, but also disfellowshipping him because of his "spirit of apostasy and dissension."[20]

George A. Smith and Ezra Taft Benson wrote to Brigham Young the same day the council censured Wight in the Iowa conference. They knew Young had borne "so long with him," and might find their action hasty. They cited the pamphlet, Wight's missionaries working among the LDS faithful in the Mississippi Valley, and his attack on their own apostolic authority. The Iowa leadership "did not feel contented to let the innocent be deceived." Smith and Benson concluded by asking Young for both advice and his ratification of their action. They dispatched a second letter the next day, further justifying their actions, along with a copy of Wight's pamphlet. Hyde lampooned Wight by suggesting wryly that he commanded "all people, saints and sinners, Democrats and Barnburners, tall and short, those that live in big houses or small ones . . . and every one else, to come to his standard." Ironically, the general conference held that same day at Salt Lake Valley had sustained Wight as a member of the Twelve.[21]

---

20. Pottawatamie High Council conference minutes 1848–51, 7 and 8 October 1848, LDS archives. The Pottawatamie conference minutes, recorded in Journal History of the Church, 71:7 October 1848, 2, 3, 5, are slightly different than the original minutes. Smith's "old Lyon" comment, for example, reads as "an old lion in a mire," and Joseph Young is reported to have stated that many of Wight's followers absconded from Nauvoo with items that did not belong to them.

21. George A. Smith and Ezra T. Benson to Brigham Young, Journal History of the Church 71:7 October 1848, 6; letter to President Brigham Young and Council, Journal History of the Church 71:8 October 1848, 2; *History of the Church,* 7:528. The general conference minutes at Salt Lake City, as recorded in the Journal History of the Church, noted that Heber C. Kimball successfully offered Lyman Wight's name to the conference as a member of the Twelve, stating that Wight and his followers were doing well with their mills among the Comanche. Two pages later, the record tersely notes that fellowship had been withdrawn from George Miller and Lyman Wight, although the Pottawatamie High Council conference minutes are clear that fellowship had been withdrawn only from George Miller.

Brigham Young, having not seen *An Address* and possibly still unaware of the action at Winter Quarters, had decided to resolve issues with Wight. On 9 November 1848, he directed Preston Thomas to take William Martindale with him on a mission to Texas, one of their objectives being "to go and hunt up Lyman Wight. We want to know what he is doing, for it is all we can to get the people to hold on to him by faith and prayer. . . . Learn his purposes and intentions, and if he does not come up right soon," Young continued, "the spirit of the Lord will say, 'Clip the thread and he will go down at once.'"[22]

Thomas, Martindale, and James McGaw, during their trip to Texas by way of St. Louis, met with Lucius Scovil in the early part of December. Informed that they were to interview Wight at Zodiac, Scovil told them that Haws and Woodworth "had just returned from Lyman's camp." George Miller had left Wight and taken some people with him, it was reported, indicating dissension was occurring at Zodiac. Thomas and Martindale reached Zodiac the evening of 31 December 1848, and lodged with Wight. Thomas's journal entries recorded much more than did his letter to Orson Hyde of 14 March 1849, to whom he underplayed the real bitterness Wight felt for the Twelve.

The first evening, Wight seemed reluctant to talk. Instead, Thomas and Martindale met with the High Council of Zodiac and discussed the events at Council Bluffs. Wight "was perfectly sober and free from the influence of ardent spirit, a thing we hardly expected to find from what several persons had told us," recorded Thomas. He was "in feeble health. . . . We had several interviews and much conversation with him, in all of which it was evident to us that he was alienated in feeling entirely from his quorum and the Church, pronouncing them all Apostates." Wight talked spitefully about Brigham Young. "In all our interviews with Elder Wight," continued Thomas, "he never expressed any good feelings toward any of the Church, except Elder Geo. A. Smith." Wight was unaware of Smith's letter to Parley Pratt accusing Wight of alcoholism, which would be published that week in the *Millennial Star.* [23]

22. "Preston Thomas: His Life and Travels," folder 1:32, 41.
23. Elder Lucius Scovil to Elder Pratt, Journal History of the Church, 72:11 December 1848; Hawley, "Autobiography of John Hawley," 7; "Preston Thomas: His Life and Travels," folder 1: 75, 76; George Albert Smith to Parley P. Pratt,

The following morning, Martindale and Thomas met again with Wight. The old apostle, "when hardly pressed by us concerning some passages in his pamphlet . . . would try to equivocate and put entirely a different construction upon them from the ideas the passages would naturally convey." How could the Twelve have identified themselves as the "Aspirants" or "Bigots" mentioned in the pamphlet, Wight argued ingenuously, for "he considered the Twelve of heaven and not of earth and therefore, he could not of meant them." The Wild Ram was semi-playfully butting the younger ones around. Then he grew more serious. He did not want fellowship with anyone who fellowshipped with Orson Hyde and W. W. Phelps, and he found offensive Brigham Young's remarks that he was a coward for leaving Nauvoo in 1844. More importantly, Wight believed that Young had "usurped" the presidency of the church. Later in the day a feast was served, attended by several local Germans. This must have been a break from unpleasantness, for Thomas felt the Pedernales River, flowing by the community's feast held on its banks, was "a beautiful pure clear mountain stream" because its rock foundations gave "great water power" for the mills.[24]

A community/church meeting was held that evening. Wight preached on the common-stock principles of Zodiac, with side remarks directed against Young, the Twelve, and storekeepers in general. Thomas and Martindale, when they spoke to the audience, remarked that the real issue remained Wight's unwillingness to follow the Twelve's counsel. Taking the bit in their teeth, they informed the audience that *An Address* "did not meet the mind of the church, neither the mind of the Lord." Wight had to come to Salt Lake City "and be united in feeling and hope." The unspoken threat was clear. Wight exploded, vehemently asserting that

> he was not going to take that wild goose chase away to Salt Lake City to please them, no he would see them all damned to the lowest hell before he would do it. He could not see why they did not let him alone and mind their own business and let them do so too.

---

postscript dated 31 October 1848 to letter dated 20 October 1848, *Latter-Day Saints' Millennial Star*, 1 January 1849, 14.

24. "Preston Thomas: His Life and Travels," folder 1:42–43.

> He had his bark afloat already rigged with the rudder fixed, and he meant to run it into heaven and would if [the Twelve] did not run their big Steam Boat in his way.

The following day, before their departure, Wight told Thomas and Martindale that because of his age he considered himself president of the Twelve, and that they should come to him for counsel. Wight stated in the presence of others that he thought "them all apostates."[25]

In March 1849, Thomas wrote to Orson Hyde about the visit. He did not describe the level of Wight's bile, for the point was moot. Orson Hyde appended to the Thomas-Martindale report his own summation to Young, simply repeating that Lyman Wight was disobedient, and that the Texas Ram had no use for either Hyde or Young, denying that the latter had the right to rule the Church.[26] The letters sent from Council Bluffs to Salt Lake City the previous October, describing Wight's behavior and accompanied by a copy of his pamphlet, finally moved Brigham Young to decisive action. On 3 December 1848, at Fort Douglas, John Smith, uncle of Joseph Smith Jr. and the senior member of the Fifty, announced publicly in the presence of President Young and Apostle Amasa Lyman that Wight and Miller were cut off from the Church, losing both their offices and their church memberships.[27]

These dismissals, along with the earlier excommunications of apostles John Page and William Smith as well as other lesser leaders, removed all remaining major opposition to Young's succession. Cutting off Wight and Miller also put all members of the Fifty on

---

25. Ibid., 43–45. Wight may have been basing his argument on the fact that not only was he the oldest among the active apostles, but also that he had been appointed to fill David Patten's office, who at the time of his death had been the senior apostle by age. Apostle Orson Pratt argued many years later that age among the Twelve did not equate with seniority. According to Pratt, the apostasy of Thomas Marsh, the oldest and senior member of the original Twelve, and the death of David Patten, to whose office Lyman Wight was appointed in 1841, did not give Lyman Wight the right to preside over the Twelve: "'You shall be equal, showing respect to the oldest.' They were arranged according to their ages, while all their successors were arranged, according to the date of their respective ordinations" (O. Pratt, *Journal of Discourses,* Vol. 19:5 October 1877, 119).
26. Hyde commentary to Thomas and Martindale, Journal History of the Church, 73:14 March 1849, 2.
27. Roberts, *Comprehensive History* 2:414, 416n436.

notice that they were expected to support President Young's vision. Peter Haws, still a supporter of the Fifty's prerogatives, complained at Council Bluffs in January 1849, following the Wight excommunication, that Wight held more power than the other apostles "did, ever did, or ever will. . . . Twelve men had swallowed up thirty eight," a bitter reference to the emergence of the Twelve over the Fifty. A struggle, at times bitter in tone, ensued during the next two months in the high priest quorum meetings at Council Bluffs, as apostles Orson Hyde, George A. Smith, and Ezra Taft Benson forced the rebellious elements of the Fifty to heel.[28]

By March 1849, in little more than a year, Brigham Young had emerged successfully as the powerful leader of Mormonism's largest sect. He had ended the apostolic interregnum and organized a new First Presidency. He had excommunicated apostles and others who opposed him. He had welded together a Twelve supporting his vision. His followers overwhelmed any in the Fifty who dared to challenge him. Young deferred the succession rights of Joseph Smith Jr.'s sons for the time being to the Twelve. Wight, now a minor irritant, appeared more than ready to remain outside the Utah church for the rest of his life, and, indeed, for years his followers were isolated in the wilds of the Texas frontier.

---

28. Quinn, *The Mormon Hierarchy*, 200; Pottawatamie High Council conference minutes 1848–1851, 20 January 1849, 6; George A. Smith and Ezra T. Benson to Brigham Young, Journal History of the Church, 71:7 October 1848, 6; Letter to President Brigham Young and Council, Journal History of the Church, 71:8 October 1848, 2; George A. Smith and Ezra T. Benson to Brigham Young, Heber C. Kimball, and Willard Richards, 27 March 1849, LDS archives. "An Epistle of The Twelve," as well as "First General Epistle of the First Presidency . . . ," Journal History of the Church, 73:9 March 1849, and 74:9 April 1849, respectively, mention that Lyman Wight had been disfellowshipped rather than excommunicated. See the full proceedings of the Pottawatamie High Priest quorum minutes, LDS archives, for the concerns expressed by certain high priests and the church mandates required of them during the January, February, and March 1849 meetings. For example, in Journal History of the Church, 73:20 January 1849, 1, the following is recorded: "Brothers Haws and Woodworth professed to have greater power than another [*sic*] persons in the Church and would be subject to the authority thereof. The [Pottawatamie High] council decided that they be notified that unless they met with the council at its next sitting, they would be dissatisfied." The council included apostles Hyde, Smith, and Benson, as well as Joseph Young, a brother of Brigham Young and one of the seven presidents of the Quorum of Seventies, all having been active in opposing Lyman Wight and his Texas mission.

7

Independent Mormonism in Antebellum Texas

Brigham Young would have to be a completely different man to have any kind of influence on us.

—Lyman Wight

The Wightites had found 1848 to be an eventful year. It included the coming and going of George Miller, the departure of the Zodiac apostates, the issuance of *An Address* and its rebuttal by Orson Hyde, the visit of Thomas and Martindale, and Wight's excommunication. In the midst of all this, Wight had been writing to William Smith about the post-Joseph church. In July, he informed Smith, "I have no other calling to attend to: but according to all lineal rights you are left as Patriarch of the Most High God; and Young Joseph to preside over the church." On 22 August 1848, Wight wrote Smith that he and his followers considered Smith as "Patriarch of the whole church," with "the blessing of Prophet and Seer to rest upon Joseph's eldest son if he will receive it." Leyland, Wight's scribe, noted in his journal that Wight's activities in Texas pleased the Smith family. William Smith made Wight an apostle in his church.[1]

Wight's "calling" involved a resolution of community strife in Zodiac. William Leyland noted in his journal that certain members

1. Lyman Wight to "Mother Smith," 21 August 1848, *Melchizedek and Aaronic Herald* (Covington, KY), May 1849, 4; William Leyland journal, in H. H. Smith, "The Lyman Wight Colony in Texas," 22; Lyman Wight to William Smith, 22 August 1848, *Melchizedek and Aaronic Herald* (Covington. KY), May 1849, 1; and H. C. Smith, "Lyman Wight on Succession," 1.

had left the church during the summer of 1848, and had been spreading "false stories." Leyland did not elaborate on the nature of the stories. The dissenters may have been dissatisfied with Lyman Wight's leadership, or disliked the common-stock economy that prevented the accruing of an individual or family surplus, or not approved of plural marriage. Apparently this dissent, surprisingly, had little to do with George Miller, Leyland's hated stepfather. Leyland certainly would have included that fact in his journal. Miller, after his return to Zodiac, still held considerable influence, by virtue of his previous roles in the church and his guidance of his party across the wilderness to Texas.[2]

Wight knew his refusal to go to Salt Lake City would mean excommunication. Thomas and Martindale wrote to Orson Pratt in April 1849 that though the Wightites were living in a "very reduced condition," their leader had "far from a humble heart." He remained unfazed and set about reorganizing Texas Mormonism into branches at Zodiac and at Grape Creek. He also completed the finishing of the Zodiac Temple on 17 February 1849. The two-story building of huge oak timbers measured seventy-two feet by eighteen feet. RLDS historian Heman Hale Smith incorrectly wrote that the building was a temple in name only, for primary sources clearly document the Pedernales temple was the first such active Mormon temple built west of the Mississippi River.[3]

Wight's dismissal from the Utah church did not alienate his followers. They aligned themselves formally with their leader in awaiting the longed-for succession of Joseph Smith Jr.'s posterity to the prophetic mantle of Mormonism. At a Zodiac conference held in August 1849, the Wightites solemnized their religious beliefs and future goals. In the words of William Leyland, they committed themselves to accept Joseph Smith III as church president when he presented himself as such. They also sustained "Wight and Miller in the

---

2. William Leyland journal, in H. H. Smith, "The Lyman Wight Colony in Texas," 22.
3. Orson Spencer to Orson Pratt, Journal History of the Church, 74:10 April 1849; Miller, *Correspondence of Bishop George Miller*, 44; William Leyland journal, in H. H. Smith, "The Lyman Wight Colony in Texas," 21; building description in "The Mormon Colony (Zodiac) Near Fredericksburg, Texas."

Council of Fifty; to uphold the Twelve; to sell the mills and return to Jackson County, Missouri," and to permit Miller to "have wagons and teams to carry him and others to Jackson Co. (or some other place)." The resolutions defined Wightite beliefs and concerns. The conference committed to patrilineal, not apostolic, authority as the rightful path for Mormonism, yet the roles of the Twelve and the Fifty were sustained as necessary quorums of church government. They recognized the temporary nature of the church at Zodiac, and that the eventual gathering of all Latter Day Saints would be in Jackson County, Missouri. The conference offered a way to soothe troubles between Wight and Miller, permitting the latter to not "go out empty" when he departed for Jackson County.[4]

The August conference at Zodiac committed its members to alternatives other than Utah Mormonism. William Smith and Lyman Wight continued to write. This resulted, on 3 October 1849, in the Wightite branches sustaining, without a dissenting vote, William Smith "as Prophet, Seer, revelator and translator, untill [*sic*] some one of the posterity of Joseph Smith his deceased brother shall come forward and take [one word gone, hole in paper] lace."[5] The Wightite branches turned away forever from Brigham Young.

The merger of the William Smith and Lyman Wight groups was convenient. The combined organizations offered a way to unblock the patrilineal succession of Joseph's sons. William Smith and several of his followers filed the *Petition of Smith, Sheen, et al.*, with the federal Committee of Territories on the last day of 1849. This petition reveals not only the incongruity of the liberties taken by various sides of Mormonism when describing their opponents, but also the relationships of the followers of Wight and Smith. The petition opposed Young's attempt to organize Utah as the State of Deseret. Smith et al. argued that "Salt Lake Mormonism is diametrically opposed to the pure principles of virtue, liberty, and equality," and maintained the leaders of Utah Mormonism were "enemies of our government."

---

4. Lyman Wight to William Smith, 25 July 1849, quoted in H. C. Smith, "Lyman Wight on Succession," 1; William Leyland journal in H. H. Smith, "The Lyman Wight Colony in Texas," 22; Miller, *Correspondence of Bishop George Miller*, 46–47.
5. H. C. Smith, "Lyman Wight on Succession," 3 October 1849, 1–2.

The petition further alleged hypocritically that Brigham Young's followers "teach and practice polygamy, and thereby treating with contempt the bonds of wedlock, placing themselves on a level with brute creation." For additional measure, Utah Mormonism engaged in all varieties of iniquity, including "murder, treason, adultery, fornication, robbery, counterfeiting, swindling, blasphemy, and usurpation of power." Young, the petition alleged, tried to have William Smith, who claimed to be "the true and lineal successor in the presidency" of the Church, killed, as well as taking Smith's printing press and real estate in Ohio.[6]

Some of the signers of the petition were associated with Wightism. James Goudie, Silas Caldwell, and George Bailey were enumerated at Zodiac in the census of 1850. Otis Hobart's daughter, Mary Ann, was a plural wife of Lyman Wight, and Hobart had served as the clerk of the Black River Falls branch in 1844. William Smith surely was aware the Wightites practiced polygamy; he himself had more than one wife at times. Whether Lyman Wight realized that William Smith considered himself, rather than his own nephews, the "true and lineal successor" to Joseph Smith Jr. is uncertain.

In the spring of 1850, the Texas church sent delegates to a conference held by William Smith at Covington, Kentucky. They included Otis Hobart, Stephen Zeloutus Curtis, Joseph D. Goodale, and Silas Caldwell. Otis Hobart, according to the conference minutes, had been "gathered unto the Lord," dying almost immediately before the opening meeting. He was to "be interred with his robes on him," a reference to the holy garments that he had worn as part of the endowment ceremony in the Zodiac temple. William Smith presided over the conference, which began 5 April 1850 with Joseph D. Goodale of Zodiac giving the invocation. The conference ratified

---

6. *Petition of Smith, Sheen, et al.*, signed by William Smith and Isaac Sheen and countersigned by church members at Covington, Kentucky, including James Goudie, William and Silas Caldwell, George Bailey, Otis Hobart, Samuel Heath, and Joseph C. Hobart, filed 31 December 1849 with the Committee on Territories, quoted in *Journal of History*, 7, no. 4 (October 1914): 454, 455, 457; Turk, "Mormons in Texas", 49–50; population schedule, census of 1850, Zodiac, Gillespie County; Sanford, "The Mormons of Mormon Coulee," 134. William Smith failed to note that he had been practicing polygamy since the early 1840s.

Joseph Smith Jr.'s approval of Wight's Texas mission to establish a gathering place for the church. The Texas Mormons were called on to raise funds to move the Smith family to Zodiac that fall. The Kentucky congregation decided that it, too, would immigrate to Texas, where, according to an earlier revelation given to William Smith on 20 March 1850, the members would receive "endowments and blessings" in the Texas temple. The next church conference would convene in Texas on 23 December 1850, the birth date of Joseph Smith Jr.

Several doctrinal issues other than polygamy were discussed at Covington, including the proper economic system that church members should follow. Tithing, titled the United Order of Property, was instituted as the economic pattern of the church, although the church would accept private property holders if they obeyed the church rules. Smith quoted from Sections 103 and 107 of the *Book of Commandments*, an earlier version of the *Doctrine and Covenants*. The record did not register the reactions of the Zodiac delegates about the failure to include the common-stock property ordinances of the Texas community. It is difficult to imagine that Lyman Wight would accept economic rules excluding the system he believed was instrumental in religious salvation, both on earth and in heaven.

The conference called for reform in church leadership, asking Joseph Smith III to step forward and be ordained as his father's successor. Smith III, however, would have to receive the ordination from his uncle, William Smith, who had been chosen as president of the church, with Isaac Sheen and Lyman Wight as his counselors. The three of them constituted the Quorum of the First Presidency, having the right to administer all of the affairs of the church. A Quorum of the Twelve Apostles was chosen also, including seven Wightites and five from the Covington branch. The Texans included William P. Eldridge, Andrew Ballantyne, Spencer Smith, Joseph D. Goodale, Stephen Curtis, Orange L. Wight, and Irvin Carter; from Kentucky were selected George Bailey, Nathaniel T. James, Henry Nisonger, Edwin Cadwell, and Alva Smith. Stephen Curtis and J. D. Goodale were called on missions, the former to Pennsylvania and the latter to Michigan. On the final day of the conference, Silas Caldwell was called to be a teacher. A new stake would be located at Palestine,

Illinois, probably to provide a location for those gathering to go to Texas.[7]

James J. Strang, not surprisingly, deprecated the unification between William Smith's and Lyman Wight's organizations, arguing that Smith had only twelve followers total, and that the succession to church leadership could not pass by patrilineal descent. In 1848, Strang had described Wight's position in the *Voree (WI) Gospel Herald:* "Lyman Wight seems to cherish the idea that is ignorantly held out by some others that Joseph, the Prophet's son, will yet come up and take his father's original place in the church." In July 1850, Strang notified the world as well as Wight that a Strangite conference had voted to take "the Priesthood of an apostle [meaning Wight] . . . from him and given to one that will fill the calling." The *History of the Reorganized Church of Jesus Christ of Latter Day Saints* records that most of the Smith-Wight apostles did not assume their appointments, although some members of the Covington church did immigrate to Zodiac in the summer of 1850.[8]

John Hawley, William Curtis, and Andrew Hoffman were detailed to go to the Gulf Coast and meet the first (and apparently only) group of Covingtonites at Port Lavaca. During the trip to the coast, Hawley and his comrades helped pull a whiskey trader's mule from the mud. The travelers then celebrated their effort with some of the trader's wares, which, according to Hawley, was a transgression of Wight's rule, although many in the colony used alcohol, including

7. *Melchisedek and Aaronic Herald* (Covington, KY), April 1850; Hawley, "Autobiography of John Hawley," 7–8; William Leyland journal, in H. H. Smith, "The Lyman Wight Colony in Texas," 25. Roberts, *Comprehensive History*, 2:434, was not certain if Wight approved of or affiliated with this conference and its results.

8. *Gospel Herald* (Voree, WI), 31 August 1847; *Gospel Herald*, 30 May 1850, 989; *Beaver Island (MI) Record*, 9 July 1850, 69; manuscript of Strang conference, Beaver Island, 6 July 1850, RLDS archives; William Leyland journal, in H. H. Smith, "The Lyman Wight Colony in Texas," 25; Hawley, "Autobiography of John Hawley," 7. *Reorganized History*, 3:34, states that Aaron Hook was the first counselor to William Smith, with Lyman Wight as second counselor. They served pro tem, i.e., until Joseph Smith III would step forward to assume the mantle of leadership. Compare name listings in Turk, "Mormons in Texas," with the conference minutes in the *Melchisedek and Aaronic Herald* (Covington. KY) and the population schedule of the census of 1850 at Zodiac.

Wight. Hawley believed that the arrival of a Comanche band wandering nearby was the direct result of their sinful imbibing. He and the others knew some of the natives from the various clans, but not any from this party. The spirit of prophecy came on Hawley, and he prayed for forgiveness for his behavior. The Comanches apparently forgave Hawley and his fellows as well, for they did not attack them. The Wightites completed their mission, delivering the Smith party safely to Zodiac.[9]

The Smith-Wight organization fell apart before the end of the year. The conference at Zodiac was not held. Lyman Wight, however, still supported the patrilineal succession of the Smith family. On 8 December 1850, he recorded in his journal that he had always born testimony "that Joseph Smith appointed those of his own posterity to be his Successor." His daughter Anna Wight Smith and Rebecca Jane Connyers Ballantyne, both young wives in the colony, recalled more than fifty years later the events of a Christmas feast held at Zodiac in 1850. According to Anna, Wight prophesied the day would come when Joseph Smith III would succeed to the church leadership. Wight corroborated further his testimony by telling the community of an incident at Liberty Jail, when in Wight's presence, Joseph Smith Jr. had placed his hands on his son's head and "blessed him as his successor in the prophetic office." Rebecca J. Ballantyne, in a sworn affidavit in 1908, testified that Wight had told her that he had assisted Smith Jr. in ordaining Joseph Smith III as his successor shortly after Smith and Wight were released from Liberty jail. Smith and Wight, according to her testimony, laid their hands on the head of the young boy, and Smith reportedly blessed his son to become his "successor when I depart." The only important discrepancy in the testimony of the elderly colonists is whether the blessing occurred in the jail or shortly thereafter. Joseph Smith III himself remembered that he had been ordained when his father was still in jail.[10]

The interpretation of Wight's testimony and the elderly women's recollection of the events of that Christmas feast are subject to the vagaries of age, bias, and selective perception. The ladies, each

---

9. Hawley, "Autobiography of John Hawley," 7–8.

10. *Reorganized History,* 2:789; 3:506; H. C. Smith, "Succession in the Presidency," 5, 6, 8.

more than seventy years of age, were recounting events more than a half-century old. The elderly women had been committed to the RLDS church and its principles for more than forty years. Rebecca, with her new husband Andrew Ballantyne, were among the first, if not the first, Wightites to leave Texas and move to Iowa before the Civil War, and were quick to join the Reorganized church. The RLDS historian who aided the ladies in their depositions was Heman C. Smith, a grandson of Lyman Wight and a son of Anna Wight Smith. He himself had been born in 1850 at Zodiac, and joined the RLDS church with his father's family. His father, Spencer C. Smith, had been a missionary to Texas in 1865, and was instrumental in converting a great majority of the remaining colonists to the RLDS faith.[11]

Wight's journal entries support the vigor of the evidence given by Rebecca Ballantyne and Anna Smith. Two days after Christmas, Wight wrote, "I have stood for the Smith family for twenty years, and am abundantly able to stand for them twenty years more. No man wishes more than I do to see them have their rights, and I shall be found standing for them when some who now think they are a long way ahead of me will be found somewhere else." It is clear Wight supported the Smith family's rights of patrilineal succession, rather than a continuing apostolic presidency or a reorganization of the First Presidency without Joseph Smith III at its head. He was committed explicitly to Joseph Smith III. To stand the commitment on its head, reconciliation with Brigham Young, James Strang, or William Smith was impossible.[12] Wight's commission to Texas still burned bright in his heart. In 1851, the day after Christmas, he wrote in his journal his reasons for rejecting Strang, William Smith, and Young:

> I was sent with this company, to this place, by Bro. Joseph in his lifetime. Brigham offered to revoke it on his own responsibility, and appoint me a new mission. Mr. Strang offered to let me go on, provided I would give strict adherence to his mandates. William Smith proffered to receive me as I was, provided I would receive him as

---

11. Turk, "Mormons in Texas," 20, 34; Black, *ERLDS*, 1:261, 262, 263.
12. H. C. Smith, "Lyman Wight on Succession," 8 December 1850 and 27 December 1850, 2; H. C. Smith, "Succession in the Presidency," 5–6; *Reorganized History*, 3:506.

president of the church and Joseph Wood as God's spokesman. For absolute refusal I was disfellowshipped by all three."[13]

Then he recorded what he thought should have been the proper procedure for choosing Joseph Smith Jr.'s successor:

> The fifties assembled should have called on all the authorities of the church down to the lay members from all the face of the earth, as much as was convenient and after having taken sweet counsel together, in prayer and supplication before God, acknowledged our sins and transgressions which had caused our head to be taken from our midst: and then have called on Young Joseph, and held him up before the congregation of Israel to take his father's place in the flesh.[14]

The growing numbers in, and strength of, the Utah church began to dull its worry about Wight's disaffection. The authorities in Salt Lake City continued their polemical warfare against Wight in a lighter spirit. Part of the discussion at the general conference in September 1850 had revolved around the issue of dissident and disobedient authorities. Brigham Young noted, to the laughter of the audience: "When we have an apostle abroad, who has not the power to deal with a conference, we call that man home, or send him to Texas to join Lyman Wight, and then we will put another man in his place."[15] In another conference, Young stated, with wisdom and solid insight on what the probable results would have been if the Nauvoo church had moved to an area where they would have eventually been outnumbered:

> A great many wanted to go to the Gila River; that was proposed when we first came to this valley. It was said to be a lovely country, and that men could live there almost without labor. What if we had

---

13. Lyman Wight's journal, in *Reorganized History*, 2:791 and 3:34.
14. Lyman Wight's journal, under the date December 1851, in *Reorganized History*, 2:791.
15. General Conference minutes, Journal History of the Church, 82:7 September 1850.

> gone there? You see what has followed us here; but what would have been the result, if we had gone there? Long before this time we would have been outnumbered by our enemies; there would have been more against us than for us in our community. Suppose we had gone to Texas, where Lyman Wight went? He tried to make all the Saints believe that Joseph wanted to take the whole Church there. Long before this, we would have been killed, or compelled to leave the country. We could not have lived there.[16]

Just as Young separated his people and doctrines from those of the Texas Mormons, so did Wight continue to encourage the world to understand that he and his people did not follow Brigham Young. In 1852, in a *New York Sun* article, the Texas patriarch advertised his new mills at Hamilton Valley in Burnet County. He wrote to let the world know his followers were not affiliated with the Utah Mormons, whose doctrines he alleged were in no way connected with those taught by the late Joseph Smith.[17] Wight never changed his feelings regarding Brigham Young, personally or publicly. Letters to Sanford Porter in 1855, his nephew Benjamin Wight in 1856, and an exchange of letters beginning with one to Brigham Young himself in 1857, convey two major points: first, his anger, resentment, and intense dislike to, for, and about Young; and second, his commitment to his own principles.[18]

Two weeks before he died in 1858, the *Neu Braunfels (TX) Zeitung* reviewed a quarrel Wight had been pursuing with the *San Antonio Herald.* Wight accused the editor of associating him and his followers with Brigham Young. The editorial was concerned that Wight was leaving the state, either going to the North or to Utah. The implication was clear that Wight would give support to northern enemies or, ironically and somewhat confusingly on the part of

---

16. B. Young, *Journal of Discourses,* 4:344.
17. "The Mormon Settlement," *New York Sun,* 10 February 1852 (photocopy), LDS archives.
18. Lyman and Harriet Wight to Sanford Porter, 7 December 1855, and Lyman Wight to Benjamin Wight, 12 January 1856, postscript 3 April 1856, postscript 26 April 1856, both in the Lyman Wight letterbook; Lyman Wight to Brigham Young, 2 March 1857; Wilford Woodruff to Lyman Wight, 1 July 1857, and Lyman Wight to Wilford Woodruff, 24 August 1857, LDS archives.

the editor, to Utah—because the Utah Mormons had been resisting Colonel Albert Sydney Johnson and one-third of the standing federal army since the previous fall. Wight informed the *Galveston (TX) Weekly News* that

> We never had such intentions. I believe that we have provided ample proof for a long time that we have totally broken away from Utah. We abhor the life and behavior of Brigham Young as much as we abhor hell, and we regard it as an act of defamation if our names and his are mentioned in the same newspaper. Already twenty years ago we were so much against their principles as any sect can be, and now we appeal to those who know us best and can say what character we have. I was never against it that the *News* wrote against Brigham Young. The editor of the *Herald* knows that we subscribe to the *News* and that we were not against an article concerning Brigham Young. Brigham Young would have to be a completely different man to have any kind of influence on us.[19]

Lyman Wight's alienation from most of the Mormon world was complete. This process took nearly a decade, with roots as early as 1841, and led to his excommunication and removal from the Twelve by Brigham Young. Some Utah leaders, such as Orson Hyde and Joseph Young, demonstrated real animosity toward the Wild Ram. Others, including those who dominated church councils—Brigham Young, Heber C. Kimball, and George A. Smith—seemed motivated by real concern for Wight as a person as well as for the protection of their authority. Wight held to the principles that he believed governed his mission to Texas. He believed that he was answerable only to Joseph Smith Jr. He believed he was the co-equal to any and all of the Twelve. He believed that common-stock principles, which he had followed as early as 1829, should govern the economy of a religious community. He believed that the prophetic mantle of Mormonism should pass only through the Smith family. He held true to his beliefs for the rest of his life. The unquestioned fact remains that

19. Lyman Wight to the editor, *Weekly News* (Galveston, TX), quoted in *Neu Braunfels Zeitung* (New Braunfels, TX), 19 March 1858 (photocopy), Sophienburg Museum and Archives.

if he convinced no one else in the larger community of Mormonism, he had good success with influencing his own followers. Most of the survivors of Zodiac eventually joined the Reorganized church under Joseph Smith III.

8

Polygamy and a Temple on the Pedernales

So we built a good little Temple to worship in.
—John Hawley

The intrinsic cultural patterns of Zodiac included polygamy, temple ritual, and socio-economic communitarianism, and, as such, they reflected antebellum Mormonism. RLDS president Joseph Smith III, in a letter to Joseph Davis of the Utah church in 1899, wrote, "nearly all the factions into which the Church broke had plural marriage in some form" in the post-1844 era before the Civil War. His father had been gathering concurrent wives as early as the Kirtland years. Joseph Smith Jr. further refined the practice at Nauvoo, moving it from private to doctrinal grounds. By 1860, plural marriage was an integral part of Mormonism in Utah Territory, Michigan, Wisconsin, Iowa, Illinois, and Texas.[1]

---

1. Joseph Smith III to Mr. Joseph Davis, 18 Oct 1899 (copy), 406, Francis M. Lyman 1901–1903 letterbook, LDS archives; Todd Compton, "Fanny Alger Smith Custer: Mormonism's First Plural Wife," *Journal of Mormon History* 22, no. 1 (Spring 1996): 174–207; see Quinn, *The Mormon Hierarchy*, 87–89, 146–48, for an overview of the early years of Josephite polygamy among other LDS members in Ohio. For brief, competent comments about Joseph Smith Jr. and his responsibility for the institution of Latter Day Saint polygamy, as well as the attitudes of Emma Smith and Joseph Smith III (his wife and son), see Richard S. Van Wagoner, *Mormon Polygamy: A History*, 2nd ed. (Salt Lake City: Signature Books, 1989), 77–81; B. Carmon Hardy, *Solemn Covenant: The Mormon Polygamous Passage* (Urbana: University of Illinois Press, 1992), 47–48, 255–56, 289–90. For developments in recent RLDS revisionism of Joseph Smith Jr. and his role in polygamy, as well as those of his wife and son, and

Temple ritual and some form of economic cooperative also distinguished most of these groups from other American denominations. Just as Joseph Smith built and used temples and subjected his followers to the Law of Consecration and, later, tithing, so did temple building and forms of economic cooperation characterize the churches of Brigham Young, James Strang, William Smith, Alpheus Cutler, and Lyman Wight, who built the first Mormon temple west of the Mississippi.

James Strang took his first plural wife in 1850 at Beaver Island, Michigan. George Miller reinforced and continued the practice when he and his polygamous family joined the Strangites later that year. Plans were drawn in 1847 for a Strangite temple, and construction was underway in September 1849 on two and a half acres. However, the design, with its incorporated twelve towers and a Great Hall, was never finished. William Smith, the only surviving brother of Joseph Smith Jr. and a man whom Orson Hyde described as one who used the priesthood as a vehicle for "sensuality, avarice, and ease," organized a church in 1847. It had failed by 1851, because of its polygamous practices. William Smith's attempt to merge his church body with that of Wight included encouraging the Covington membership to emigrate to Texas. There they could join the Wightites and receive "endowments and blessings" in the Zodiac Temple.[2]

Alpheus Cutler, an intimate of Joseph Smith before his murder in 1844, and a member of the Fifty as well as a leader at Winter Quarters, led the Church of Jesus Christ (Cutlerite) from 1853 until his death in

---

in its historical interpretation in the RLDS church, see Linda King Newell, "Emma Hale Smith and the Polygamy Question," *John Whitmer Historical Association Journal* 4 (1984): 3–15; Alma R. Blair, "RLDS Views of Polygamy: Some Historiographical Notes," *John Whitmer Historical Association Journal* 5 (1985): 16–28; and Richard P. Howard, "The Evolving RLDS Identity," *John Whitmer Historical Association Journal* 14 (1994): 3–10. See Todd Compton, *In Sacred Loneliness: The Plural Wives of Joseph Smith* (Salt Lake City: Signature Books, 1997), for the definitive work on Smith and his wives.

2. Miller, *Correspondence of Bishop George Miller*, 151, 152, 155; David Rich Lewis, "'For life, the resurrection, and life everlasting': James J. Strang and Strangite Mormon Polygamy," *Wisconsin Magazine of History* 66 (Summer 1983): 274–91; Quist, "Polygamy Among James Strang and his Followers," 31–48; *Frontier Guardian* (Kanesville, IA) 1 (7 February 1849): 2; Quinn, *The Mormon Hierarchy*, 224; revelation to William Smith, 20 March 1850, *Melchisedek and Aaronic Herald* (Covington, KY), April 1850; *Reorganized History*, 3:35.

1864. Excommunicated in 1851 by Brigham Young, Cutler and his followers lived their own form of Mormonism, first in Mills County and then Fremont County, Iowa. Eschewing polygamy, although Cutler himself had practiced it earlier, the characteristics of the Cutlerites, as with other branches of the Mormons, included a form of economic communitarianism and the practice of sacred rites.[3]

The environs of a temple were not required for Mormon ritualism at this time. Thus, the practice of sacral ceremonies outside of a temple was not uncommon among the various factions. The Cutlerites practiced them in Iowa, and the Wightites, discussed below, did the same in Texas before they built the Pedernales temple. Brigham Young, at the request of many of the LDS at Winter Quarters, Iowa, years before the Endowment House was built in Salt Lake City, approved the performance of eternal sealings, marriages, and adoptions.[4]

The Cutlerites' Order of Enoch was a common-stock proposition organized and directed by its church corporation. However, it did not function well, and participation by the membership remained optional. According to Danny Jorgensen, Cutler temple ritualism "involved a secretive initiation, assignment of a sacred personal identity, passwords to the spirit world, endowments (or blessings), ritual cleaning by water and anointings with oil, the receipt of a sacred undergarment, and ritual reenactment of sacred myths." Other ordinances included baptism by proxy for the salvation of the dead, as well as monogamous marriage for eternity. The Cutlerites, even those who had earlier practiced polygamy, had abandoned the practice by 1853. The endowment of the first generation, coupled with the quickly decreasing numbers of followers after the death of Cutler in 1864, limited ordinances to the ritual baptism for the dead.[5]

Temple ritualism, economic exclusiveness, and plural marriage fused the sacred and the secular at the Zodiac community. From its early beginnings in Wisconsin, this community defined its familial and individual concerns in religious terms. Apostle Lyman Wight,

---

3. See Danny L. Jorgensen, "The Fiery Darts of the Adversary: An Interpretation of Early Cutlerism," *John Whitmer Historical Association Journal* 10 (1990): 67–83, for a fascinating study of Alpheus Cutler.
4. Bennett, *Mormons at the Missouri*, 189–91.
5. Jorgensen, "The Fiery Darts of the Adversary," 67–70, 74, 75–76, 83.

as the community prophet, patriarch, and leader, offered direct, authoritarian guidance. The rituals of the Pedernales temple delineated the focus of family and individual goals. Temple ritualism bound the community together: husbands and wives, parents and children, leaders and followers. It gifted (endowed) families with continuity that sublimated mortal death to eternal life, and unraveled the bindings of secular time and space. Those at Zodiac believed their temple work gifted them beyond the grave with everlasting exaltation—for themselves, their families, and their familial dead. Levi Lamoni Wight wrote years later that the Zodiac years had presented his people with the opportunity to worship "according to our desires, unity, peace, and harmony prevailing."[6]

John Hawley recorded that "Lyman told us we must build a house for to attend to the baptism for the dead and also the ordinance of washing of feet and a general endowment in the wilderness. So we . . . built a good little Temple to worship in. . . ." Completed on 17 February 1849, the first Mormon temple west of the Mississippi was a large, two-story log building that functioned as a multi-purpose center for Zodiac, with a company storehouse as well as an upstairs room for temple ritual. One of the two Mormon schools enumerated in the Census of 1850 met in the building. The Zodiac High Council gave permission for William Leyland to hold his classes in the large room on the second floor.[7]

Various ordinances performed in the Zodiac Temple involved married and unmarried individuals. Ceremonies included baptism for the dead; washings of feet, head, and body; a general endowment; various anointings; adoptions; the sealing (marriage) of men and women for time and eternity; and the setting apart of kings, queens, and priests for eternity. Temple ritualism at times reorganized families, as well as saving them. When George Miller returned to Zodiac in early 1849, his Leyland stepchildren, who hated him, used the temple and its ceremonies to separate themselves from his

6. L. L. Wight, "Autobiography of L. L. Wight," 265.
7. Hawley, "Autobiography of John Hawley," 7; "The Mormon Colony (Zodiac) Near Fredericksburg, Texas"; William Leyland journal, in H. H. Smith, "The Lyman Wight Colony in Texas," 21, 25; social statistics schedule, census of 1850, Gillespie County.

rule. William Leyland recorded that on 8 April 1849, he received the endowment portion of "the washing of feet under the hands of the Twelve High Counsellors and their presidents along with sixteen elders and their presidents and on the 9th received the washings of the body and anointing." The following month, William Leyland and his sisters Sophia, Sarah, and Eliza were adopted into the Lyman Wight family. Although the girls were only "adopted until they were of age," William wrote that he was "adopted under the oath and covenant of the priesthood unto my salvation or damnation until I could save my father and raise him to be a king and priest."[8]

John Hawley was one of few individuals to experience the endowment ritual in both the Wightite and Utah branches of Mormonism. He celebrated the ceremony at Zodiac (1851) and later in Utah (1857). In 1893, under sworn oath in the Temple Lot Case, he compared and contrasted the ordinances and clothing associated with these rituals. According to him, Young and Wight both believed they had the authority to seal men and women together for time and eternity. Unlike the Utah Mormons, the Wightites wore their religious garments only for special occasions, including sealing ceremonies and for burial. The temple robe was supposedly patterned on that worn by the angel Moroni, an angelic messenger who Joseph Smith claimed had visited him. This outer garment was a loose frock without markings, being described by Hawley as an "entire covering of linen," leaving bare only the hands, feet, and head. An apron, a facsimile of those allegedly worn by Adam and Eve, was as bare of markings as the garment. In contrast, the Utah garment was always worn by the initiated, who were counseled never to take it off, even to the

---

8. William Leyland journal, in H. H. Smith, "The Lyman Wight Colony in Texas," 21–22. John Hawley either considered the type of ceremony in which Leyland participated as not an endowment, or was unaware that Leyland had received anointings and washings without the sealing ceremony to a woman for time and eternity. Hawley, *Temple Lot Case,* 455, carefully distinguished the difference between the first ordinances and marriage sealing, noting that while in Salt Lake City young men could receive the first part of the endowment without the sealing ceremony for time and eternity, such was not the case at Zodiac. Hawley's temple experiences are recorded in three different documents: John Hawley to Bro. Joseph, *Saints' Herald (True Latter Day Saints' Herald)* (Lamoni IA), 28 June 1884, 412; Hawley; "Autobiography of John Hawley," 7; and Hawley, *Temple Lot Case,* 451–62.

act of leaving one leg in the garment while washing. The apron and the tight-fitting Utah garment, joined together at the waist and legs to make one piece of clothing, had special markings. The temple clothing also included a robe with a "bandage" that came down from the shoulders, moccasins, and a cap.[9]

Hawley testified in the Temple Lot Case on behalf of the RLDS church, which defended Joseph Smith Jr. well into the twentieth century against the charges that he was the foundation of Mormon polygamy. Hawley testified that he encountered endowment practices first in Zodiac, and that "Lyman Wight was the first person that taught [to Hawley] anything about endowments according to my best recollection." The Zodiac endowment, he alleged, involved only matrimonial concerns, the sealing of a man and women "together in order to enjoy each other society in eternity." He described this as "spiritual wife marriage," a negative term used in that era to attack the marriage practices of Utah Mormonism, the language of which was guaranteed to offend LDS sensibilities. Hawley testified further that sealings for time and eternity were performed for monogamous as well as polygamous couples at Zodiac.

Nonetheless, having more than one concurrent wife, according to Hawley, led to the accrual of extra spiritual advantages: "Those that were in spiritual marriage were said to be in polygamy, as well as those that were not. The understanding was that they would enjoy the same glory as others, but the ones that had more than one wife would enjoy a greater portion of it." He further offered that it "was not a necessary and logical sequence" that those that had been married for time and eternity would have to practice the doctrine of plural marriage. If a man took more than one wife, according to Hawley's understanding, then his "glory which was in eternity would be greater" than the husband who had only one wife.[10]

---

9. John Hawley to Bro. Joseph, 412; Hawley, "Autobiography of John Hawley," 6–7; Turk, "Mormons in Texas", 44–45, 46–47, incorrectly dates George Hawley's marriage to Ann Hadfield as either in 1848 or 1849; Hawley, *Temple Lot Case*, 452, 453, 457.

10. Hawley, *Temple Lot Case*, 453–56. In his autobiography, Hawley was writing of his endowment ceremony to his first wife, Harriet Hobart, performed near Austin in 1846. In the Temple Lot testimony, Hawley was referring to the endowment with his second wife, Sylvia Johnson, performed in 1851. Hawley's

Wight was always concerned that the rite of eternal marriage orders, or patriarchal marriage, be correctly performed, and that couples were married for eternity as well as time. He earlier had ordained Pierce Hawley, John's father, as a patriarch because, in Mormon theology, this office had the spiritual authority and power to discern an individual's family line. Pierce Hawley discovered that his son was from the tribe of Ephraim, and of the royal blood and lineage of Joseph of Egypt. Eternal marriage under the Wightite system, like other Mormon factions, did not always have to be performed in a temple.[11]

Wightite marriages were often arranged. Lyman Wight and Pierce Hawley had made the selections for John Hawley (Harriet Hobart), Priscilla Hawley (John Young), and George Hawley (Ann Hadfield). On 4 July 1846, with Pierce Hawley and Otis Hobart officiating, John Hawley was ordained a king and priest, and anointed with oil after having his feet washed. John then washed Harriet's feet, anointed her head with oil, and ordained her a queen. Lyman Wight then sealed John and Harriet for time and eternity. Hawley testified that the use of "the power of the priesthood" differentiated sealings from civil rites. The Mormons used them "instead of the legal form of marriage and at that time we looked upon it as being more binding for eternity than the other form of marriage." His later marriage to Sylvia Johnson was monogamous. Harriet had left John sometime during the summer of 1848. Wight decreed that John had been divorced because of Harriet's desertion.[12]

Hawley testified that the Utah ceremony at the Endowment House was "not the same endowments that I took under Lyman Wight's administration." The Zodiac endowment consisted of only

---

anti-LDS bias is also revealed, in that his writings never mention that he officiated as a counselor and presiding elder of the LDS church in Pine Valley, Utah Territory, during the 1860s; see Journal History of the Church, 173:22 March 1863; 180:8 May 1864, 3; and 198:31 December 1866, 2.

11. Hawley, "Autobiography of John Hawley," 6, 7.

12. Turk, "Mormons in Texas", 43, 52, 83; Hawley, *Temple Lot Case*, 452; Hawley, "Autobiography of John Hawley," 6, 7, 10–11. Hawley's testimony, *Temple Lot Case*, 454, revealed that at Zodiac "Lyman did the sealing and my father was a high priest in the church in old Joseph's time and he did the washing of the feet and the anointing of the head." Hawley, "Autobiography of John Hawley," 9, wrote concerning Harriet: "But let me say she was of a quiet disposition and made me a good housekeeper. Lyman said we was entirely divorced from each other and I was at liberty to marry again."

the one ceremony, including the following ordinances: the washing of feet, an anointing with oil, and the ordaining of the initiates as "kings, queens, and priests," which Hawley averred comprised "the sum and substance" of the Zodiac endowment. His testimony cited that "Wilford Woodruff did the anointing and washing and Brigham Young did the sealing" for Hawley and his wife in the Endowment House. Unlike the Zodiac endowment, the couples in Hawley's ceremony at Salt Lake City were separated by gender in different rooms. The Utah endowment involved the washing and anointing with oil of the entire body and feet of the initiate.

The Utah ceremony also differed from the Texas one in that it involved the swearing of oaths "to avenge the blood of the prophets," and included resurrection ordinances as well as ones for marriage. The penalty for revealing the "grip and oath" associated with avenging the Smiths' murders "was disembowelment." The candidate then received "a name we would be called for from the grave by." Hawley stated that the Utah endowment did not include ordinations as kings, queens, and priests. Brigham Young had added a second endowment, wrote Hawley, that included "an anointing and setting apart for the resurrection, and" a power to be called "to rise from the dead, and to raise others."[13]

Young spoke to an audience in 1853, describing how Utah Mormonism felt about the deaths of Joseph and Hyrum. Asking if the blood of Joseph "had been atoned for," Young answered that no "nation of men, without the Priesthood, has the power to make atonement for such sins. The souls of all such, since the days of Jesus, are 'under the alter,' and are crying to God, day and night for vengeance. And shall they cry in vain? God forbid! He has promised He will hear them in His own due time, and recompense a righteous reward."[14]

---

13. Hawley to Bro. Joseph, 412; Hawley, *Temple Lot Case*, 453, 454, 457, 458. Captain James Brown, during the first Mormon Battalion Reunion, held in Salt Lake City in 1855, told the audience that the members of the battalion "have got the spirit of revenge, to avenge the blood of the prophets shed in Carthage Jail, and we shall do it," never to "give up till the blood of the prophets is avenged upon those who dwell on the earth"; see David L. Bigler and Will Bagley, eds., *Army of Israel: Mormon Battalion Narratives* (Logan: Utah State University Press, 2000), 432.
14. B. Young, *Journal of Discourses*, 2:6 April 1853, 232.

The desire for vengeance by the Utah Mormons, and the blood-curdling oath of the Utah ceremony, must be set in the context of the place and time. The journal entries of Allen Stout, a worker in the Wisconsin pinery with the Wight and Hawley families, and a follower of Brigham Young across the western plains, reflect the horror and desire for vengeance that many Mormons held for the rest of their lives. Stout wrote, years after the murders, that

> their beloved forms, reposing in the arms of death engendered such feelings as I am not able to describe. . . . I there and then resolved in my mind that I would never let an opportunity slip unimproved of avenging their blood upon the head of the enemies of the Church of Jesus Christ. . . . I feel like cutting their throats yet. And I hope to avenge their blood; but if I do not I will teach my children to never cease to try to avenge their blood and then teach their children and children's children to the fourth generation as long as there is one descendent of the murderers upon the earth.[15]

Not only were the individuals who killed the Smiths held liable, but the United States and its people also remained guilty of the crimes and would be punished eventually by God. President J. M. Grant, second counselor to Brigham Young, preached that "it is a stern fact that the people of the United States have shed the blood of the Prophets, driven out the Saints of God, rejected the Priesthood, and set at naught the holy Gospel. . . . The result of rejecting the Gospel has been, in every age, a visitation from the chastening hand of the Almighty." God's "chastisement," Grant believed, would "be administered in proportion to the magnitude and enormity of their crimes." Consequently, he expected God "to use His whip on the refractory son called 'Uncle Sam.'"[16]

The issue of privacy also differentiated the endowment ceremonies of Zodiac and Utah. Hawley testified that at Zodiac, anyone could attend. At Salt Lake City, "it was done secretly and no one was

---

15. Journal of Allen Joseph Stout (photocopy), 13–14, Utah State Historical Society archives.
16. J. M. Grant, in B. Young, *Journal of Discourse*, 2:148.

permitted to see them only the officers and the ones talking the endowments. No one else was present or permitted to be present simply because no one else had any business there and they were not permitted to be there." The availability of facilities was probably one reason for the difference in the practices. Zodiac was a frontier community with a two-story structure, the village's only major community building besides the mill, and it served as a temple as well. The Endowment House in Salt Lake City had, according to Hawley, "a good many departments" with "a reception room, a small stairway to the veil, and it was pretty much all on the ground floor. Had dressing rooms, washing rooms, a prayer circle, and an altar."[17] The Utah Mormons had the time, the opportunity, and the security to build a private structure in which to house a much more polished ceremony than that at Zodiac.

Ordinances continued at Zodiac from 1849 to 1851. Shortly before the colony moved to Burnet County in 1851, several sessions in February and March celebrated baptisms for deceased family members. On 10 February 1851, Lyman Wight signed an attestation of purpose concerning the principle of such baptism. Convinced by scripture, the words of Joseph Smith Jr., and "twenty years in the cause of God," the Zodiac leader wrote "that baptism for the dead is one of the most essential ordinances given to us by Christ our redeemer." Only a covenanted people, he declared further, dedicated "even unto the principle of all they have and being placed under the controll of the Almighty God" could build an appropriate house and font for the sanctification of God's followers. Wight averred that never before, in his opinion, had a site been worthy of such an edifice and the rites held within it. According to him, "the Lord Almighty [had] accepted" the Zodiac Temple. Stephen Curtis baptized Lyman Wight as a proxy candidate for his grandfather Levi Wight and Harriet Benton Wight as a proxy for Levi Wight's wife, Susanna Wight. Official witnesses were Pierce Hawley, Sarah Schroeder, Joseph D. Goodale, and George Hawley.[18]

Half a dozen more sessions were held from 11 February to 11 March 1851. The women normally used their maiden names, rather than those of their husbands. Recorders included John Young and

---

17. Hawley, *Temple Lot Case*, 454, 456.
18. Lyman Wight, "Revelation on Baptism for the Dead," 10 February 1851, Iowa State Historical Society archives.

Stephen Curtis, with Andrew Ballantyne, Stephen Curtis, and J. D. Goodale as the persons conducting the baptism. Proxy candidates included Pierce and Sarah Schrader (Schroeder) Hawley; George Montague Sr. and his plural wife Eliza Segar; Stephen Z. Curtis; John F. Miller and Margaret Frances Andrews; Ralph Jenkins and Verona Brace; Irvin Carter and Mary Ann Six; and Jennet Turnbull and Andrew Ballantyne. Witnesses included George Hawley, John Hawley, Priscilla Hawley, I. F. Carter, Spencer Smith, Rodney Bray (Brace), Andrew Ballantyne, George W. Bird, Pierce Hawley, E. W. Curtis, Eber Johnson, William Ballantyne, Alaxe St. Mary, (Marion) Frances Andrews, J. S. Goodale, and Margaret Ballantyne.[19]

Lyman Wight's attestation of baptism for the dead at Zodiac clearly demonstrates his rejection of the post-Joseph churches of Nauvoo and Salt Lake City. It also clearly rebuffs the authority of Brigham Young and the rites performed in the Nauvoo temple after Joseph Smith Jr.'s death. Thus, according to Wight, the Nauvoo temple was not worthy as a site for religious rituals, thus underlining the futility of its ordinances before the Lord and the world. The implications of the Texas directive are clear: only a covenanted, common-stock people, who had dedicated all they owned and who had been accepted and directed by the Lord God Almighty, could perform according to the worthiness of such rites. The conclusion of that train of logic was clear. In this case, Lyman Wight, not Brigham Young, was the Lord's appointed messenger. Obviously some form of common-stock association was necessary, rather than the stewardship and tithing programs of Utah Mormonism. The inferences of the document of 10 February 1851 clearly reflect that Lyman Wight believed only he could officiate in such a position and that only those at Zodiac could build an acceptable temple and worthily perform its rites.

The writings of John Hawley and William Leyland, and the records of baptism for the dead, reveal the extent of Zodiac temple activities, including the wearing of garments, the receiving of endowments, and the performance of other religious rituals. In light of the contemporary records that have been discovered, it is reasonable to think other Zodiac members, who believed that baptism for the

19. Administrative records for baptism of the dead (February and March 1851), Lyman Wight records in Zodiac, RLDS archives.

dead was "one of the most essential ordinances given to us by Christ" (indicating other equally essential rites existed), used the temple. It is equally reasonable to conclude that many men and women at Zodiac were sealed to one another for time and eternity, and participated in the various rituals associated with temple Mormonism. The often extra-judicial nature of marriage arrangements in Wight's colony characterized the communities of the Mormon dispersion. Winn, in *Exiles in a Land of Liberty*, argues that "Mormonism" was not simply an extension of Christian primitivism in the United States during the nineteenth century. Instead, this society "was a religious revolt, not simply a social protest movement." Unable to separate "the secular from the religious elements in early Mormonism," the followers of the Mormon Restoration refused "to bifurcate their lives into separate spheres of the sacred and the profane."[20]

Other scholars have crafted similar observations. Lawrence Foster, for example, in *Religion and Sexuality*, believes the various Mormon groupings sacralized marriage and divorce as ecclesiastical rather than secular procedures, which thus were beyond the realm and arm of secular society. The result separated the Mormons from the larger non-Mormon community. Foster wrote that often "Mormon arrangements were not fully in harmony with local marriage regulations or mores." Joseph Smith and his first counselor Sydney Rigdon, neither of whom were ordained to perform secular marriages, both had troubles with civil governments as a result of their efforts to regulate Mormonism's social and religious affairs when they intruded into the profane world. Control of divorce, marriage, and personal and family salvation (whether at Salt Lake City or Nauvoo or Beaver Island or Zodiac) provided these communities' leaders with the key to regulate the lives of their members. Because polygamy was not a sanctioned form of marriage in the many civil jurisdictions of North America, the practice further isolated them from the larger population.[21]

Polygamy was even more characteristic of Mormonism than temple ritualism. The unpublished 1987 manuscript of Toni R. Turk, "Mormons in Texas: The Lyman Wight Colony," was the first to reveal

---

20. Winn, *Exiles in a Land of Liberty*, 9.
21. Foster, *Religion and Sexuality*, 135, 136.

the extent of Zodiac polygamy. A short history prefaces a genealogical index of many of the colony's members. Turk notes that information about the colonists remains incomplete and at times inaccurate; the spellings of names, not only in the last century but also by later descendants, vary.[22] Determining the extent of Wightite polygamy is further complicated by the scattering and destruction of some primary sources. Such sources for Zodiac polygamy are not generous, due to contemporary reticence. RLDS historians, the last to have access to the writings of Lyman Wight, do not quote the apostle on the subject. Other examples indicate Wightite reluctance to discuss the institution. John Hawley wrote unenthusiastically about marriage practices in his own autobiography but far more fully in other forums when discussing the endowment ceremonies and temple garments. Hawley's comments are apologetic in nature, a defense of the RLDS Church, and are not complete. One example is that he mentions Brigham Young and Lyman Wight by name as teaching and practicing the doctrine, yet he refrains from noting that his sister, Mary Hawley, was a plural wife of Lyman Wight.[23] He does not mention that his second wife, Sylvia Johnson, earlier may have been a second wife to Newell Drake, her sister Cynthia's husband. He does not discuss the fact that his brother George Hawley took as his plural wife a woman already plurally married to Orange Wight—Ann Hadfield, a sister to his own wife, Sarah Hadfield Hawley. George Hawley never mentions this fact, either, nor does his obituary. The obituary, interestingly enough, insists that George Hawley, a member of the local RLDS Stake High Council, had condemned Brigham Young as the author of polygamy.[24]

Those who lived in the various Wight households were later as loath to mention their marriage practices as those from the Hawley homes. Orange L. Wight briefly mentions his own plural marriages but, understandably, does not discuss losing his second wife to

---

22. Turk, "Mormons in Texas," 85–89, 96.
23. John Hawley to Bro Joseph, 412; Hawley, *Temple Lot Case*, 451–62.
24. *Journal of History*, 5, no. 2 (April 1912): 235; subject name listings in Turk, "Mormons in Texas"; subject name listings in the Newell Knight journal and autobiography 1800–1847, provide only conjecture, until definitive evidence is produced, for the polygamous relation of Sylvia Johnson and Newell Drake. It is known, however, that the Drakes and various Johnson relatives traveled in the party of the polygamous bishop George Miller.

George Hawley. Levi Lamoni Wight never speaks about polygamy in his father's colony, although he and his wife both were children and stepchildren of polygamous parents. Gideon Carter, who lived in Wight households, openly talked about the philosophy and practice of Zodiac polygamy, but he, too, restricted identifying polygamous participants to only Lyman Wight and Orange L. Wight. Carter's two sisters, Matilda and Rosilla, were Orange's first and third wives.[25]

The Wight colonies were polygamous villages, from Mormon Coulee in Wisconsin (1844) to the final trek in Texas (1858). Where the prophet Joseph Smith Jr. led, apostle Lyman Wight followed.[26] In a sworn statement to Utah historian Brigham H. Roberts in 1894, Gideon H. Carter explained plural continuity in Wight's community. Carter, a son of a Danite killed during the Mormon-Missouri civil war, grew to manhood and lived for twenty years in the homes of Lyman Wight and Orange Lysander Wight. Carter went with the Wights to Texas. He averred that both Wights taught and practiced the doctrine, and Orange Lysander Wight married the two Carter sisters. He also avowed that both Lyman Wight and Joel S. Miles took plural wives during the trek. [27]

Not only had Joseph Smith taught the principle to Wight, Carter said, but Smith had also given Wight authority to perform such marriages, as well as other ceremonies of the church. Wight supposedly issued a pamphlet explaining the principle, with many special regulations on how to live the doctrine. Lyman argued that (1) it was of God; (2) Joseph Smith Jr. bore testimony of it; and (3) the practice of it could bring "wisdom, truth, and virtue capable of bringing great good to the world." Wight's teachings and this publication apparently caused a stir among the surrounding population, and the pamphlet was withdrawn. Not only were non-Mormons upset with the pamphlet, but polygamy within the colony also caused some agitation at Zodiac. Younger members in Wight's group, "who found no warrant for it in

---

25. Sworn statement of Gideon H. Carter to Brigham H. Roberts, 27 February 1894; O. L. Wight, "Recollections," 4, 5; L. L. Wight, *Reminiscences*, pp. 11, 12; Hawley, "Autobiography of John Hawley," 10.
26. A reading of Lyman Wight's *An Address* clearly reveals the admiration and sense of discipleship that Lyman Wight had for Joseph Smith Jr.
27. Sworn statement of Gideon H. Carter to Brigham H. Roberts, 27 February 1894, 1, 2.

the Book of Mormon and the Doctrine and Covenants," opposed the doctrine. This outcry may have risen from the fact that single, marriage-age females were few at Zodiac. Wight, according to Carter, discontinued performing plural marriages because of the local prejudice against it and because the "people were not pure enough." Those men who already had plural wives continued to live with their wives and support their families.[28] Just when Wight discontinued the practice is not clear. Hawley mentioned in his autobiography that one reason the sect left Zodiac in 1851 was due to some neighbors' unrest over polygamy. In addition, some at Zodiac were questioning the necessity and scriptural basis for it. For example, Richard Hewitt, in an addendum to a letter in 1849 to James Strang, queried the Beaver Island leader and wanted to know "your mind . . . about men having the priesthood having more wives than one. The principle is taught amongst all that I have been with. . . . If it is consistent I want you to let me know . . . so Bro. Miller and myself will know what to do." George Miller allegedly had told Hewitt that the Zodiac polygamists would go to hell with "their whoring." Either Hewitt did not know that Miller himself had three wives, or Hewitt was convinced that Wight's teachings about the practice were wrong. Hewitt did not like the practice, writing that "I don't find such things in the Book of Covenants, nor in the Book of Mormon, nor in the writings of the apostles, and I don't want to be deceived nor flattered any more." The fact that Hewitt counseled with Miller instead of Wight, as well as his plaintive lament to Strang about the need for trusting his leaders to tell the truth, clearly suggests that Hewitt, and perhaps others, were not only questioning the principle of polygamy, but also Wight's leadership as well.[29]

Polygamy came to the Wightite world, and indeed to the world of all Mormons, through Joseph Smith Jr. He started it, taught it, lived it, and, in part, died of it with his brother on a warm, muggy June evening at Carthage Jail. Orange L. Wight, unlike most members of his father's colony, rejoined the LDS Church later in life and died a testifying member. He stated in his memoirs that his father, Joseph Smith Jr., George Miller,

---

28. Ibid., 3–4.

29. Hawley, "Autobiography of John Hawley," 10; George Miller to James J. Strang, 12 June 1849, with addendum by Richard Hewitt, quoted in H. H. Smith, "George Miller," 230–31.

William Clayton, David Clayton, bishop Isaac Higbee, and John Higbee had taught him the principles of polygamy as a young man. The faithful believed God ordained the practice, and Joseph Smith directed it. Orange Wight wrote that Lyman Wight believed Joseph Smith to be "a Prophet, seer and revelator inspired by God," remembering that "plural marriage was practice[d] and taught by the Prophet and Apostles of that day. In all of this time I did not hear Pres. Brigham Young's name mentioned in connection with plural marriage." Wight was not slighting Brigham Young, whom his father resented and eventually grew to hate. Instead, Orange Wight was protecting Young and the LDS Church from the assertions by RLDS apologists, such as John Hawley,[30] that Joseph Smith Jr. never practiced plural marriage and that such doctrines began only with Young, Wight, and others. The internal contradictions of Hawley's sworn testimony in the Temple Lot Case in 1893, when compared to his letter of 26 June 1884 to Joseph Smith III and Hawley's 1889 "Autobiography," reveal either that his mind was beginning to lose its full faculty or that he was making a stumbling attempt at perjury on behalf of his church.

Table 8, next page, identifies twelve marriages contracted by Wightites from February 1844 to July 1846. Five were certainly polygamous. It seems that such relationships could have been hidden only shortly from the rest of the small community. Hawley did write that he had no idea that the young woman he had been courting during the journey to Texas (probably Patience Curtis) had become the spouse of a married man just a short time earlier, "and of course I dropped her mighty quick. That was the first intimation that I had that there was anything of the kind practiced. That was the first case of spiritual marriage that ever came to my knowledge."[31]

Certain social benefits accrued because of these marriages. Strong, cohesive internal bonds developed among the community's members, through the linking of various family groups into family-kin framework relationships. Lyman Wight's three polygamous wives were daughters or sisters of several of the more important colonists (Andrew Ballantyne, Otis Hobart, and Pierce Hawley),

---

30. O. L. Wight, "Recollections," 5–6; William Leyland journal, in H. H. Smith, "The Lyman Wight Colony in Texas," 22; Hawley, *Temple Lot Case*, 451–62.
31. Hawley, *Temple Lot Case*, 455.

TABLE 8

WIGHT COLONY MARRIAGES FROM 1844 TO 1846

** Plural Marriage*

Year	*Bride and Groom*	*Place*
6 February 1844	Rosina Minerva Wight to John F. Miller	Black River Falls, WI
6 February 1844	Anna Christina Wight to Spencer Smith	Black River Falls, WI
6 February 1844	Matilda Carter to Orange Lysander Wight	Black River Falls, WI
7 February 1844	Sarah Hadfield to Orange Lysander Wight*	Prairie La Crosse, WI
Early 1845	Mary Hawley to Lyman Wight*	DuPage, IL
Spring 1845	Patience F. Curtis to Joel S. Simonds*	Unknown (during trek)
27 September 1845	Bernice Monroe to Charles Bird	Near Mound City, KS
27 September 1845	Eliza Curtis to George W. Bird	Near Mound City, KS
27 September 1845	Marion Sutherland to William Curtis	Near Mound City, KS
4 July 1846	Priscilla Hawley to John Young	Austin, TX
4 July 1846	Ann Hadfield to George Hawley	Austin, TX
4 July 1846	Harriet Hobart to John Hawley	Austin , TX

binding them to Wight in family and religious links. Andrew Ballantyne was the millwright, the master artisan of the company. Otis Hobart clerked for the church at Black River and Zodiac. Pierce Hawley served as a counselor to bishop George Miller and became the colony's patriarch. Orange L. Wight's marriages to Sarah Hadfield and Matilda Carter at Black River, Wisconsin, further attached the Hadfield and Carter family members to his father's group. Lyman Wight's marriages also helped to sublimate ethnicity in the colony. Through Wight's wives, the Scots Ballantynes were linked familially to the American Hawleys. Plural marriages linked the community's families more closely because the practice itself isolated them from the much larger monogamous society of the United States.

The strong influence of plural marriage in Zodiac's social relationships can be inferred by examining the twenty-one families that made the trek to Texas in 1845. Although only three heads of household—Lyman Wight, Orange Lysander Wight, and Joel Simonds Miles—were known to be plurally married, more than sixty percent of the families, more than forty percent of the adults, and more than fifty percent of all community members had relatives in one of those three families.[32]

32. "Andrew Ballantine," population schedule, census of 1850, Gillespie County; Turk, "Mormons in Texas," 49; L. Wight, *An Address*, 2; Hawley, "Autobiography of John Hawley,"6, 7.

From 1848 to 1850, plural families came and went at Zodiac, and other polygamous marriages were made. The families of Lyman Wight, Orange Wight, and Joel Simonds Miles arrived with the original company. George Miller and his three wives (Mary Catherine Fry, Elizabeth Boughton, and Sophia Wallace Leyland) came to Zodiac in February 1848. George Montague Sr. married Nancy Daniels Richardson the following year. George Miller departed the colony in 1849, and neither Joel S. Miles nor his wives Patience and Delia were recorded as living at Zodiac in the census of 1850. It is known that Montague and John F. Miller (an original colonist, a son of George Miller, a son-in-law of Lyman Wight, and possible polygamist) remained at Zodiac after George Miller's departure.[33]

Of the ten known couples wedded at Austin and Zodiac, all identified in Table 9, next page, five were monogamous, four polygamous, and one possibly polygamous. Jenette Sutherland, in April 1847, became the second concurrent wife of Ezra Alpheus Chipman, joining Malinda Porter, Ezra's early sweetheart and wife. Marion Sutherland, the former monogamous wife of William Curtis (married in September 1845), joined Ezra, Malinda, and Jenette in the Chipman household as a third plural spouse about 1850. George Montague Sr., as noted above, married Nancy Daniels Richardson. That same year Orange L. Wight took his third wife, Rosilla Carter, sister to his first wife, Matilda. A possible plural marriage occurred between Margaret Francis Andrews and John F. Miller in late 1849 or early 1850.

Identifying the polygamous households in 1850 at Zodiac is problematic. Turk recognizes the plural relationships of Lyman Wight, Orange Wight, Ezra Chipman, Joel S. Miles, George Montague Sr., George Miller, and the possible polygamous situation of John F. Miller, although Turk believes that Miller was not married to Margaret Francis Andrews before the death of Rosina Minerva Wight. By 1850, known plural households at Zodiac included those of Lyman

33. William Leyland Journal, in H. H. Smith, "The Lyman Wight Colony in Texas," 14–15, 21; H. H. Smith, "The Lyman Wight Colony in Texas," 20; L. L. Wight, *Reminiscences*, 12; Turk "Mormons in Texas", 58, 64; "John Miller," res. 261 and "George Montague," res. 262, population schedule, census of 1850, Gillespie County.

Table 9
Wight Colony Marriages 1847 to 1851
** Plural Marriage ** Possible Plural Marriage*

Year	*Bride and Groom*
16 April 1847	Jenette Sutherland to Alpheus Chipman*
—— 1848	Ann Hadfield to George Hawley
—— 1849	Rosilla Carter to Orange Lysander Wight*
—— 1849	Nancy Daniels Richardson to George Montague*
22 October 1849	Sylvia Johnson to John Hawley
About 1849	Marion Sutherland to Ezra Alpheus Chipman*
1849/1850	Margaret Francis Andrews to John F. Miller**
1849/1850	Emeline Curtis to Meacham Curtis
1849/1850	Elizabeth Hewitt to E. B. Hewitt
15 August 1850	Maria Henrietta Racig to William Curtis
—— 1848	Ann Hadfield to George Hawley
—— 1849	Rosilla Carter to Orange Lysander Wight*

Wight, Orange Wight, George Montague Sr., and Ezra Chipman, a total of four men and sixteen wives.[34] Joel S. Miles may have been living at Grape Creek. The households of John F. Miller and Abraham Moncur as well may have also been polygamous by 1850.

County and census documents support the assumption that John Miller's household in 1850 was monogamous. A Gillespie County mortuary schedule penciled on an "Assessor's Guide Book—Gillespie County" for 1850 notes that Roseanna Miller, age twenty-three and born in Ohio, died on 26 March 1850 from a two-day illness, resulting from a "mortification" of the chest. Undoubtedly still weakened from the birth of daughter Rosina Romilia on 6 February 1850, the young mother could not withstand the pleurisy or pneumonia that struck her down. The population schedule for Zodiac in 1850, from information gathered during the late summer, enumerates Frances Miller, a female eighteen years of age, living with John Miller and his three children, the oldest being four years of age. This teenage girl was Margaret Francis Andrews, a daughter of Nancy Daniels Richardson, the plural wife of George Montague Sr. Mother and daughter lived next door to one another. A Wightite justice of the peace, Ralph Jenkins, married Margaret and John on 11

34. Turk "Mormons in Texas," 85–87; subject name listings in Turk, "Mormons in Texas."

July 1850.[35] Without further evidence, it remains speculative whether they had privately and polygamously married before the death of Roseanna Miller.

The confusion as to the extent of polygamy at Zodiac is extended by the subterfuge of plural wives giving varying names to the census taker. Two of Lyman Wight's wives (Residence 243) were enumerated as Margaret Ballantyne and Mary Hawley; a third, Mary Ann Hobart, used the first name of her father (thus Mary Ann Hobart Otis). Sarah Hadfield and Rosilla Carter maintained their maiden names in Orange Wight's residence (No. 257), as did Nancy Andrews in George Montague's home (No. 262). In the Ezra Shipman (Chipman) household (No. 265), the act of protecting plural wives enters the realm of the strange: although plural wife Janette Sutherland maintains her maiden name, her sister Marion, Ezra's third wife and the former monogamous wife of William Curtis, is enumerated under the name of her first husband.[36]

Once the reader is aware that Zodiac wives were willing to deceive the outside world about their marriage relationships, then the probability increases that the Scots shoemaker, Abraham Moncur, was the polygamist husband of Jane V. Ballantyne Moncur and her sister, Ellen Bell. Ellen Bell, listed as thirty-seven years of age with seven-year-old daughter, Janeth, was actually Hellen Ballantyne (age 41), the sister of Abram's first wife, Jane Ballantyne. Hellen earlier had been married on 14 November 1843 at Nauvoo to William Bell. He may have begun the trek from Wisconsin to Texas, but he did not complete it, leaving his wife with Janeth. In 1850, Ellen Bell was living in the Moncur household with her daughter.[37]

---

35. Assessor's Guide Book—Gillespie County, 1850, Texas State Library, Austin, TX, with manuscript copy at Gillespie County Historical Society Archives; Black, *ERLDS*, 4:438; "John Miller," res. 261, and "George Montague," res. 262, population schedule I, census of 1850, Gillespie County; Gillespie County Commissioners' minutes, A (1850–1856): 3, Gillespie County archives, Fredericksburg, TX; Gillespie County marriage record, 1:11 July 1850, 1, Gillespie County archives.
36. "Lyman Wight," res. 243, "Orange Wight," res. 262, "Ezra Shipman," res. 265, population schedule I, census of 1850, Gillespie County.
37. "Abraham Moncur," res. 255, population schedule I, census of 1850, Gillespie County.

The immediate family members of the sisters Moncur-Ballantyne are recorded in the Ballantyne home (No. 259): brother Andrew "Ballantine," age thirty-six, a millwright, as head of household; their mother, Janet Turnbull "Ballantine," age 64; three more unmarried brothers—William (26), a carpenter; James (23), and Robert (age 21), both herdsmen; as well as the family of another sister without a husband, Jeanette Ballantyne Hay and her three children. The immigrant Scots family members obviously lived together when unmarried, reinforcing Jane Margaret's and Jane V.'s plural relationships to Lyman Wight and Abram Moncur. The only family member not living at home is Hellen Ballantyne, who with her daughter resided in the Moncur household. That she was a plural spouse seems likely.[38]

George Hawley was married to the sisters Ann and Sarah Hadfield concurrently after 1852. This caused community tension, for Sarah had been the second wife of Orange L. Wight. Ann Hadfield bore George Hawley a daughter, Martha A. Hawley, about 1849 at Zodiac. Sarah Hadfield bore Orange Wight four children, the last at Hamilton Creek, Burnet County, Texas, in August 1852. Although it is known that she subsequently left Wight and went to Hawley, the immediate circumstances of the triangle are unknown. Ann Hadfield bore George Hawley a daughter on 30 March 1859 in Washington County, Utah. Turk only notes that Sarah married George Hawley before 1859. The actual date was probably in 1852 or 1853, before most of the Hawley clan left Mormon Mills in Hamilton Valley and moved on to Indian Territory. This included George Hawley and his two wives, with Sarah's children by her first marriage to Orange L. Wight. There they reconverted to the LDS faith and moved on to Utah Territory. Sarah Hadfield Hawley died in 1864 and was buried at Pine Valley, Washington County, Utah. Her husband and her sister later moved to Galland's Grove, Iowa, where they joined the RLDS faith.[39]

---

38. "Andrew Ballantine," res. 259, population schedule I, census of 1850, Gillespie County; Turk "Mormons in Texas", 20–23.
39. Hawley, "Autobiography of John Hawley," 6–7, 12–13; Turk "Mormons in Texas", 43, 44–45, 46–47; Black, *ERLDS*, 3:372. See the journal of Henry W. Miller and Elmira Pond Miller, 8–27, for the Hawley sojourn in the Cherokee Nation. See "Journals from the Life and Times of Joseph Ira Earl and His

Why, then, do early contemporary sources identify only a few individuals who practiced the doctrine? Gideon Carter, according to Heman Hale Smith, testified in a California court in 1874 that only Lyman Wight and Orange Lysander Wight practiced plural marriage in the Zodiac community, which is consistent with his sworn statement to Brigham Roberts twenty years later. Several other known Wightite accounts of Zodiac events disappeared while in the care of RLDS historian Heman C. Smith. A diary by Spencer Smith, Lyman Wight's son-in-law, and journals by Wight and his scribe, William Leyland, were destroyed in a fire. Those parts from the destroyed works that are quoted by Heman Hale Smith in "The Lyman Wight Colony" fail to mention, perhaps not surprisingly, the practice of polygamy at Zodiac.[40]

Contemporary non-Mormon accounts of early Texas Mormonism downplay polygamy as a feature of Wight's communities. Noah Smithwick, a friend of the Wightites for at least fifteen years, denied knowledge of polygamous activity among them. Samuel E. Holland, a contemporary of Lyman Wight in Burnet County from 1851 to 1853, never mentioned any practice of polygamy. Early secondary commentaries are also inaccurate. Don Biggers and J. Marvin Hunter, good amateur historians of the Texas Hill County, further confused the subject. Biggers, quoted by Hunter, recorded in 1925 the general belief that "no one knows whether they practiced polygamy." Hunter, following the lead of Heman Hale Smith as well as Biggers, wrote that Lyman Wight was the "only one of the colony who followed" the practice, and that "[a]ll of the other men, except one, were young men and loyal to their wives." Historian C. Stanley Banks, in "The Mormon Migration into Texas," handled the problem of polygamy in the Lyman Wight colony by simply ignoring it.[41]

Wives: Elethra Calesta Bunker and Agnes Viola Bunker," compiled by Owen Ken Earl (typescript manuscript, ca. 1986), 19, 20, 37–38, 235, LDS archives, for commentary about the Hawleys' role in the founding of the Pine Valley lumber mission in Utah.

40. H. H. Smith, "The Lyman Wight Colony in Texas."

41. Smithwick, *Evolution of a State,* 228; M. G. Bowden, "History of Burnet County" (master's thesis, University of Texas, 1940), 45; Don Biggers, quoted in Hunter, *The Lyman Wight Colony in Texas,* 2, 36; Banks, "The Mormon Migration into Texas," 233–44. See also Heman Hale Smith, office of the historian, RLDS church offices, Lamoni, Iowa, to Charles W. Ramsdell, 20 July 1920.

Biggers and Hunter may actually have believed what they wrote, or they may have been influenced by the fact that they had life-long acquaintances with many Wightite descendants in the Hill County. For example, Ezra Alpheus Chipman, the last polygamous patriarch from Wight's colony, died on 3 June 1913 in Bandera County, at the age of ninety-five.

Hunter relied on Noah Smithwick's statements, suggesting that Smithwick's veracity was strengthened because of his lack of a vested concern in the Mormons. Smithwick, to the contrary, had possessed specific interests in them since 1846, when they arrived at Austin and he vouchsafed their presence and conduct. He also bought their mill and property on Hamilton Creek in 1853. Five families remained at the mill and worked for him, while three of those families emigrated to California under his guidance in 1861.

The Wightite families at Smithwick's mill had close connections to polygamy. Several of the Hawley clan, including the family of John Hawley, stayed for a time. Mary Hawley, daughter of Pierce and sister to John, was the fourth and final wife of Wight, and the first to die, at the age of twenty-two. John F. Miller was a son-in-law to Lyman Wight and a son of George Miller, the leading polygamists in the colony. Smithwick, through the normal congress of friendly and employee relations, would have known the convoluted marital relationships of the Wightites. Smithwick, however, had the best of reasons not to discuss the matter. Many were his friends.[42]

RLDS historians continued to underplay the extent of the practice at Zodiac. Heman Hale Smith, in a letter of 1920 to Charles Ramsdell, made some corrections "in the Lyman Wight article," referring to his manuscript titled "The Lyman Wight Colony 1846–1858," that he earlier had sent to the Texas historian. Smith informed Ramsdell that the practice of plural marriage among the Wight colonists "was not general . . . there being no evidence of it outside the indiscretions of Lyman and his son Orange." Smith supported his assertion by citing Gideon Carter's testimony at San Bernardino in 1874: that

---

42. Hunter, *The Lyman Wight Colony in Texas*, 36; J. Hawley to Lyman Wight, August 28, 1853, Lyman Wight letterbook; population schedule, census of 1860, Burnet County, Texas, "East Texas Research Center"; Smithwick, *Evolution of a State*, 228; Turk "Mormons in Texas", 31, 43, 57–61, 81.

Lyman Wight had three wives; that Orange Wight took a plural wife at Prairie La Cross, Wisconsin, a sister of Gideon Carter; and that he had married another Carter sister in 1849 at Zodiac.[43]

Gideon Carter apparently answered the questions of the court strictly, not volunteering any more than what was asked. Although he boasted that he never joined the Mormon church, for nearly thirty years he had lived and associated with men who participated in the inner life of the community. Carter knew far more than that to which he testified. In 1858, he was selected, for example, for grand jury duty for Bandera County. Ten fellow members of that jury were members of the former Wight colony: I. F. Carter, E. A. Chipman, O. L. Wight, William Ballantyne, Andrew Hoffman, William Curtis, Charles Bird, B. F. Bird, George Hay, and O. B. Miles. These men were linked in plural relationships. I. F. Carter was Gideon Carter's brother; their sisters had been plurally married to Orange Wight. Ezra Chipman as well as Orange Wight had been plurally married. At least one of William Ballantyne's sisters, and most likely three, had been plural wives. Andrew Hoffman's wife was the niece of the three Ballantyne sisters. George Hay was a brother-in-law to Andrew Hoffman and nephew of the Ballantyne sisters. William Curtis's first wife, Marion Sutherland, had divorced him and plurally married Ezra Chipman. Charles and B. F. Bird were brothers-in law of their brother George's wife, Eliza Curtis, the sister of William Curtis. Only Orlando B. Miles is the possible exception in the juror list; he cannot be linked definitely to a plural relationship, plural relative, or knowledge of the practice. He may have been, however, a brother or cousin to Joel S. Miles, an original Wight colonist with two wives.[44]

Why, then, did Heman Hale Smith, the great-grandson of Lyman Wight, indicate a limited practice of polygamy at Zodiac to Dr. Ramsdell? Smith's grandparents were Spencer Smith, a relative of Joseph Smith Jr., and Anna Christina Wight, a daughter of Lyman Wight by his first wife, Harriet Benton Wight. Spencer Smith was an original follower of Lyman Wight, who attempted to force Spencer into plural

43. Herman Hale Smith to Charles W. Ramsdell, 20 July 1920.

44. Turk "Mormons in Texas", 42; Bandera County district minutes, fall term, 1858, 26:1 August 1858, Bandera County archives, Bandera, TX; see subject name listings in Turk, "Mormons in Texas."

marriage in 1848 to Sophia Leyland. Heman C. Smith, son of Spencer and Anna Smith and father to Heman Hale Smith, was born at Zodiac at 1850. Spencer Smith and Heman C. Smith later joined the RLDS church, in which Heman C. Smith was raised, serving the Reorganized church as a general authority and church historian.

Heman C. Smith's denial of extensive polygamy at Zodiac makes sense when the reader realizes that Joseph Smith III, the first president of the Reorganized Church of Jesus Christ of Latter Day Saints and son of Joseph Smith Jr., notoriously and steadfastly denied to his death, in the face of obvious and contrary evidence, that his father was its genesis in origin and practice. Heman Hale Smith succeeded his father as RLDS church historian. Historian Smith's assertion to Professor Ramsdell that Zodiac polygamy was limited becomes understandable in light of the way that he vigorously defended his church's positions: namely, that polygamy began with Brigham Young, and that Brighamite polygamy affected only two men at Zodiac. The weight of the entire evidence—the fact that both Heman Smiths were immediate relatives of polygamists, the fact that they supported the RLDS denials about polygamy, and the fact that important journals, diaries, and memoirs of the Zodiac community disappeared while in their keeping—inevitably leads to the belief that their writing concerning Texas polygamy should be evaluated very carefully.[45]

Temple ritual, a communal economy, and polygamy were integral keys to Wightite socialization. The operations of each created a cohesive yet isolated community in the larger Hill Country society. Texas polygamy functioned not only along the frontier, but beyond the mainstream of Hill Country custom. The practice bonded its membership into a cohesive, mutual organization, aloof from the 'foreigners' who surrounded them. As in other Mormon communities, Wightite polygamy, although it had not led to the wellsprings of murder as in Nauvoo, still contained the seeds of its own demise and a denial of its own history.

---

45. See several of the examples listed in footnote 1 at the beginning of this chapter for the difficulties that the RLDS church and Joseph Smith III faced in the growing evidence that his father was the fountainhead of Latter Day Saint marriage practices.

9

The Mormon Millers of Hamilton Valley

I had begun to disbelieve much that was said

—John Hawley

Lyman Wight and most of the colony moved about fifty miles from Zodiac, to Hamilton Valley in Burnet County, during the first half of 1851. Several reasons were responsible—disease, floods from the Pedernales River, massive thunderstorms, jealousy from the larger non-Mormon community, and economic difficulties. John Hawley also mentions "outsider" concern about polygamy; that remains a problematic assumption. He was the only contemporary Wightite source to make the claim, whereas no mention of this exists in non-Mormon sources.

One major reason for Zodiac's demise was a common one—the jealousy of the larger non-Mormon community, reflecting similar earlier experiences in Ohio, Missouri, and Illinois. Wightite political strength strained relations with the local Germans. Wightite hard work in electing sympathetic religionists to county and local offices resulted in a backlash at the polls.[1] Political power flows from economic strength, and Wight's followers pursued both goals in Gillespie County. Although some Texans, like Alta Holland Gibbs of Burnet County, thought later they were "politically unknown,"[2] the Wightites were always involved with county political affairs. This common practice among the Mormons resulted in confrontations in Ohio,

1. Hawley, "Autobiography of John Hawley," 10.
2. Bowden, "History of Burnet County," 45.

Missouri, and Illinois. These conflicts schooled them in the concept that domination of local electoral processes was necessary for the protection of Mormonism's unique habits and customs. In Gillespie County, the success of Mormon political involvement partly required them to move on from Zodiac.

Potential Mormon political strength motivated George Miller, even after all his problems with Wight, to try and lure the Texas colony to Michigan. Wightite voters would add weight there in the local elections. On 19 January 1854, Miller wrote to Wight to let him know that he would be in Corpus Christi, Texas, on business. He reminded Wight of earlier conversations and again advised him to move to Michigan, asking for the names of family heads for the upcoming Michigan census. Inflating the census outcome would give the Strangites at least one senatorial and three representative seats in the state legislature. Wight ignored Miller's letter.[3]

Wightites had been involved in Gillespie County politics since their arrival. Voting in Precinct 1 in June 1848, they elected co-religionists John Young and Ralph Jenkins, respectively, as the county clerk and Zodiac's justice of the peace. William P. Eldridge became the county's first commissioner in 1850, shortly before he died. Irwin Carter was elected to succeed him, John F. Miller (a Wight son-in-law) became the precinct constable, and Jenkins was re-elected as justice of the peace. Wight himself was elected to the office of the chief justice of the county in the fall of 1850, an office best described as the head of the county commissioners' court as well as probate judge.[4] Wight had received fewer votes than his German opponent but successfully challenged him on the grounds that he was a German alien, not a citizen. This upset the majority element in the county.

The Mormons, sixteen percent of the population, held the county offices of chief justice, commissioner, and probate judge, as well as Zodiac's precinct positions of constable and justice of the peace. These office holders fused secular with religious power, enabling Wight to exercise political and religious control over his own followers. As justice

---

3. George Miller to Lyman Wight, 19 January 1854, Lyman Wight letterbook.
4. Texas Historical Records Survey, *Inventory of County Archives of Texas, No. 86, Gillespie County (Fredericksburg)*, 4; Gillespie County marriage records 1:1, 2; Gillespie County Commissioners' minutes: 10 and 14 September 1850, 2, 3, 4, 7, 9; Hunter, *The Lyman Wight Colony in Texas*, 2.

of the peace, Jenkins performed and recorded marriages, and determined misdemeanor infractions in his jurisdiction. This included resolving minor infractions, like theft or public intoxication, with fines or other punishment. He referred more grievous crimes to the equivalent of a grand jury, binding the accused over to the sheriff and forwarding any charges found appropriate to the district court. Constable John Miller, Zodiac's police authority and holder of a county sheriff's warrant for that part of the county, enforced Jenkins' authority. Jenkins, with all the county's justices of the peace, reported directly to Chief Justice Wight, who was his religious and political superior. Chief Justice Wight directed the executive and legislative functions of the county. He supervised not only the justices of the peace, but also directed the probate court, which had primary jurisdiction in matters of wills and other affairs dealing with probate. He now combined political and police powers in the county with religious supremacy over his flock at Zodiac.

The population of Fredericksburg resented the concentration of power in Wight's hands, as well as his overturn of the ethnic majority's electoral will. The mixture of ethnicity, religion, politics, and the competition for army contracts aggravated relationships between the two communities.

Several special elections were held early in 1851, each more confusing than the one before it. Finally, amid accusations of electoral irregularities, the Germans conquered the polls. Although Wight remained chief justice, he was plagued with both county politics and internal dissension at Zodiac. He stopped attending the commissioners' court meetings. Three commissioners—Schmidtzensky, Mosel, and Jordan—met on 2 June 1851 and ordered Wight to appear before them "to settle and close up all matters with the county as chief justice and probate judge." They ordered Christian Gartner, constable of Precinct 2, to serve the summons, understanding that Constable John Miller of Zodiac would probably not serve the writ on his father-in-law. Wight failed to appear, and a special election to replace him, on 7 July 1851, revealed that W. G. Thomas won all thirteen votes in Precinct 1. These very votes indicated that the Mormons were moving or had already moved to Burnet County. Commissioners' actions during the next two years demonstrated that the Mormons had no further interest in Gillespie politics: the township had been placed in different precincts at least twice, and A. Erlenmeir became the area's election officer.[5]

Some sources indicated disease was a major motivation for the Wightite move, but in fact it played only a minor role for their exodus. Local historian Don H. Biggers, in 1925, correctly discounted "newspaper romancing" that the Mormons moved because they "nearly all died during the cholera epidemic. There is no foundation for such stories; the epidemic was over before the Mormons came to the county." They had arrived, in fact, at the height of the epidemic in 1847, but it did not spread to them. A Wight letter in July 1851 indicates that illness was only a minor motivation, preventative rather than curative, for moving. Although Gillespie County mortuary schedules in 1850 clearly showed that cholera was still a local health problem (almost twenty died of it in June and July alone at Fredericksburg), the half dozen deaths at Zodiac were attributed to "chills and fever." Birth and death rates at Zodiac, analyzed earlier in a previous chapter, document that the community's health had not suffered during these years.[6]

One important reason for the move was the economic devastation wrought upon the common-stock cooperatives of Zodiac. First, the army post had stopped contracting locally, which hurt both German and Mormon communities. Second, a series of storms in the summer of 1850, each more powerful than the one before, battered the county. A major gale that November destroyed the mill and flooded some of the cropland. The Mormons pitched in and made the repairs. The following February, however, a tempest far more powerful than those of the previous year delivered the final blow. The deluge wrecked the mill, buried the millstones somewhere in the river, flooded out the homes on the old Austin road, and, more significantly, destroyed the arable land.[7]

---

5. Gillespie County Commissioners' minutes: 2 June 1851, 9; 10 June 1851, 10; 7 July 1851, 11; 12 October 1852, 42; 9 November 1852, 43; 8 December 1852, 46; 4 April 1853, 50.
6. Biggers, quoted in Hunter, *The Lyman Wight Colony in Texas*, 2–3; Lyman Wight to Mr. Van Duevee, 23 July 1851, Lyman Wight letterbook; "Persons Who Died During the Year–1850," annotated in Assessor's Guide Book—Gillespie County.
7. Banks, "The Mormon Migration into Texas," 239; H. H. Smith, "The Lyman Wight Colony in Texas," 26; Jermy Benton Wight, *The Wild Ram of the Mountain: The Story of Lyman Wight* (Star Valley, WY: Llama Star Press, 1996), 273.

A mill could be rebuilt. New millstones could be refashioned. Houses could be cleaned and repaired. Only God or Nature could repair the earth in the miraculous way required by Lyman Wight and his people. Neither power intervened. This disaster destroyed the Wightites economic power. From that time on, the colony never again reached the rustic splendor it possessed at Zodiac.

Perhaps the comfort the Wightites had known since 1849, when they voted in conference to return someday to Jackson County, Missouri, may have mitigated the mixed feelings they felt when departing Zodiac. As the main body of Latter Day Saints under Brigham Young moved to the Rocky Mountains, Lyman Wight's people must have realized that Zodiac would not be their permanent home. Where they finally would settle remained an unknown element in their lives. Wight discussed Old Mexico at times (much to the consternation of the Hawley clan), and as late as 1855 considered California.[8]

Less than six months after Bartlett wrote his glowing description of Zodiac, the Mormons were trekking to Burnet County. Stephen Curtis, Meacham Curtis, Ezra Chipman, Joseph Goodale, and Orange Wight rode to the northeast and found a good location on Hamilton Creek near Marble Falls, where the first mill west of Georgetown would be constructed. The scouting party included the colony's various economic and social interests. Goodale and both the Curtises were monogamous; Chipman and Wight, polygamous. Goodale was the colony's senior millwright and expert on grist milling. All were strong in matters of faith and committed to Wight personally. Joseph Goodale, Stephen Curtis, and Orange Wight had been chosen the year before as apostles in the Smith-Wight church. Chipman had been Wight's friend and follower for nearly twenty years, and he would protect his chief's interests.[9]

The growing season compelled the Wightites to move in time to plant a crop and then have the mill up and running for the

---

8. William Leyland journal, in H. H. Smith, "The Lyman Wight Colony in Texas," 22; O. L. Wight, "Recollections," 41; Hawley, "Autobiography of John Hawley," 11; Eliza Wight to Sister Miller, 8 April 1855, *Northern Islander* (Voree, WI), 31 May 1855, 90.

9. Bowden, "History of Burnet County," 47, 53; population schedule, census of 1850, Zodiac, Gillespie County; *Melchisedek and Aaronic Herald* (Covington, KY), April 1850, 3; L. L. Wight, *Reminiscences,* 19.

harvest. On 23 July 1851, Wight wrote to a Mr. "Van Duevee" (Logan Vandeever), whom he incorrectly believed to be the land's owner, and apologized for the presence of his people, explaining they had been searching for a new home. He stated that they had been cutting timber for animal pens. Instead of reciting the real reasons for leaving Zodiac (economic difficulty and political strife), Wight astutely suggested that illness and several deaths had prompted them to search for a healthier location. He also claimed the Zodiac mills had been rented out, a blatant falsehood. Afraid that Vandeever might be hesitant to sell or lease land if he had known their economic straits, Wight was trying to make a bad situation better. He continued in his letter that several of "our best examined the falls minutely . . . [and found it] rather a slimy prospect" because of the capital needed. Still, Wight offered to buy the site. Vandeever passed on the letter to the rightful owner, William Magill, a farmer and resident of Burnet County, who sold the land to Wight.[10]

The county's largest settlement north of 'Mormon mill' was known first as Hamilton, and later as Burnet. Hamilton had been founded immediately after the end of the Mexican War. Fort Croghan (Smithwick refers to it as "Fort Croggin") provided the local settlers with an outlet for possible economic development and community growth. Smithwick worked as the post's armorer, and noted that Logan Vandeever and William McGill (Magill), both veterans of San Jacinto, were among the area's first arrivals, having obtained a military contract for furnishing supplies to Fort Croghan. The business firm of Boland & McKee operated the first mercantile outlet in the area. W. H. Dixon, a graduate of Oxford, presided over a one-room schoolhouse.[11]

Although Wight's residence may have changed, he still maintained distrust of the outer world. By the end of 1850, he recorded in his journal that he doubted if the church could survive in the wicked world. Among his musings were: "The church now stands

---

10. Lyman Wight to Mr. Van Duevee, 23 July 1851; Bowden, "History of Burnet County," 41; Burnet County deed records, A:253, Burnet County archives, Hamilton, TX; Burnet County deed records, F:577; population schedule, census of 1860, Burnet County; population schedule, census of 1860, Burnet County.
11. Smithwick, *Evolution of a State*, 221–22.

rejected together with their dead. The church being rejected now stands alienated from her God in every sense of the word." The leadership of Brigham Young, James Strang, or William Smith, as far as the Wild Ram was concerned, offered no hope. Despair emanates from his entry as he continues: "This being the case, what should now be done?" He laments that the Fifty did not uphold the rights of Joseph Smith III, which would have resulted in the church moving "smoothly on, and onward, until the final redemption of Zion, and the building of the great temple therein." He ignored the probable reality of a child church president in a regency torn apart by the invariable conflict of various councils and quorums struggling for power. William Smith, aware that the Wight colony was still the only viable alternative for building an opposition church that could compete with those of Brigham Young and James Strang, summoned Wight once more to a new conference, this time at Palestine, Illinois, in April 1851. None of the Wightites attended. Wight turned his attention more fully to Joseph Smith Jr.'s posterity as the true hope for the church's survival.[12]

Wight continued to instruct that only the children of Joseph Smith Jr. could be the true successors to church leadership. He recorded in his journal on 5 October 1851 that he had called a meeting for that evening, "and I lectured to some considerable length on the subject of a successor to Bro. Joseph Smith, endeavoring to show the impropriety of these being one aside from the fruit of his loins." Only a son, not a brother or a cousin, certainly not a Young or a Strang, could succeed Joseph Smith. Wight would never swerve from these beliefs, and never again affiliated with any other group of Mormons.[13]

The mill spot was one of the most picturesque locations in Burnet County. By 1851, the Anglo-European settlements had been steadily pushing the native buffalo culture further west, but bear, javelina, and cougar still prowled the terrain. The *Burnet County History* notes that the headwaters of the creek, four to five miles above Hamilton Valley, drew drainage from the adjacent cedar breaks and flowed down from the upper valley. At one point, it dropped

12. *Reorganized History*, 3:34–35, 790–91.
13. H. C. Smith, "Succession in the Presidency," 5.

twenty-eight feet into a pool about two and a half acres in size, with a depth of up to sixty feet. Heavy rainfall would transform the normally slow-moving stream into a torrent. The stream quickly flowed between the tall walls of the gorge, then turned ninety degrees and plunged over the falls to the pool below.[14]

This was a mill man's dream come true. There, Wight and his millers built a three-story mill structure. The upper floor had a small corn-cracker feed mill (also known as a cracker mill or grinding mill) for animal fodder. The second floor stood at the foot of the falls, and was level with the stream. A gang-way flume passed the water along to the twenty-six foot overshot water wheel, which drove the machinery on the ground floor. The main machinery powered an up-and-down sash saw, an advantage over weaker, circular saws which could not handle large timbers.[15] The feed-cracking and lumber-milling operations worked well, but the marble replacements for the original millstones, buried in the sand of the Pedernales, had to be dressed often to do other milling than cracking feed. This was the genesis of Smithwick's story about colonists' credulity in Wight as he led them in a vision quest to find (successfully) the lost mill stones.[16] Smithwick's interest in the Wightite mill was simple; he wanted to buy it.

The Wightites, along with their feed, grist, and lumber operations, had set up a turning lathe and were soon producing household furniture for the entire county. They seeded a crop for a new farm, and the women engaged in handicrafts, including making "very pretty willow baskets." Despite their energy, Smithwick noted that the Wightites did not achieve the prosperity they had once enjoyed at Zodiac. The houses were primitive and small, "and their furnishings meager," indicating they were selling their products to their neighbors and not using it for their own needs.[17]

The colonists built their cemetery across the creek, about a half-mile distant from the community. There, Smithwick wrote, "not withstanding the miraculous . . . powers" of Wight's faith healers, "a comparatively large number of the saints had ended their early

---

14. Debo, *Burnet County History*, 28.
15. Ibid., 26, 28.
16. Smithwick, *Evolution of a State*, 223, 225.
17. Ibid., 225.

pilgrimage within 'a neat wall of red sandstone,'. . . each grave being marked with a headstone of the same." Non-Mormons were buried outside the graveyard wall. A later, local diary notes that at least fourteen of the colony were laid to rest there. Although factual errors exist in its accounts, the accuracy still is remarkable for a journal relying on oral tradition and folk memory.[18]

Wight tried to improve the colony's prospects in the *New York Sun*, which was notified that the new mill at Hamilton Valley was larger and better than the one at Zodiac. Burnet County offered opportunity for immigrants, he asserted, for it had been organized for the betterment of its citizens. He also made sure to let the world know that his colony had nothing to do with Utah Mormonism, and that his people had nothing to do with the doctrine of the late Joseph Smith Jr.[19] Since polygamy was the only doctrine the rest of the non-Mormon world had any interest in, Wight was suggesting by inference that it was practiced only in Utah. This creative and false campaign was the only time in public that Wight denied Joseph Smith's influence on the Texas colony.

Nannie Mae Kinser, who lived at or near Hamilton Mills for more than sixty years (1871 to the 1930s), was told by both L. W. Coon and Samuel E. Holland that the Mormons did not practice polygamy in Burnet County. Polygamy, however, remained part of the Mormon society at Hamilton Valley, and was practiced at least in the homes of Lyman Wight, Orange Wight, and Ezra Chipman, and possibly Abram Moncur. They took care to hide it away from the rest of the county. As noted below, the issue of plural spouses became a cause for schism at the mills.[20]

The Wightites participated in Burnet County political matters, but did not elect their own as office holders. They may still have been leery from the German reaction in Gillespie County, or they may have just been too busy with building a new community. In December 1851, petitioners from the area requested the state legislature to create a new county and a new county seat "near the center of said proposed new county." Forty-one petitioners were members

18. Ibid., 229. Also see Debo, *Burnet County History*, 29.

19. "Mormon Settlement," *New York Sun*, 10 February 1852.

20. Smithwick, *Evolution of a State*, 228; "Nannie Make Kinser, Statement," *Ghost Towns of Texas* (pamphlet, ca. 1933 or 1934), copy at Chamber of Commerce, Marble Falls, TX.

of the Mormon mill community. Governor P. H. Bell approved the legislation on 5 February 1852, recognizing Burnet County.[21]

The Mormons established their community school as soon as possible. The *Burnet County Bulletin* reported that the schoolmaster was an itinerant journeyer named Abijah Hopkins. He wandered the frontier from Texas to Wisconsin and back, never spending more than six months in a spot. Smithwick wrote that Hopkins's "hobby was mathematics, which he had for the most part mastered unaided. He said that the first class he ever instructed was in algebra, he had to study the lesson at night he taught the day following." The teacher, mild in manner, had no trouble keeping "his . . . urchins quailing at a glance. . . . Our schools in those days were crude affairs, but the children learned more in a day than they do in a week—yes, in a month—in our modern schools. There was no red tape connected with them." Smithwick's rhetorical approval is, of course, a romantic glamorization of times past, but yet there gleams through it real respect for school men (and women) who brought education to the far frontier.[22]

A more serious issue in Hamilton Valley, or the lack of it, was the apostasy and departure of most of the Hawley clan. Patriarch Pierce Hawley's faith in Wight had been shaken. First, his daughter, Mary, the fourth and youngest wife of Wight, died in 1852 before reaching her 23rd birthday. The following year, hard feelings intensified between the apostle and the colony patriarch over who would name the newborn Hawley infants. Pierce Hawley took offense when Wight named one of his grandsons Alma, a role that he felt as patriarch he should fulfill. Wight would not relent, informing the elder Hawley, the infant's name he had chosen was the correct one.[23]

Pierce Hawley left the colony in the summer of 1853, and his daughter Priscilla and her husband, John Young, went with him. George Hawley joined his father because he took Ezra Chipman's plural wife as his own. Sarah Hadfield Chipman joined George and George's first wife, Ann Hadfield, who was Sarah's sister. This union, which produced a son in 1859 at Pine Valley, Utah, never is

21. Debo, *Burnet County History*, 331.
22. Ibid., 28; Turk "Mormons in Texas," 50. Both rely heavily on Smithwick, *Evolution of a State*, 228–29.
23. Hawley, "Autobiography of John Hawley," 11; Platt and R. Hawley, *House of Hawley*, 42.

mentioned in John Hawley's memoirs, RLDS records, or the writings or remarks of George Hawley, whose actions moved him into the ranks of the plurally married and beyond Lyman Wight's good graces. Although Chipman himself had set precedence for this type of behavior, marrying Marion Sutherland, the first wife of William Curtis, he had long been a friend of Wight, and was a senior member of the community. George Hawley sided with his father. Most of the Hawley clan journeyed across the Red River into the Indian Nations.[24]

John Hawley faced a dilemma—loyalty to his family or to his religious leader. Where Wight might be taking the colony, literally, concerned him far more than who gave babies their names. Not only was Wight pondering about taking his group into Mexico, he was beginning to talk about it. Hawley wrote, "I had begun to disbelieve much that was said and the greatest stumbling block was a revelation he received that he was commanded to go to Mexico. I thought this was not the mission to get revelations to govern the church and to lead off our Texas mission as a company to Mexico."[25] Smithwick bought the mills from Lyman Wight in July 1853, and John Hawley informed Wight on 28 August 1853 that he was working for Smithwick. He stated that he would soon join his parents, who had already left Hamilton Valley. If they returned to Wight's colony, John would also come with them. Since Wight still had wagons and cattle at the mill, he requested the use of them until he moved on. Thirty years later, Hawley recalled these events in a more negative light. He said that he notified Wight that he was leaving, "and all the property that was in my possession was at his disposal. . . . So in a day or so Lyman sent over and drove off the cows and took what company property was in my charge." John Hawley then set off to Indian Territory to find his father.[26]

---

24. Turk, "Mormons in Texas," 43–44, 77–78, Hawley, "Autobiography of John Hawley," 12. See *Saints' Herald (True Latter Day Saints' Herald)* (Lamoni IA), 1911, in which Young is condemned by the Hawleys for polygamy in the Latter-Day Saints church, in *Journal of History*, 5, no. 2 (April 1912): 235. George Hawley was a strong opponent in his later days in the RLDS community in Iowa.
25. Hawley, "Autobiography of John Hawley," 11.
26. Ibid.; J. Hawley, Hamilton Mills, to Lyman Wight, 28 August 1853, Lyman Wight letterbook.

The Hawley clan and their friends were not the only ones to leave Wight and Hamilton Mills. Others were leaving as well. Andrew Ballantyne and his wife, Rebecca Connyers, left Burnet County soon after their marriage in January 1853, because the first of their twelve children (all born in Little Sioux, Harrison County, Iowa) arrived in July 1854. The three Gaylord brothers—Lyman, Sidney, and William—left for Iowa, either with the Ballantynes (for Lyman and Sidney were later recorded as living in Little Sioux, Iowa) or perhaps even later, for William signed a taxpayers' petition in Bandera County in 1855.[27]

Wight was losing entire families during the last months of the colony's stay in Hamilton Valley. Some, like the Hawleys, had followed him since the earliest days in Wisconsin. Now members of his own family were beginning to weaken. John F. Miller, his former son-in-law, stayed to work with Smithwick. So did Rodney and Sarah Curtis Brace, and William and Maria Curtis. William Curtis later rejoined Wight in Bandera County, where he was elected sheriff in 1856. After Wight's death in 1858, the Curtises returned to Smithwick's mill.[28]

The group with Pierce Hawley, who lived in the Indian Nations during 1855 and 1856, became the battleground for contesting Mormon missionaries. Strangite Jacob Prindle and LDS follower Henry W. Miller strived for the right to convert the one-time Wightites.[29] Miller, the former chief of sawmill operations in Wisconsin, had been chosen by Brigham Young to be the President of the LDS Cherokee Nation mission. Miller converted the Hawley families, with the exception of Pierce Hawley, his wife Sarah, and Joseph Goodale. Goodale would not let Miller baptize him because of Miller's addiction to tobacco. Therefore, Miller ordained John Hawley an elder, so that the latter could baptize Goodale. Hawley believed, "if my memory serves me correct," that Goodale was in the church about eight hours. Goodale, after being confirmed a member of the church, "knelt in prayer

27. Subject name listings in Turk, "Mormons in Texas"; [RLDS membership records] Galland's Grove [Iowa], Org. 21 1859 [local juris. #136; MRB A: 191] and Little Sioux [Iowa] Org. [local juris. #146 & 146.4 O/S MRB A], RLDS archives.
28. Subject name listings in Turk, "Mormons in Texas"; Black, *ERLDS*, 2:409, 412.
29. Journal History of the Church, 154:31 August 1860, 2.

and asked for a witness whether Brigham was the lawful successor of Joseph. God did not tell him. Because he got no witness, he told the church they could erase his name from the record which we did . . . [and] his wife's name also."[30]

The converted Hawley families prepared to move on to Utah Territory to join the rest of the Latter-day Saints. Pierce Hawley would not go with his sons' families. He still held a grudge against Brigham Young for taking his property "in Lee County, Iowa . . . and all this stuck in [his] craw" because he believed that the sons of Joseph Smith Jr. should inherit the leadership of the church. The captain of the Utah-bound wagon train, Jacob Croft,[31] an LDS convert and sawmiller himself from Houston, Texas, wrote to the elderly Hawley, asking him to reconsider and join them. Hawley wrote back informing Croft that he believed the truth was not with the Utah faction, and that its leader was a pretender, an imposter. Hawley advised Croft to go to Nebraska Territory, "till the Lord raises up the man to lead us to sion [*sic*]." Hawley died two years later in Indian Territory.[32]

The members of the wagon train ignored the old man's counsel, and on 23 June 1856 they moved out. The train consisted of sixty-five people and was organized with Jacob Croft, captain; William Slade, chaplain; John Hawley, sergeant of the guard; and S. A. Duggans, clerk. Once they arrived in Salt Lake City, they were rebaptized and tithed. They then deeded over their excess property for consecration. They also were reunited with their Wightite neighbor from Texas, John Taylor. Brigham Young was aware that many "of this Texas company are from Lyman Wight's company."[33]

Being good millers with plenty of experience, John Hawley, George Hawley, and some of their relatives were sent to the Pine

---

30. Hawley, "Autobiography of John Hawley," 12, 13.
31. Jacob Croft, in East Texas Sawmill database project, Texas Forestry Museum, Lufkin, TX.
32. Hawley, "Autobiography of John Hawley," 12, 13; Pierce Hawley to Jacob Croft, 6 June 1856, folder 3, George Wise Cropper Collection 1823–98; Platt and R. Hawley, *House of Hawley*, 49.
33. Journal of Henry W. Miller and Elmira Pond Miller, 27; Hawley, "Autobiography of John Hawley," 13; council minutes, historian's office, Journal History of the Church, 123:4 October 1856.

Valley mission in southern Utah. There, in September 1857, they observed the wanton aftermath of what is known as the Mountain Meadows Massacre. Local Mormon militia units, perhaps with the assistance of some local Indians, destroyed a wagon train a few miles north of Pine Valley, and butchered 120 of the California-bound immigrants. John Hawley angrily argued against the killing of men, women, and children who had surrendered to the militia under the direction of local Mormon religious and military leaders. Some of Hawley's opponents wanted to kill him, and may have been planning to do so, when an express rider from Brigham Young arrived too late with instructions to let the wagon train pass unmolested.[34]

This group of former Wightites joined other Mormon settlers at the community in Pine Valley, a day's ride north of St. George, Utah. Among the eight families were George Hawley with his two wives, Sarah and Ann; John and Sylvia Hawley; and Jeannette Goudie and Joseph Hadfield, who had married in 1857 at Pine Valley. John Hawley, for almost fifteen years, was an important person in the area. Some former Wightites intermarried with the earlier settlers. One was Harriet Wight, a daughter of Orange Wight and Sarah Hadfield, who came with her mother and stepfather, George Hawley, to Pine Valley. Harriet married Wilbur Bradley Earl in 1867, one of three brothers who spent their lives on the Utah-Nevada border. All three brothers practiced polygamy. Harriet was the second wife in the family, joining Mary Langley, Wilbur's first wife. Harriet was one of several former Wightites, including children of John Taylor in Weber County, who are known to have entered polygamy. It was to Harriet Wight Earl's home that her father, Orange Lysander Wight, would come in the late 1890s after a lifetime on the American frontier. He rejoined the LDS Church in Utah.[35]

---

34. Hawley, "Autobiography of John Hawley," 12, 13; John Hawley to Bro. Joseph, 412. The definitive history of this evil tale of American terrorism is Will Bagley, *Blood of the Prophets: Brigham Young and the Massacre at Mountain Meadows*. University of Oklahoma Press, 2002.
35. Turk "Mormons in Texas," 43, 77–78; "Journals from the Life and Times of Joseph Ira Earl and His Wives," 19, 20, 37–38, 235; O. L. Wight, "Recollections," 5. The *Index of the Annals of the Southern Utah Mission*, LDS Genealogy Library, St. George, UT, documents John Hawley's public and church life in Pine Valley: constable, 39; presiding elder, 1 October 1860, 51; road supervisor, 47; presiding elder, 1866, 243; 1st counsellor to Bishop Wm Snow, July

The remaining Wightites moved on from Burnet County late in 1853. The reasons were similar to those that caused them to depart from Zodiac. Alta Holland Gibbs recorded that Indian depredations, debts, and non-Mormon discontent forced them to leave. However, the prevailing reason, L. L. Wight felt, was the increasing Indian raids against their livestock. The German immigrant treaty with the Comanche had broken down because of two incompatible cultures fraying against one another. In addition to losing livestock, several of their neighbors had been captured and killed by the raiders.[36]

Economic frustrations, along with the raids, encouraged the Wightites to resettle. Jermy Wight, in *The Wild Ram of the Mountain: The Story of Lyman Wight*, believed that difficult terrain and poor economic outlets contributed to the Mormons' difficulties. Rocky soil prohibited gathering the large crops of corn they had enjoyed at Zodiac. The scrub cedar that inhibited farming also provided only a mediocre source of lumber. Southern pine was available in only limited quantities. Additionally, the Wightites did not have a local community the size of Fredericksburg in which to market their produce and milled products. Unable to secure the corn contracts at Fort Croghan, the small contracts they did have with Fort Gibson (lumber and shingles) and Fort Belknap (shingles, lumber, and hay) were not enough to make the community economically viable. Smithwick also believed military corruption complicated the situation. According to him, the officers at Fort Croghan were taking kickbacks from non-Mormon suppliers, who were returning this money for underweight bags of corns supplied to the post.[37]

Earlier, on 25 June 1853, John Young had written to Lyman Wight that economic matters were a concern. He couched the letter as an

---

1866, 252; called on mission to relatives, 265. The mission to his RLDS relatives in Iowa was the beginning of the end for the Hawley presence in Pine Valley. See the discussion by Jesse L. Embry, "Josephites at the Top of the Mountains: RLDS Congregations in Utah," *John Whitmer Historical Association Journal* 16 (1996): 57–71, concerning this little-known facet of RLDS reconversion among the members of Utah Mormonism.

36. Debo, *Burnet County History*, 28; L. L. Wight, *Reminiscences*, 266.

37. J. B. Wight, *The Wild Ram of the Mountain*, 365; Orange Wight, Fort Gibson, to Lyman Wight, 9 September 1852, Lyman Wight letterbook; John Young to Lyman Wight, 25 June 1853, Lyman Wight letterbook; Smithwick, *Evolution of a State*, 222–23.

expression of the comprehension and will of the "brethren" at Hamilton Creek. He noted that the potatoes were growing well and that business at the mills and wagon shop remained busy. William Magill had told Young the previous day that he would transfer the land by deed, rather than by certificate. Although unclear whether the transfer was to be made by Wight or Smithwick, subsequent events make clear that Smithwick was negotiating for the mills. It was the will of the male members of the local church branch that Wight handle the matter of the deed. Even with the problems caused by the dissidents, Wight remained in charge of the community's cooperative economy.[38]

John A. Green wrote Wight in July 1853 that his client, Noah Smithwick, was ready to assume Wight's debts in return for the "mill property on Hamiltons Creek." In return for $5,000 to Wight, Smithwick would accept transfer of the mill, the property, and the machinery to his name. Wight agreed, and, on 12 August 1853, Magill deeded the land to Smithwick. Many years later, Smithwick recalled that the Mormons had "offered their mill for sale. Having all my life had a penchant for mills, I recognized this as 'my long lost brother,' and at once opened negotiations for it. The dream of my life was fulfilled and I was at last the proud possessor of a bona fide mill." He installed a new set of burrstones, and converted a bolting mechanism to work them. Smithwick was soon grinding not only cracker meal, but also the first cornmeal west of Georgetown.[39]

---

38. John Young to Lyman Wight, 25 June 1853.
39. Orange Wight, Fort Gibson, to Lyman Wight, 28 July 1853, Lyman Wight letterbook; Debo, *Burnet County History*, 28; L. L. Wight, *Reminiscences*, 266; Smithwick, *Evolution of a State*, 225, 226, 228.

10

The Mormon Cowboys of Bandera County

We are surprised any who was ever a Mormon should engage in hunting Indians.

—Editors, *Northern Islander*

In the fall of 1853, the locals of Bandera City had heard that Lyman Wight and his Mormon families were again on trek, heading slowly south by west out of Burnet County in their heavy wagons. Even in the far reaches of Lone Star civilization, Texans were well aware of the rumors of the supposed Mormon culture of violence. However, no one in the Hill Country feared this particular group, led by its old patriarch. Although they might be polygamous and separatist, they were not followers of Brigham Young and Utah Mormonism. Wight was simply moving his community again, as before, farther west into the Texas frontier.

Wight and his followers continued to be the supreme milling mechanics in central Texas. They had not improved as businessmen, however, and this time had to sell their mill and site in Hamilton Valley to Noah Smithwick. Several Wightite families stayed with Smithwick, while their co-religionists gathered their cattle herd grazing near Honey Creek. For several weeks the Wightites prospected near the Pack Saddle Mountains, looking for and failing to find an old Spanish silver mine. By the early part of December 1853, their wagons and herds were traveling south on the Llano and Fredericksburg roads.

Lyman Wight rode into Fredericksburg to settle some business matters with the German leaders there, and his followers rested livestock and repaired transportation, first at Cherry Springs, then at Squaw Creek. The Fredericksburg leaders wanted Wight to return and build another mill close to them, but no deal could be reached.

The Wightites made short moves during January and February, searching for better pasture and water. The pushed on by horseback, by wagon, and on foot as their herds and flocks trailed behind. Spencer Smith wrote in his journal that between marches they busied themselves with wagon repair, animal husbandry, and gathering wild honey. They began their final push to the Medina River, now their destination, on 19 February 1854. On the other side of the river the new village of Bandera, which they reached on 1 March 1854, awaited them. Levi Wight would remember later they had reached "Bandery Town" on his birthday.[1]

Relations with the Native Americans had continued to worsen during the trip. The days of amity with Buffalo Hump, as recently as 1850, were gone forever. Lamoni Wight thought of the Tonkawa as friendly pests and thieves, but he and others believed the southern Indians to be mounted raiders "noted for thievery and murdering." For instance, young Wight was chased by, in his words, a "savag," during the move to Bandera in January. Before he lost the pursuer in some cedar breaks, Wight was convinced the warrior would murder him. In later years, geography continued to define his feelings about the natives. The northern Indians were "wonderful beggars and thieves," while he described the Comanche raiders as murderers.[2]

In late February 1854, Spencer Smith's diary records that a Comanche raiding party killed a heifer, "and the meet cut off from the bones and carried off, and two others wounded, and 8 head of horses and mules gone." Nine Wightites mounted up and followed the Indians' tracks, while Spencer Smith, Orange Wight, Joseph Goodale, and Andrew Hoffman led the others on to the Medina River. By the next day, having discovered their prey, the Mormon frontiersmen used the cool foggy morning to make a rifle ambush about 100 yards distant

---

1. J. B. Wight, *The Wild Ram of the Mountain*, 381–83; H. H. Smith, "The Lyman Wight Colony in Texas," 32–33; L. L. Wight, *Reminiscences*, 16.
2. William Leyland journal, in H. H. Smith, "The Lyman Wight Colony in Texas," 25; L. L. Wight, *Reminiscences*, 2, 11, 14.

from the Indian camp, driving the Comanches into wild retreat. The whites believed they had killed at least one Comanche and wounded two more. The riflemen recovered not only their own stock, but six ponies as well, and returned with "bows, shields, lances, etc."[3]

Many of Bandera's original settlers arrived with Wight's colony, including the Chipmans, Goodales, Curtises, Carters, Moncurs, Hays, and Minears. The Mormon frontier families immediately began creating a community, first in Bandera and then twelve miles upstream, described by George Hay as a "beautiful wild country." They shucked 165,000 cypress shingles and sawed lumber at Charles DeMontel's horse mill,[4] completing 165,000 shingles in April and May. Although they still lived in tents at the end of April, Spencer Smith was teaching boys over the age of eight in a new schoolhouse.[5]

The settlers put down roots. William Curtis had earlier married Lydia Minear at Hamilton Mills, after the murder of her husband. It is unknown how many of her twelve children he sheltered after the marriage; however, they added one, and possibly two, of their own in Bandera County. After Lyman Wight's death in 1858, the families of Andrew Hoffman, Janet Ballantyne, Abram Moncur, Joseph Goodale, Meacham Curtis, and others remained in the county. This Wightite remnant provided the basis for the revival, in 1865, of the Reorganized Church of Jesus Christ of Latter Day Saints and its continuing history since then in the Texas Hill Country.[6]

Lyman Wight offered Charles DeMontel the opportunity to work together on shares. DeMontel was supposed to contribute the saws and machinery, and the Mormons the grist stones and expertise. The opportunity for machine-ground meal must have been tempting, but DeMontel, perhaps knowing how difficult the Wild Ram could be, declined.

---

3. Spencer Smith diary, in H. H. Smith, "The Lyman Wight Colony in Texas," 35; L. L. Wight, *Reminiscences*, 15.
4. "DeMontel, Charles S.," *The Handbook of Texas Online*, http://www.tsha.utexas.edu/handbook/online/articles/DD/fde35.html accessed 19 February 2004.
5. George Hay, quoted in J. Marvin Hunter, *A Brief History of Bandera County: Covering One Hundred Years of Intrepid History* (Bandera, TX: Frontier Times, 1936), 112; Spencer Smith diary, in H. H. Smith, "The Lyman Wight Colony in Texas," 36–37.
6. J. Marvin Hunter, "100 Years in Bandera, 1853–1953" (photocopy), 3, 4, 86, LDS archives.

In November 1854, Wight then moved his group upstream to a more isolated location. Medina Lake now covers the small village of rough homes once known as Mountain Valley, where they quickly constructed horse-powered mills for sawing and grinding. Soon they were selling shingles again in Castroville.[7]

While Mormons were building yet another schoolhouse, planting crops, and preparing the new homesites, they became careless with their livestock. Some of the young boys discovered one morning that natives had stolen some horses. A mounted party from Mountain Valley pursued the Indians and, on the second day, stumbled on their camp. The warriors scattered as the white men's mounted assault swept through it. Neither side took casualties, but the Mormons ran off most of the Indian livestock. The Indians had escaped into the brush, where, Levi Wight thought, they were planning "another campaign, which they no doubt completed before the next morning." His diary reflects the fact that the Comanches were indeed busy. Several weeks later, they ran off thirteen mules and horses from a night corral the Wightites had made while carrying shingles to Castroville.[8]

The material culture of Mountain Valley was primitive. In a letter from Lyman Wight to his old friend Sanford Porter in Salt Lake City, he answered some complaints of Porter's daughter, a plural wife of Ezra Chipman. Matilda Porter Chipman had earlier written to her father that she was unhappy at Mountain Valley. Wight told Porter, in wry humor, that the cabins were 100 minus 86 feet by 50 feet minus 38 feet, each with a "good door in front and an old quilt neatly hung for the back door." Wight then chastised Porter, not ungently, about questioning his leadership, Mountain Valley's economic conditions, and the Porter family's welfare there. The Wild Ram defended his "common property" stewardship of the community as "the principle of equality[,] the foundation of the celestial church." He

---

7. Charlotte H. Cates, "The History of Bandera County" (master's thesis, St. Mary's University, 1942), 19; J. Marvin Hunter, "A Bandera County Pioneer," *Frontier Times* (Bandera, TX), July 1924. 12–13; Texas Historical Records Survey, *Inventory of County Archives, No. 10, Bandera County (Bandera),* (San Antonio: Texas Historical Records Survey, Division of Professional and Service Projects, Work Project A, 1940), 11.
8. L. L. Wight, *Reminiscences,* 17–18.

believed that Joseph Smith Jr. had "commanded me to come to Texas and God commanded me to continue to preach . . . until I had finished my work and then he would take me to himself." Wight, of course, took the opportunity to dig at Brigham Young, referring to him as the eighth angel of perdition from the *Book of Revelations*.[9]

The village progressed, if slowly, with the additions of a horse-powered mill and a blacksmith shop. Fifty acres of communal gardens included corn, lettuce, radishes, and cotton. In an extended letter from January to April 1856, Wight wrote to his nephew Benjamin Wight that the colony was crafting bedsteads and chairs, 8 or 10 of the former and about 130 of the latter having already gone to market, and the furniture makers were planning to ship the same amount in about three weeks. Optimistically, if unrealistically, Wight confided his hopes that a railroad connecting Austin with the Gulf of Mexico would soon be built. His health, after some bad spells, had again improved, and his weight was up to 222 pounds, he told his nephew. He provided some insight concerning the community stewardship of the economic cooperative's procedures. He did the trading for the men, while his wife Harriet did the same for the women, revealing they still dominated the economic tasks for the community.[10]

Life continued at Mountain Valley. Levi Lamoni Wight married his adopted sister, Sophia Leyland, on 4 September 1856, his father celebrating the ceremony with Spencer Smith and Asher Gressman as witnesses. The newlyweds' home imitated the general standard of Texas frontier housing before 1900—a one-room "shanty built of split cypress board," no floor, but with a fireplace. The young couple crafted homemade furniture—a bedstead, a table, two chairs, and corner shelves. Cooking and eating utensils included dishes, two plates, two tin cups, two forks and knives each, a frying pan, one skillet, and a small fire shovel. Most of the bedding was borrowed. Levi had a gun, a cow, a sycamore fishing pole, and an axe for creating the

9. Lyman and Harriet Wight, Medina River, to Sanford Porter, 7 December 1855.
10. Lyman and Harriet Wight, Medina River, to Benjamin Wight, 12 January 1856, postscript 3 April 1856, postscript 26 April 1853, Lyman Wight letterbook.

necessities of life. In this frontier environment, Levi and Sylvia Wight would have seven children. They moved constantly, from Texas to the Cherokee Nation, to Missouri, and on to Arkansas, returning to Texas, where they lived to the turn of the century, died at Sweetwater, and were buried in its cemetery.[11]

Comanche raids continue to severely hurt Mountain Valley and its economic development. Orange Wight and his sister-in-law Eliza Wight (Lyman Lehi's wife) both wrote in April 1855 to members of George Miller's family in Michigan about their struggles with the Indians. Eliza reported that the warriors had stolen all but one of the community's mules and horses. Orange told the Millers that he had been serving with the Rangers, and had chased the natives all the way to El Paso and then on into New Mexico Territory. Catching up with one small party of Comanches, the Rangers killed five or six warriors. This setback did not stop the natives from stealing at least another twenty-nine horses from the Mormons, which, according to Ranger Wight, "has injured our circumstances considerably."[12]

The Wights' letters upset the Mormon Strangite leadership in Michigan. James Strang's newspaper editorialized against the Wightites' Indian battles, insisting all had to be startled that "any who was ever a Mormon should engage in hunting Indians." The editorial opined that the obvious reason was because the natives had not been paid for having their hunting grounds taken from them. They could not be blamed, for, "What less could the Indians do? We cannot condemn them," for they were doing "no more than any man would do under the same circumstances." This public statement, remarkably free from the era's race prejudices, infuriated the Wightite frontiersmen.[13]

Orange Wight and Lyman Wight defiantly wrote replies to the *Northern Islander* at Beaver Island, Michigan, which published only the younger man's letter. He strongly defended the settlers' actions, arguing the Mormons, as native-born Americans, had as much right

---

11. Bandera County marriage licenses, 1:No. 1; L. L. Wight, *Reminiscences*, 17–18; L. L. Wight, "Autobiography," 257, 266; Turk, "Mormons in Texas," 55, 78–79.
12. Eliza Wight to Sister Miller, 2 April 1855, and O. L. Wight to Bro. James [Miller], *Northern Islander* (Beaver Island, MI), 31 May 1855.
13. Editors, *Northern Islander*, 31 May 1855.

to the land as did the Indians. He ignored the fact that more than twenty of the adult Wightites had been born in Scotland. The Indians, Wight went on, refused to sell their land to the settlers. He concluded that self-defense was the only possible resort against a people who "will not make peace, and live on equal terms with [us]."

The *Northern Islander* published an opposing piece to Wight's opinion. It noted that "Bro. Wight is entirely wrong as to this controversy," referring to Wight's followers and others of their race as "strangers from distant climes." The editorial finished on the note that "the question at issue therefore is, not whether Bro. Wight and the rest of the Texans shall keep their possessions, and the Indians theirs, but whether the white Texans have a right to keep all they have got, and to get all they can."[14]

Lyman Wight's unpublished comments strongly rebuked the Strang-Miller combination for criticizing his dealings with the Indians. What angered Wight most was the suggestion that he could prosper only if he moved off the Indians' lands. Wight warned the editors to "be careful when you handle edged tools that you don't cut your fingers." Joseph Smith himself, the Wild Ram trumpeted, had sent him to preach to and feed the Indians. He claimed that he had given them, along with the stolen livestock, beef, pork, beans, clothing, and other items. And, after all, Wight continued, the Strangites were merely apostates while he was an apostle of the Christian church (never mind Brigham Young!) and a faithful follower of Smith. The long letter recounted his triumphs and positions in the church. His role was to lead the few remaining faithful until Joseph Smith Jr.'s posterity stepped forward to lead the church. Wight sniffed he was not "the least disappointed" to have neither office nor leadership position "in the Strangite Ch[urch] or Brigham's church."[15]

Wight, in other correspondence in 1855 and 1856, continued the refrain against the local raiders. He notified Major Robert Simpson Neighbors, the federal Indian agent for the area, about the raid which Eliza Wight had written of to the Millers. In two days, the

---

14. O. L. Wight to the Editors, *Northern Islander*, 16 August 1855; subject name listings in Turk, "Mormons in Texas."

15. Lyman Wight, Medina River, to the editors, *Northern Islander*, Beaver Creek, Michigan, July 1855, Lyman Wight letterbook.

Comanches, he wrote, had stolen sixteen horses and twenty-five oxen, as well as butchered two steers. Sixty-six families in the area were suffering from lack of military protection. If the government was taking Indian lands, then the federals should either subsidize the natives, or send in Army troops for protection. He admitted to Major Neighbors that the Mormons were thinking about leaving Mountain Valley.

Major Neighbors replied on 26 November 1855 that as long as the U.S. Army continued, in his opinion, to war unjustly on the natives, he could do nothing to control Indian affairs. The army had patrols in Comanche hunting grounds and had driven the Lipan Apache to Mexico, where he believed they were plotting with Mexicans against the Americans north of the Rio Grande. He could offer no relief to the Wightites.

The major had served the Republic of Texas as an army officer from 1836 to 1844. Afterward, he served both the Republic and the United States as an Indian agent. He spent more time than probably any white man on and beyond the frontier, among the Lipan Apache and the Comanches. He served the state and the federal government continually until 1859, not only as an Indian agent, but also as a state commissioner, a legislator, and a presidential elector. Most Texans who lived on the frontier or traveled beyond it despised him for his 'pro-Indian' beliefs. A man whom he probably did not know, Edward Cornett, killed him from behind at Fort Belknap on 14 September 1859.

The Comanches continued raiding on into the following year, and neither Major Neighbors nor the federal army could control them. On 7 March 1856, Wight wrote to the governor of Texas that the Indians had stolen $3,000 of his stock since 1851. Only the previous Tuesday, they had taken the last of the horses, which put idle his grist mill, sawmill, and turning lathe. He could not buy more horses. Wight asked if the state government could provide some type of redress for the community. Other than sending a few Rangers, Texas could give no aid to Wight and his people.[16]

---

16. "Neighbors, Robert Simpson," in *The Handbook of Texas Online*, http://www.tsha.utexas.edu/handbook/online/articles/NN/fne8.html, accessed 19 February 2004; Lyman Wight, Medina River Camp, to Major Neighbors, 18 March 1855, Lyman Wight letterbook; Robert S. Neighbors, Indian Agent, to Gentlemen c/o San Antonio, 26 March 1855, Lyman Wight letterbook; Lyman

Despite Indian and government problems, Lyman Wight's folks once again demonstrated a sophisticated management of frontier community politics. They dominated the process in Bandera County even more thoroughly than at theocratic Zodiac. The Mormons controlled all aspects of county administration until they abandoned Mountain Valley in 1858.

As usual, Mormon bloc voting brought disproportionate public power. The first county election (March 1856) resulted in a sweep of Wightite candidates—Orlando B. Miles (chief justice), William Ballantyne and William Curtis (county commissioners), Andrew Hoffman (sheriff), and Irwin Carter (assessor/collector of taxes). That November, Gideon Carter was elected the county treasurer. The next spring, George Hay became deputy county clerk, while the ten-member county road committee included seven Wightites. Ezra Chipman served briefly as county commissioner, and later as a deputy sheriff under William Curtis. Meacham Curtis was Mountain Valley's justice of the peace.[17]

Wightite political influence dominated the juror selections for 1857 and 1858. In 1857, nine of the eighteen grand jurors were Mormon; in the spring of 1858, seven of twenty were Mormon; and in August of 1858, after Wight's death, another twelve of his former followers were elected. Finally, at this time, William Bell became the first non-Mormon elected to county office as county commissioner. He joined Mormons O. B. Miles and Ezra Chipman on the commissioners' court.

The greater irony of Mormon politics in Bandera County was that it signaled the death knell of the common-stock association, which ended Lyman Wight's economic power over his people. No evidence exists that disaffected members had organized an immediate or direct conspiracy against him. Apparently, the growing privatization of property was at first indirect and incremental; however, it also

---

Wight "To His Excellency the Governor of the State of Texas," 7 March 1856, Lyman Wight letterbook.

17. Commissioners' Court minutes, 1, 2, 7, 9, 10, 13, 16, 17; Debo, *Bandera County History*, 309; [Bandera County unmarked register] 1856:5, 9, 11, 10, 20, 23, 30, 31, 35, 36, 42, 43, 44, Bandera County archives; Bandera County probate and wills 1:6, 7, Bandera County archives; Bandera County district minutes, Spring and Fall terms, 1857 and 1858, 14, 22, Bandera County archives.

undermined Wight's spiritual as well as fiscal power. Changes began when Andrew Hoffman, Abram Moncur, and eight other colonists independently registered livestock under their own brands rather than that of Lyman Wight & Co. Colony members registered four more brands before L. Lehi Wight registered his father's brand, Aries, the mark of the Ram of the Zodiac, for the church cooperative.[18]

Some in the colony, however, continued to follow Wight's leadership. In 1857, Lehi Wight sold 100 cattle to John Vance on "behalf of the company with me as there [*sic*] legally authorized agent to transact all business pertaining to said company, and for myself," for $700. Four months later, the first overt economic competition within the colony became evident. David Monroe and Charles Bird registered their mark for Monroe Bird & Co., challenging Lyman Wight & Co. The religio-economic bonds of familial and in-kin ties forged by Lyman Wight were now being further sundered through the transfer of community property to private holdings.

The economic change transcended age, gender, family, and in-kin relationships. Those who registered private brands/marks included Moncur, a brother-in-law to Lyman Wight; Sheriff Hoffman; William Ballantyne, another brother-in-law to Wight and county commissioner; William Curtis, county commissioner; O. B. Miles, the chief justice; and Gideon Carter, a former Wight family ward and current county treasurer. Others included Rosilla Carter, plural wife to Ezra A. Chipman; George Hay, the deputy county clerk; Irwin Carter, county assessor/collector and another former ward of the Wight family; and Benjamin F. Bird. When Ezra A. Chipman, Wight's companion and supporter for twenty years, registered his brand, the old order had broken down for good. The registration of brands and marks by young men who had grown to manhood in Wight's colony—David Monroe, Charles Bird, Joseph David Sutherland, and George Montague Jr.—gave further evidence the old order was over.

Later in the fall of 1856, the change to private property evolved further when a majority of the colonists bought Bandera City real property. Families were moving out of Mountain Valley to live in the village. On the 18th and 19th of September, the following bought

18. Bandera County deed record, 9 May 1857, Bandera County archives.

town lots in Bandera: Orlando B. Miles, William Ballantyne, Irwin Carter, William Curtis, Abram Moncur, Ellen Bell, Gideon Carter, Andrew Hoffman, Jenet (Jeanette) Hay, George Hay, and B. F. Bird. Most property buyers were family heads. When Ezra Chipman bought a lot in December, the last of the polygamous males—other than Lyman Wight—deserted Mountain Valley.[19]

Wight's remaining power naturally was focused within his immediate family. Only Aaron Hawley, who neither registered a private brand nor bought a town lot, was unrelated by blood to Wight; however, a sister had been Wight's youngest wife until her death. Others included his son-in-law Spencer C. Smith and three of his sons—Lyman Lehi Wight, Loami Limhi Wight, and Levi Lamoni Wight. Orange Lysander Wight, Lyman's eldest son who long disagreed with his father's autocratic ways, had left the colony more than a year earlier.[20]

The secularizing process of transforming former Wightites into citizens in the larger community continued. Private matters, once handled within the community, were now sent to the district court for resolution. The fall 1857 term of the District Court of Bandera County heard the case of *Amasa Clark vs. Frances Clark.* The husband accused his wife of adultery and sued for divorce. Seven members of the jury—former Wightites Marion Andrews, William Curtis, Cyrus Isham, Aaron Hawley, William Gaylord, John Gressman, and George Montague—formed a majority. The jury found for the plaintiff—awarding him custody of the child, all of his property before the marriage, and half of the property acquired after the marriage. Miles and Curtis were directed to inventory the property and report their findings, which were two cows, two calves, and one unimproved town lot in Bandera City.

Former Wightites persisted in the use of the secular legal system to resolve family and social problems. One example was that of Petronella Kindla, the ward of John Kindla. Several citizens of Bandera County—including William Curtis, William Ballantyne, Gideon Carter, and Amasa Clark—accused John Kindla of misusing his ward. His offense is not clear, but court records suggest a

---

19. Bandera County deed records, A (transcribed in A-3/B-2):17, 18, 20–21, 23–24, 26–27, 29–30, 33–34, 35, 38–39, 40–41, 42–43, 49–50, 53; O. L. Wight, "Recollections," 12.

20. [Bandera County] brand record, 1, 2, 3, Bandera County archives.

dark undertone to the entire incident. Consequently, the court transferred the guardianship of Petronella Kindla to David Monroe. Lyman Wight would not have permitted the introduction of non-Mormons into his followers' families without his permission. Now he had no say at all.[21]

The former colonists' economic inclusion, as well, into the larger secular community is further demonstrated by an examination of Abram Moncur's 1859 probate record. The estate had grown steadily during the three years since the former tailor's assistant and miller had bought two town lots in 1856. Irwin Carter and Benjamin F. Bird appraised his property as follows: a wagon valued at $40; a yoke of oxen, $100; horses, $75; sixty-nine acres, $265; houses and lots, $100; cattle and other stock, $168; a bed stead, $12; chests and contents, $6; a cupboard, $10; table and chairs, $3 each; a clock, $5; a plow, $6; thirty to forty hogs, $45; cash, $138; and a gun and six-shooter, $12 and $25 each, a total value of more than $1,000. Moncur had become a small, apparently prospering stockman and farmer. He and his Wightite neighbors had evolved, and spun a peculiar and communal colony of religionists into the vital, dynamic fabric of the whole cloth that made up frontier Texas.[22]

An interesting part of this emerging order was increased opportunity for women. Ellen Bell, the unacknowledged plural wife of Abram Moncur, was the first woman in Bandera County to record land in her own name. She bought a town lot in Range 8, several spaces from that of Moncur. Her sister, Jenet, bought her own property the same day. Jenet Hay's home, with cypress floors, was quickly completed and became a political, economic, social, and religious center for the town. At various times, her home served as courthouse, boarding house, school, store, church, and post office. Contrary to local legend, it never served as the town jail.[23]

The economic and personal developments shrinking Wight's remaining followers into a rump quorum weighed heavily on the old

---

21. Bandera County district court register, Fall term, 1857, 14–15, Bandera County archives; Bandera County probate and wills, 1:6, 7.
22. Ibid., 21 and 28 May 1860, 11, 13.
23. Bandera County deed records, A (transcribed in A-3/B-2):18, 20–21, 42–43; Debo, *Bandera County History*, 386.

man's mind. Early in 1858, he declared that the colony should move on to Jackson County, Missouri. He had been pondering for some time the possibility of leaving Texas. Nearly two years earlier, he had written to Salt Lake City (while being unable to resist making the comment that he still thought Utah Mormonism an abomination, comparing its fair city with Sodom) to inform a nephew that, while praising the Lone Star State for its religious toleration, he wanted to see Jackson County again, which he considered part of his inheritance.[24]

Another factor influencing Wight's decision was that the role of Texas as a gathering place for Zion had been unnecessary for almost a decade. The Mormon majority was affiliated with Brigham Young in Utah's valleys. The LDS leader's preeminence as greater Mormonism's recognized leader continued to irritate Wight. He picked at it as if it were a scab. In 1857, the Wild Ram wrote a bitter letter to Young. Unwilling to salute him as president, Wight addressed Young as governor. Still upset after eight years about Thomas's and Martindale's allegations of his excessive drinking, Wight told Young that Haws and Woodworth had said in front of fifty witnesses that "it would take ten yoke of oxen to draw enough alcohol over the mountains to keep brother [Willard] Richards drinking one year and that it cost more to support Brigham Young alone than it did any other hundred men in the church." Wight, finally removed of a burden that weighed heavily for years, then dismissed Young and the entire matter.[25]

Sixty-two and in poor health, Wight had little to hold him to frontier Texas. He would not leave much of worth. The Comanche and Apache raids had crippled Lyman Wight & Co. His former followers had taken most of the cooperative's remaining assets for their private livestock and farming operations. Finally, Wight wanted to join with those other co-religionists in Missouri and Iowa who were opposed to Brigham Young, and were also creating Josephite religious alternatives. Wight was interested in joining those encouraging Joseph Smith III to assume his father's mantle and step forth to lead the entire Restoration.

---

24. Lyman Wight, Mountain Valley, to Benjamin Wight, 12 January 1856, postscript 3 April 1856, postscript 26 April 1856, Lyman Wight letterbook.
25. Lyman Wight to Brigham Young, 2 March 1857.

Other reasons were more personal. Along with his wife, Harriet, the old Wild Ram wanted to visit the scenes associated with his vigorous manhood, where he with Joseph Smith Jr. defended and suffered for their common faith. This time he set out on what would be his final trek; eighty men, women, and children followed him. The major in-kin and family groups, although represented in the final following, no longer supported him. The final membership of this group reflected how much the original colony dynamics had deteriorated. Numbers now were counted only in scores, not hundreds; the households no longer were counted in dozens, but on two hands.

The immediate households included those of his three surviving wives (Harriet, Jane Margaret, and Mary Ann) and their younger, dependent children. Next were two of his married sons, Lyman Lehi Wight and Levi Lamoni Wight, with their families, and that of his son-in-law Spencer Smith and wife, Anna Wight Smith. Other households included James and Abigail Andrews Ballantyne, William and Lydia Curtis, Aaron and Ann Hawley, and George and Eliza Curtis Bird. Neither of the remaining polygamous patriarchs—Ezra Chipman and Orange Wight—joined the caravan. Chipman would remain in Bandera County until he died in 1913, while the younger Wight had earlier left Mountain Valley sometime in 1855.[26]

The small band set off for Jackson County, Missouri. The next day, 31 March 1858, the Moses of the early Texas Mormons died at Dexter, a few miles west of San Antonio. A fatal seizure felled him, caused in part because of years of alcohol abuse and the medicinal opium he used to treat earlier illnesses. Ninety-one-year-old Virginia Minear Hay Garland (interviewed by Garland E. Tickemeyer) recalled, in May 1935 at a Bandera reunion, that she had been a thirteen-year-old girl in the wagon train when Wight became ill. She remembered him as a short, fat man who drank too much and used opium.

It should be noted that the drug's use in the West was legal and not uncommon, sold over the counter in Texas before the Civil War. Its value was measured on a small set of scales, balancing equally

26. Turk,"Mormons in Texas", 62; O. L. Wight, "Recollections," 12; L. L. Wight, *Reminiscences*, 20. O. L. Wight later wrote that he had left the community two and a half years before his father's final journey.

an amount of the powder against the weight of a gold dollar. Davis Bitton has written, in his annotated edition of Levi Wight's *Reminiscences*, that the circumstances of Wight's death require

> further exploration, but it should be stated here that opium derivatives were used in many medicines during the nineteenth century (including soothing syrup for babies), that it was possible for addicts to function normally for many years, and that Lyman Wight seemed to have been a man of great energy and stamina.

No record is extant that Wight used it recreationally. Thus, the role of opium in Wight's death does not reach the opprobrium associated with modern standards.[27]

With his interment the next day, Wight and Wightism were buried forever in the cemetery of Zodiac.

27. Garland E. Tickemeyer notes, interview with Virginia Minear Hay, May 1935, in "Lyman Wight (a Description)," (photocopy of reconstructed typescript manuscript, 1961), RLDS archives; L. L. Wight, *Reminiscences*, 87–88n9. The extensive interview was typed by Tickemeyer and sent to Sam Burgess, an RLDS historian at Independence, Missouri. This transcript has been destroyed, misplaced, or lost. Tickemeyer, in 1961, prepared a two-page summary from memory, highlighting particularly the death of Lyman Wight.

Conclusion

The Way of All Flesh

When the clods fell upon his coffin, they obliterated his mistakes in life.

—Levi Lamoni Wight

The company disbanded, and the survivors split the property and goods. Some, like Orange Wight who had earlier left the colony, did not receive a share. Harriet Benton Wight and several of her family endured the frontier hardships of the Civil War at Bandera, Fredericksburg, and Marble Falls. Others returned to Bandera County to join their former neighbors from the colony. Many lived in Texas for the rest of their lives, including Ezra A. Chipman, the last polygamist, who died in Bandera County in 1913 at the age of ninety-five.[1]

The Civil War caught up the former Bandera Mormons, as it did with the citizens of the various states. The issues of secession and unionism sweeping Texas in 1860 and 1861 affected the sixty-odd voters in Bandera County. John Bell's Constitutional Union Party carried the county in the presidential election, suggesting that the male adults were uncomfortable with the idea of leaving the Union. Three months later, however, the secession referendum carried Bandera County by one vote, thirty-three to thirty-two. Since the former Wightites could have cast as many as thirty votes, they most likely

1. O. L. Wight, "Recollections," 12; population schedule, census of 1860, Gillespie County; L. L. Wight, *Reminiscences*, 20, 27, 28, 112; Bandera County district minutes, Fall term, 1 August 1858, 26; subject name listings in Turk, "Mormons in Texas."

TABLE 10

VOTING IN SELECTED HILL COUNTRY COUNTIES IN THE ELECTION OF 1860 AND THE SECESSION REFERENDUM OF 23 FEBRUARY 1861[2]

County (Year of Establishment)	*Dominant Cultural Group*	*Actual Voting % of the Electorate*		*% of Vote Against Secession in 1861*
		1860 National Election	*1861 Secession Referendum*	
Gillespie (1848)	80% German	20.6%	62.6%	96%
Kerr (1856)	55% German	59.4%	67.5%	43%
Medina (1848)	30% German	41.8%	76.3%	60%
Bandera (1856)	Former Wightite / 20% German	35.8%	61.3%	49%

chose secession. The local ethnic groups, such as the immigrant Poles and Germans, who were noted for having federal sympathies, probably cast their votes against leaving the Union.[3]

Researching the secession question in the Hill Country of 1860 and 1861, however, does caution against historians' assumptions. The table above indicates the peril in attempting to interpret too minutely the voting patterns of the German frontier in Texas. These immigrants as a group seemed to oppose separation, but solid pockets of secessionism did exist among them. Gillespie County voted overwhelming (96%) for the Union, yet in Kerr County, where the electorate also had a German majority, 60% voted for secession. The counties where former Wightites lived during 1860 and 1861 are also difficult to analyze. For instance, Medina, with a sizeable German minority, voted to stay in the Union. Bandera, with an electorate split almost exactly in half between former Wightites and Germans, voted by the slightest of majorities to leave the Union.

2. Compiled from Glenn S. Gilbert, "Origin and Location of German Speakers," in *Texas and Germany: Crosscurrents,* ed. Joseph Wilson (Houston: Rice University, 1977), 25–27; Walter L. Buenger, *Secession and the Union in Texas* (Austin: University of Texas Press, 1984), 5; Timmons, "The Referendum in Texas on the Ordinance of Secession," 15–19; Jordan, *German Seed in Texas Soil,* 184; Randolph B. Campbell, *An Empire for Slavery: The Peculiar Institution in Texas, 1821–1865* (Baton Rouge: Louisiana State University Press, 1989), 264–65.

3. Joe E. Timmons, "The Referendum in Texas on the Ordinance of Secession, February 23, 1861: The Vote," *East Texas Historical Society* 11 (February 1973): 12–15; James A. Baggett, "The Constitutional Union Party in Texas," *Southwestern Historical Quarterly* 82, no. 1 (January 1979): 263.

Other Wightites had taken the opportunity earlier to leave Texas. The families of William Curtis, John Miller, and Rodney Brace left Burnet County for California in 1861 with Noah Smithwick. Smithwick, a Jacksonian Democrat, explained many years later why he left the party: "and when the term Democrat was made to mean secessionists I could go with the party no further." After being told by one rabid secessionist, who had come to Texas only after the Mexican War, to "wait until we get things fixed and we'll attend to your case," Smithwick and company left for the West and never returned to Texas. They all eventually settled at or near San Bernardino, California.

Smithwick, in his memoirs, wrote that it was the threat of death that forced him and others to leave Texas.

> When after the close of the war we established communications with friends in Texas, I learned of the fate of many of my Union friends, among them my nephew, John Hubbard, who was waylaid and shot down, his body being riddled with bullets. I felt it would be unwise for me to return, as I should feel an uncontrollable desire to avenge his death. And yet up to the time I left Burnet County there had never been a murder in the county. But the dogs of war were literally turned loose, and the devil concealed in men, unchained. . . . For the cowards who, taking good care to keep out of harm's way, hunted down and murdered defenseless Union men—well, I have never been a believer in the orthodox hell, still, when I think of those wretches, I am forced to concede that it was an oversight in the plan of creation if hell was left out.[4]

Levi Lamoni Wight described the tumultuous times: "[S]uppresion of rebellion was on one side, and Indians on the other, and in the midst disloyal citizens and bushwhackers, governor against lieutenant governor . . . father against son, son against father, brother against brother, all in wonderful commotion. We [the former Wightites] took largely of the spirit of rebellion." Reinforcing Wight's opinion, Smithwick remembered that Mormons in California favored the spirit of secession. He found the Latter Day Saints there all "without an exception" supported the South, although, in

4. Smithwick, *Evolution of a State*, 250, 262–63.

his opinion, southerners were more intolerant of Mormonism than were northerners, and Mormons felt little "sympathy with the peculiar institution of the South." He believed his Mormon friends wished the South well in its insurrection, so that the principle of secession might apply to Utah Territory; therefore, the Mormons could shake off the federal government.[5]

Smithwick's assertion has some merit. Although many Wightites, Cutlerites, RLDS, and Strangites had little use for Brigham Young and Utah Mormonism, as a group they had an even healthier dislike of the federal government, which refused to protect them from their enemies in Illinois and Missouri. Utah Mormons certainly had no love lost for the Union. In 1857, President Franklin Pierce had sent a third of the United States Army, under the command of Colonel Albert S. Johnston, to suppress a rebellion and restore federal authority in the territory.

Most Bandera Mormons and their neighbors served the South, defending the Texas frontier after the withdrawal of federal troops. Robert Ballantyne organized Ballantyne's Minutemen, a state militia unit often incorrectly identified as Texas Rangers. George Hay and Joseph Lyman Sutherland rode with Ballantyne against the Comanches and the local draft resisters. Ezra A. Chipman, forty-five years old, along with two of his sons and a future son-in-law, also served in the state forces. Private Orange L. Wight soldiered with the Mountain Guards of Burnet County, and later enlisted in the 3rd Frontier District. Private Loami Wight marched in Captain Charles DeMontel's Ranger Company G (later D) in the Frontier Regiment. Fourth Corporal Levi Lamoni Wight served in a company guarding federal prisoners, then joined the Confederate Army. He fought against the Union at the Battle of Mansfield in 1864.[6]

Richard Bird and Gideon Hawley served the Union. Bird deserted his state unit, and crossed the Rio Grande into Mexico, where he enlisted for federal service. He shipped to New Orleans and

5. L. L. Wight, "Autobiography," 268–69; Smithwick, *Evolution of a State*, 263.

6. Bandera County History Book Committee, *History of Bandera County, Texas* (Dallas: Curtis Media, 1986), 267, 309, 385, 543–43; subject name listings in Turk, "Mormons in Texas"; records of the Civil War, Texas State Library, Austin, TX.

fought in Louisiana. After the war, Bird returned to Bandera County to woo and marry Jenemie Moncur. They left for Iowa. Gideon Hawley joined a frontier guard unit in Iowa and served for four months in 1864. He mustered out of the Iowa guard to enlist in the Union army. He was sent south to fight against the rebellion, but was discharged again, this time for poor health.[7]

Campe Verde, north of Bandera City, was garrisoned by Texas state troops in early 1861. After the inception of the draft in 1862, resistance to it continued to grow, and measures to prevent resistance grew harsher. What happened in Bandera County to eight men who disagreed with the draft reminds the reader of Smithwick's reason to immigrate to California. Eight men and one boy, all well mounted, headed through the area in the summer of 1863 on the way to Mexico, in order to escape from the troubles of the war. According to Hill Country journalist J. Marvin Hunter, twenty-five state troopers under a Major Alexander were in pursuit, "and captured them on Squirrel Creek, about ten miles south of Hondo. On the evening of the second day's return to camp, some of Alexander's troops, probably including the Major himself, hung their prisoners. Alexander's men took 'their victims' horses, saddles, bedding, clothing and shoes' and returned through Bandera." Some of the Wightites and others, including George Hay and Amasa Clark,

> found the bodies of those unfortunate men lying just as they had been cut down, pieces of the horsehair rope around each man's neck. They had all been strangled to death by the rope being placed over a limb and drawn up, possibly by someone on horseback. One man . . . was lying face down, shot through with a wooden ramrod, which had passed entirely through his body and penetrated into the ground for at least 10 or 12 inches. It was with great difficulty that I drew out this ramrod. . . . We buried them as best we could, and in giving our verdict at the inquest we definitely placed the blame on Alexander's men, some of whom I knew, but they are all dead now. (Hay, quoted in Hunter, *San Antonio Express*)

Amasa Clark thought the victims were "deliberately murdered without being given a chance for their lives. . . . Some had been

7. Platt and R. Hawley, *House of Hawley*, 49–50; Black, *ERLDS* 1:455.

partly stripped. I heard afterward that some of the men who took part in the hanging had worn the clothes of their victims while passing through Bandera." Joseph Poor believed that robbery, under the guise of military operations, had been the sole motivation for the murders.[8]

Although none of the Bandera Mormons died serving Texas and the Confederacy, all on the frontier suffered alike from native raiders, disease, and wartime privation. The Indians had been "troblesome" and had killed some Texans, according to Levi Wight. Disease struck harshly in Bandera County. Five cousins in the Bird family, all under the age of thirteen, died from illness between 23 October and 1 December 1862. The material culture of the region was devastated by the war. Levi Wight found his family "barefoot" when he came home from the fighting, noting that "the first shoes they wore after the war closed I made."[9]

After 1865, more than 200 former Wightites were living in Texas, California, Missouri, and Iowa. Almost all had joined other branches of Mormonism. The majority, including the wives of Lyman Wight and most of the other polygamists and former polygamists, joined the RLDS church in the Upper Midwest. About twenty in number reunited with the LDS church in Utah. Within a few months of the close of the war, Andrew Hoffman and Spencer Smith, who had moved to Iowa after Lyman Wight's funeral, returned to Bandera with RLDS elder Hugh Lytle. Arriving on 14 August 1865, Lytle conducted revival services every Wednesday night and Sunday morning for a month. The meetings were held in the typical arbor-brush enclosure of the South. This was a small, open-air building, with a brush-covered roof, laid out with rough timbers. The sides remained open to whatever slight breeze might blow through to relieve the summer heat. In the arbor, by sun during the day and by torch at night, the RLDS ministers preached a message familiar to these Texans: that God had not rejected His church, that Joseph Smith III, the

---

8. J. Marvin Hunter, "Lonely Grave and Sentinel Oak Mark Grim Tragedy of Bandera Hills: Men Who Remember Incident Still Alive, but No Punishment Ever Meted Out to Those Indicted More Than Half Century Ago," *San Antonio Express*, 29 January 1922.
9. L. L. Wight, *Reminiscences*, 28, 41; subject name listings in Turk, "Mormons in Texas."

son of Joseph Smith Jr., had stepped forward to assume his rightful place at the head of his father's church, and that it was the time for the former Wightites to join the Reorganized Church of Jesus Christ of Latter Day Saints.

Lytle reported, in a letter written to the RLDS newspaper in Iowa, the *Lamoni (IA) True Latter Day Saints' Herald,* that twenty-two members of the former Wight colony, with sixteen others, had been baptized. By the beginning of winter, unusually harsh in 1865–66, almost thirty of the former colonists had converted. Lytle returned to Iowa in poor health early in 1866, leaving Spencer Smith and Andrew Hoffman to continue to minister to their former neighbors.[10]

Former Wightites cross-colonized between the LDS and RLDS branches of Mormonism after 1860. Several of the Hawley clan, which had journeyed to Utah Territory in 1856, later affiliated with the Reorganized church. Most were like John Hawley, who left Utah with his family in 1870 to join RLDS relatives in Iowa. The Utah leadership had sent him on an earlier mission to Iowa to convert his relatives, and he had ended up being converted instead by them. Before leaving Grass Valley, in Washington County, Utah, he wrote to RLDS President Joseph Smith III in June of 1870 that he enjoyed defending "the Book of Mormon, and Covenants, and the history of your father, as well as the Bible." He condemned polygamy and the Adam-as-God theory preached by Brigham Young because "there is so much proof to the contrary." This was the final move for John Hawley, after what seemed to be a lifetime, in his faith journey across frontier Mormonism. He remained active in the RLDS church until his death in 1914.[11]

Some, such as John Taylor in Weber County, joined the Reorganization in Utah and stayed to preach to their LDS neighbors, a daunting task. Alexander McCord had converted Taylor in 1863. E. C. Briggs and Taylor proselytized throughout Weber County in 1864

---

10. Subject name listings in Wight colony database; *Saints' Herald (True Latter Day Saints' Herald)* (Lamoni, IA), September 1865, 27; *Reorganized History,* 3:418, 419, 426; Black, *ERLDS,* 3:734; subject name listings in Turk, "Mormons in Texas."
11. Subject name listings in Turk, "Mormons in Texas", 33, 66, 73, 77–78, 80–81; Black, *ERLDS* 3:734; *Saints' Herald (True Latter Day Saints' Herald)* (Lamoni, IA), August 1870, 477.

and 1865. Taylor went later to Montana and Canada on behalf of the RLDS church. When he returned to Utah ten years later, in 1875, he discovered that many of his children had returned to the LDS faith, a situation he described "as a state of confusion. Darkness reigns among them; even that same mist that Nephi [a Book of Mormon character] saw his brethren go into in unbelief and hardness." At least four of his seven sons, and one daughter, were spouses in polygamous households. Taylor died in 1896 near Ogden, Weber County, Utah. None of his ten children returned to the RLDS church.[12]

By a ratio of nearly six to one, former Wightite polygamists and monogamists alike reunited with the Reorganization led by Joseph Smith III. This should be understood as more than a mere rejection of polygamy, although that certainly was part of it. Antipathy to Brigham Young had been bedrock for the Wightite colonies since Wisconsin. Lyman Wight had taught his followers for years that they had reason to dislike and doubt Young. The list of issues was long, including his supposed perfidy in the *Maid of Iowa* incident; his refusal to sanction the Texas move; his interference during the Wightite trek from Wisconsin; and, most importantly, because he assumed the patrilineal rights of Joseph Smith Jr.'s posterity. The colonists' memoirs clearly reveal both their mutual dislike, if not their outright contempt, for Young, and their commitment to Smith's sons.[13]

The Reorganization led by Joseph Smith III offered hope for polygamists and former polygamists in Mormonism's household of faith. In the first issue of the *Lamoni (IA) True Latter Day Saints' Herald*, editor Isaac Sheen suggested that Joseph Smith Jr. had been the man responsible for the doctrine and introduction of polygamy into Mormonism. More importantly, Sheen wrote, Smith had repented of his error, which permitted him to "obtain salvation and exaltation." The Wightites remembered Sheen as Lyman Wight's fellow counselor to President William Smith in the latter's short-lived church. Several of their friends and neighbors had been chosen to serve in the Twelve of Smith's organization.

---

12. *Reorganized History*, 4:357, 468; *Saints' Herald (True Latter Day Saints' Herald)* (Lamoni, IA), March 1875, 249.
13. Turk, "Mormons in Texas", 98; Hawley, "Autobiography," 6, 12–13, 17; Montague, "Reminiscences," 73.

Although Joseph Smith III and others would soon suppress Joseph Smith Jr.'s responsibility for polygamy, Sheen had planted the idea that if the prophet-founder of the Restoration could err, repent, and be forgiven for polygamy, so then could others who had followed Smith, Young, Wight, and Strang into the practice. Isaac Sheen was not alone in his belief that Joseph Smith Jr. was responsible for Mormon polygamy; it was common among members during the Reorganized church's first few decades. Alma R. Blair, an RLDS historian, has written that many early RLDS leaders "accepted as fact that Joseph Smith had indeed been responsible for the introduction of polygamy at Nauvoo." They included William Marks, Ebenezer Robinson, and Austin Cowles, who were, respectively, the stake president of Nauvoo, an editor of the church newspaper, and a member of the Nauvoo High Council. It has never been a mystery who was the fount of plural marriage in Mormonism.[14]

To overstate the influence of plural relations in the Wightite community is difficult. Table 11, next page, identifies members who lived in plural marriage at some point during the community's history. Nine of those died before the reorganization in 1860. Of the eighteen still alive in 1860, twelve former plural spouses, including all of Lyman Wight's surviving wives, joined the RLDS church. The other six rejoined the LDS church in Utah. Two of those six, George Hawley and Ann Hadfield Hawley, joined the Reorganized church after the death of his polygamous spouse, Sarah Hadfield Hawley, who was also Ann's sister.

The power of plural relations continued among Wight's followers after his death. Six children from the Wightite community entered LDS polygamy after their parents moved to Utah Territory. They included Harriet Martensia Wight Earl and five of John Taylor's children. Malinda Porter Chipman and her son Sanford Porter Chipman visited their relatives in Morgan County, Utah, and decided not to return to Texas. They lived in Porterville (named after her father, Sanford Porter) among polygamists. Malinda and her son Porter rejoined the LDS faith and received their endowments at the

14. Isaac Sheen, *Saints' Herald (True Latter Day Saints' Herald)* (Lamoni, IA), January 1860, 6, 26, 27; *Melchisedek and Aaronic Herald* (Covington, KY) (April 1850); Blair, "RLDS Views of Polygamy: Some Historiographical Notes," 19.

TABLE 11

LDS/RLDS AFFILIATION OF WIGHT COLONY POLYGAMISTS AFTER 1860[15]

Name	*Level of Polygamous Activity*	*Later Affiliation*
Chipman, Ezra A.	Certain	None: died in 1913
Chipman, Jeanette Sutherland	Certain	RLDS
Chipman, Malinda Porter	Certain	RLDS, then LDS
Hawley, Ann Hadfield	Certain	LDS, then RLDS
Hawley, George	Certain	LDS, then RLDS
Hawley, Sarah Hadfield	Certain	LDS, died in 1864
Harmon, Marian Sutherland Curtis Chipman	Certain	None: died in 1916
Jenkins, Mary Ann Hobart	Certain	RLDS
Miles, Delia	Certain	Unknown
Miles, Joel Simonds	Certain	Unknown
Miles, Patience F. Curtis	Certain	None: died in 1882
Miller, Catherine Mary Fry	Certain	RLDS
Miller, Elizabeth Boughton (Bouton)	Certain	Strangite: died 1851
Miller, George	Certain	Strangite: died 1856
Miller, John F.	Possible	Unknown: died ca. 1870
Miller, Rosina Minerva Wight	Possible	Wightite: died 1850
Miller, Sophia Wallace Leyland	Certain	Wightite: died 1848
Moncur, Abram	Probable	None: died 1858
(Moncur), Ellen (Hellen Ballantyne) Bell	Probable	RLDS
Moncur, Jane V. Ballantyne	Probable	Wightite: died 1852
Montague, Eliza Ann Segar	Certain	None: died by 1860
Montague, George Sr.	Certain	None: died by 1859
Montague, Margaret Francis Andrews Miller	Certain	RLDS
Montague, Nancy Daniels Richardson	Certain	RLDS
Wight, Harriet Benton	Certain	RLDS
Wight, Jane Margaret Ballantyne	Certain	RLDS
Wight, Lyman	Certain	Wightite: died 1858
Wight, Mary Hawley	Certain	Wightite: died 1852
Wight, Matilda Carter	Certain	None: died 1870
Wight, Orange Lysander	Certain	LDS
Wight, Rosilla Carter	Certain	RLDS

15. Subject name listings in Turk, "Mormons in Texas"; subject name listings, ancestor family index, LDS archives.

Endowment House in Salt Lake City. She died in 1870, but lived long enough to know her son had married in the Endowment House three months earlier.[16]

Harriet Martensia Wight Earl and her father, Orange Lysander Wight, both died in the LDS faith. She married in 1867 as a polygamous spouse of Wilbur Bradley Earl, at Pine Valley, Utah. Her father, after his mother and last wife died, joined her household as an old man and re-converted to the church of his youth. He wrote in his memoirs that Joseph Smith Jr., not Brigham Young, had started Mormon polygamy. Wight concluded, "all the fore going is . . . to show or prove to you that plural marriage was practice[d] and taught by the Prophet and Apostles of that day. In all of this time I did not hear Pres Brigham Young name mentioned in connection with plural marriage." Several years earlier, Gideon Carter, raised to manhood in the Wight colonies from Mormon Coulee to Mountain Valley, told LDS historian Brigham H. Roberts the same story. According to Carter, Lyman Wight had taught that he had received the order of plural marriage from Joseph Smith.[17]

In conclusion, had Lyman Wight and his plural spouses remained at Mountain Valley, the colony would have still been foredoomed to extinction. Nature and the Native Americans interfered with the colonists' mechanical establishments. The personality and vision of Lyman Wight remained so intense that he could not—or was not permitted to—stay long in one place. Major family leaders (John Ballantyne, Phineas Bird, Jacob and Jeremiah Curtis) had died or, like Pierce Hawley and Andrew Ballantyne, had abandoned him. Social pressures building within the community itself—the desires for economic and individual freedom and opportunity—proved its ultimate undoing.

The restricted and unbalanced mating pool created by polygamy had been another major source of internal friction. Of those who

16. Nathan Tanner Porter, "Reminiscences," 244, 246, 247; subject name listings in Turk, "Mormons in Texas"; subject name listings, ancestor family index.

17. Subject name listings in Turk, "Mormons in Texas"; "Journals from the Life and Times of Joseph Ira Earl and His Wives," 19, 20, 37–38, 235; O. L. Wight, "Recollections," 4; sworn statement of Gideon H. Carter to Brigham H. Roberts, 27 February 1894.

lived in the community at one time or another, only thirty-one of the forty-eight adult males were married, compared to almost every woman over fifteen being a wife. At least seven men, and possibly two more, had plural wives. Everyone in the community was aware of the developing difficulties relating to age, gender, and marriage. In light of the unavailability of prospective spouses within their own religious grouping, younger males either searched outside the colony for spouses or challenged the older, polygamous males by courting their wives. The Mormon polygamous stronghold of Mountain Valley was doomed to failure, particularly with the demise of the economic cooperative, as younger members increasingly began marrying outsiders.

The impact of Lyman Wight and his colonists, was, on balance, positive. As a visionary patriarch without peer on the Texas frontier, his personality was singular. C. Stanley Banks wrote that Wight "was one who had always been in the midst of struggle and hardships, one who had repeatedly braved persecution and oppression, one to whom life was hard and cruel, but was never discouraged and who 'calculated to continue till I lose the horse or win the saddle.'"[18] The *Galveston (TX) Weekly News*' obituary acknowledged the accomplishments of Wight and his followers. In part, it declared the entire community of Texas was no

> doubt greatly indebted to the deceased leader for the orderly conduct, industry, sobriety, and enterprise of his colony. Wight first came to Texas in November 1845 and has been with his colony on our extreme frontiers ever since, moving still farther west as settlements formed around him, thus always being the pioneer of advancing civilization, affording protection against the Indians. He has been the first to settle five new counties and prepare the way for others.[19]

Wight's character and personality can be evaluated. Understanding his struggles with authority is not difficult. His allegiance

18. Banks, "The Mormon Migration into Texas," 244.
19. *Weekly News* (Galveston, TX), probably April 1858, quoted in H. H. Smith, "The Lyman Wight Colony in Texas," 48–49.

was always to Joseph Smith Jr. and his family, instructing his followers that the LDS apostolic presidency could only be an intermediate step before Smith's sons came of age and relieved Young and his peers from their duties as the head of the church. The Zodiac resolutions of 1849, while recognizing the Twelve and the Fifty, subordinated church leadership to the principle that Smith's posterity would assume the mantle of their father's authority. Wight had flirted with William Smith and his church only as a temporary, intermediate regency as the church waited for the Smith boys to reach adulthood.

Wight remained consistent, to his death, in believing that neither Brigham Young, nor James Strang, nor William Smith, nor any other Mormon leader could permanently replace the Smith family patrimony. Wight's refusal to subordinate his authority to those at Nauvoo, or Beaver Island, or Salt Lake City, or Covington was founded on his belief that only Joseph Smith Jr., "the seventh angel," could remove him from the Texas mission. As the oldest apostle in the Twelve and in the Fifty, he considered himself at least equal, if not senior, to his apostolic peers. His defiant letters became increasingly exasperated with those who tried to direct him or question his leadership. Coupled with his autocratic nature, these traits meant that no one could control him after Joseph's death.

Lyman Wight, had he lived, would have thrown his oar on the bark of Joseph Smith III and the Reorganized church. Joseph Smith III would certainly have had difficulties with Wight's drinking, opium use, and plural wives. The Wild Ram would probably have not taken the temperance pledge; many of the Mormons of the first generation drank until the day they died. There is no way to evaluate his continued usage of opium: it was legal, and the extent of his use is unclear. Whether the Texas Ram would have given up his plural wives to join the Reorganized church is problematic. However, considering his dislike for Brigham Young and Orson Hyde, it seems inconceivable that he would have found sanctuary in Utah to protect his families. Wight's fervid, contrary testimony that Joseph Smith Jr. was the founder of Mormon plural marriage, and had practiced it with many women, would have rocked the religious worldview of Joseph Smith III.

The actions of his followers are measures, too, of Wight's personality and character. They lived peaceful, industrious, and sober lives for the most part, blazing the trail for other pioneers. These Texas Mormons had completely belied the German concern about their alleged "wild and unlawful behavior."[20] They never fought with their non-Mormon neighbors: no gun battles took place, no mobs rampaged, no barns or dwellings were burned. The lack of violence manifests Wight's influence, guiding hand, and maturity as a disciplined leader. He had directed, in part, the violence in the Missouri civil war. He witnessed the aftermath of the murder of Joseph Smith Jr. He ensured that similar matters did not occur in Texas. He literally turned his cheek and, instead, moved his people. Thus, the Wightites won the trust, and sometimes the affection, of their neighbors. If their ways disturbed others enough, they moved further along their peculiar path. The former colonists and their descendants lived profitable lives in Texas, Iowa, Missouri, and California. This was, in part, because their characters were forged in the crucible of the incredible experience that was the Texas frontier, and by the hand of Lyman Wight's guidance.

Some may suggest that Mormonism lost an excellent opportunity in Texas because of Smith's murder and Young's refusal to take the church into the Old Southwest. Although Joseph Smith Jr. had been certainly considering moving the church to the southern borderlands, Young came to realize this would have been a great mistake, perhaps a fatal one, for the church. He knew that he could not create a Mormon nation in Texas. For that is what he wanted to do, to create his own country where the Mormons could live according to their dictates without interference from disagreeable outsiders.

Brigham Young envisioned an empire in the West. He was attracted by the lack of settlements along the Great Salt Lake and Utah Lake. Apostle Parley Pratt thought the Rocky Mountains would be a stronghold from which the Mormons would extend their control to California and the Pacific Ocean. Pratt wrote to Isaac Rogers, "When we arrive there [in the Rocky Mountains] we will have land without buying it. And we will have liberty without asking a set of corrupt office holders for it." In 1857, Young noted that some had wanted the Mormons to settle in California years earlier but he would not do

20. Solms-Braunfels Archiv, 9:52.

it, believing "we cannot stay there over five years." Apostle Wilford Woodruff remembered that Young reached out and struck the soil with his cane in the Great Salt Lake valley. Young said, "I am going to stop right here. I am going to build a city here. I am going to build a temple here, and I am going to build a country here."[21] Only in the vast isolation of the Rocky Mountains could the Mormons have built their settlements, constructed their temples, created their unique culture, and lived their lives so differently from the rest of their American counterparts. As a religious people and nation, they would have been destroyed in Texas, California, or Oregon, where soon they would have been outnumbered in the flood of immigration. Only in the Rocky Mountains could they have made a sacred place for their lifestyle without being destroyed by the American majority.

Lyman Wight's own strength, prejudices, and character molded a frontier people in his likeness. More than half of the survivors affiliated with the RLDS church, and, although this is not a brief for the Reorganized church, it is one for the powerful and antagonistic effect the Wild Ram had on his followers about the leadership of Utah Mormonism. Ironically, Heber C. Kimball, who truly liked the Texas prophet, commented during a prayer breakfast in 1859: "I always believed Lyman Wight would be saved. I never had any but good feelings toward him."[22] His comments reveal as much about the LDS leaders' naiveté regarding the depth of Wight's hostility toward the Twelve as it reflects Kimball's warm feelings toward Wight.

His followers carried the old patriarch's remains to the cemetery at Zodiac, nearly seventy miles distant. They laid him close to his daughter Rosina Minerva and infant granddaughters, Sarah and Mina. His faithful scribe and adopted son, William Leyland, rested nearby. Orange Lysander Wight, his oldest son, was living forty miles away when he received the news. He wrote that he "went to the place

---

21. Brigham Young to Addison Pratt, 22 August 1845, Brigham Young Papers; P. P. Pratt to Isaac Rogers, 6 September 1845, LDS archives; B. Young, *Journal of Discourses*, 5:13 September 1857, 231–32; Wilford Woodruff, *The Discourses of Wilford Woodruff*, ed. G. Homer Durham (Salt Lake City: Bookcraft, 1969; reprint of 1946 edition), 322–23.
22. Journal History of the Church, 142:23 February 1859, 3.

and assisted in the last rites and returned home." The final rites consisted of washing and anointing the body from head to foot, then dressing it in holy garments—the cap, loose-frock robe, apron, and moccasins associated with the ritual of the Zodiac temple. A brief service of hymns and speeches would have been held. Then the coffin was lowered into the freshly dug grave waiting for it.

Levi Lamoni Wight—devoted son and family man, Indian fighter and frontiersman, Confederate veteran, and RLDS missionary in his old age—as other historians have noted before, eulogized his father best. He wrote that his father "had many noble virtues to commend him and whatever may be his foibles I have no desire to make a record of them. When the clods fell upon his coffin, they obliterated his mistakes in life."[23] And there Lyman Wight rests until this day in Zodiac's city of the dead, secure in his firm belief that on Resurrection Day he will be called forth by the angel of the seventh dispensation, Joseph Smith Jr.

History ever informs us in strange and interesting ways. With Warren Jeffs, the prophet of the Fundamentalist Mormons, followers of the restoration doctrines of the first Mormon, Joseph Smith Jr. (including patriarchal leadership fusing the sacred with the profane, polygamy, common-stock economic cooperatives, and separatism from non-members), once again return to Texas. With local superiority in the electorate, the FLDS undoubtedly will try to take over the county government and local police forces, in order to protect Jeffs and their own unique ways of living. Unlike Wight's day, modern Texas has no other frontier for the FLDS to flee to from the pursuits of a secular and sectarian world far different from their own. Mainstream Texans have not had to deal with restoration Mormonism since 1858, and the outcome is not really possible to predict. Which road will Jeffs and the FLDS take when push comes to shove with Lone Star law and customs and mainstream religions?

23. L. L. Wight, *Reminiscences*, 28; see the conclusion of J. B. Wight's *The Wild Ram of the Mountain*, 424–26, for a fine creative description of Wight's seizure, final hours, and interment.

Bibliography

Archives and Libraries

Bandera County Courthouse, Bandera, TX.

Burnet County Courthouse, Burnet, TX.

Center for American History, University of Texas, Austin, TX.

East Texas Research Center, Ralph Steen Library, Stephen F. Austin State University, Nacogdoches, TX.

Church of Jesus Christ of Latter-Day Saints:

Church Historical Library, Church Office Building, Salt Lake City, UT.

Church Historical Archives, Church Office Building, Salt Lake City, UT.

Family History Library, Salt Lake City, UT.

Frontier Times Museum, Bandera, TX.

Gillespie County Courthouse, Fredricksburg, TX.

Gillespie County Historical Society, Fredricksburg, TX.

Graceland College, DeRose Room, Lamoni, IA.

Harold B. Lee Library, Brigham Young University, Provo, UT.

Institute of Texan Culture, San Antonio, TX.

Iowa State Historical Society, Des Moines, IA.

Reorganized Church of Jesus Christ of Latter-Day Saints Archives, Independence, MO.

Sophienburg Archives and Museum, New Braunfels, TX.

Texas Forestry Museum, Lufkin, TX.

Texas State Library, Austin, TX.

Utah State Historical Society, Rio Grande Depot, Salt Lake City, UT.

Western Historical Manuscripts Collection, University of Missouri, Columbia, MO.

Wisconsin State Historical Society, Madison, WI.

Public Records

Bandera County Archives, Bandera County Clerk's Office, Bandera, TX. District Court minutes, various terms of 1857 and 1858, events in which several members of the colony participated.

Bandera County Library, Bandera, TX. Includes "An Act To Create The County Of Bandera," 26 January 1856. More than twenty names of the petitioners are from the Lyman Wight colony.

Burnet County Archives, Burnet County Clerk's Office, Hamilton, TX. Deed records, in which transactions of land for Wight's cooperative take place.

"Daviess County Records, Book A, 4 December 1839," *U.S. Works Project Administration, Historical Records Survey Missouri 1935–1942*, 53, microfiche copy, folder 6523, Western Historical Manuscripts Collections.

Gillespie County Archives, Gillespie County Clerk's Office, Fredericksburg, TX. Includes County Commissioners' minutes, deed records, and marriage records.

Manuscript Census of 1850, Texas. East Texas Research Center.

Manuscript Census of 1860, Texas. East Texas Research Center.

Testimony of Chipman, Ezra, and testimony of Porter, Malinda. Cause 91, State of Missouri vs. Jos. Smith et al., 12 and 13 November 1838, folder 8, Eugene Morrow Violette Collection, 1806–1921, Western Historical Manuscripts Collection.

Testimony of Samson, Avard. Cause 91, State of Missouri vs. Jos. Smith et al., 12 and 13 November 1838, folder 2: 5, 16, Eugene Morrow Violette Collection, 1806–1921, Western Historical Manuscripts Collection.

Unpublished Manuscripts

Administrative Records for Baptism of the Dead, February and March 1851. Lyman Wight records in Zodiac. RLDS archives.

Bitton, Davis. "The Ram and the Lion: Lyman Wight and Brigham Young." Unpublished manuscript, 1996. Typescript copy in author's possession. Compare with Bitton, Davis. "The Ram and the Lion: Lyman Wight and Brigham Young." Paper presented at the symposium "Pioneers of the Restoration," Foundation for Ancient Research and Mormon Studies, Provo, UT, 8 March 1997.

Carter, Gideon H. Sworn statement of Gideon H. Carter to Brigham H. Roberts, 27 February 1894. LDS archives. Carter testified that he had never joined the church.

Dixon, Herschel Harry, Jr. "Charles Louis Klein (Kelty)." Unpublished manuscript, May 1995. East Texas Research Center.

Earl, Joseph Ira. "Journals from the Life and Times of Joseph Ira Earl and His Wives: Elethra Calesta Bunker and Agnes Viola Bunker," compiled by Owen Ken Earl. Unpublished manuscript, ca. 1986. LDS archives.

Hartley, William G. "The LDS Church in Texas." Unpublished manuscript. LDS archives.

Hawes Family Patriarchal Blessing Book. RLDS archives.
Hawley, John Pierce. "Autobiography of John Hawley." Unpublished manuscript, 1889. RLDS archives. An autobiographical work detailing Hawley's experiences as a member of the Church of Jesus Christ of Latter Day Saints in Illinois, Wisconsin, and Utah, including his firsthand observations concerning the Mountain Meadows Massacre in southern Utah in September 1857; the Wight colony in Wisconsin and Texas; and his affiliation and experiences with the Reorganized Church of Jesus Christ of Latter Day Saints.
Hawley, Pierce. Pierce Hawley to Jacob Croft, 6 June 1856. George Wise Cropper Collection 1823–98, LDS archives. Hawley affirms that he and Croft would be better off waiting for the patrilineal successors to Joseph Smith Jr. to assume leadership of Mormonism than to follow the lead of Brigham Young.
Hoffman, August. Memoirs, 6 October 1925. Barker American History Center, University of Texas.
Isom, Richard Lamb. "What Became of Joseph Smith's Early Associate Lyman Wight." Photocopy, typescript manuscript, n.d. LDS archives. Purports to be a "creative history" of the Lyman Wight colony.
Journal of the Branch of the Church of Christ in Pontiac, Michigan, Huron Branch, 1834. Handwritten manuscript. LDS archives.
Journal History of the Church collection of clippings, records, and notes. LDS Archives.
Kimball, Heber C. Journal. LDS archives.
Knight, Newell. Journal and autobiography, 1800–1847. Manuscript, LDS archives.
Lyman, Francis. Francis M. Lyman 1901–1903 letterbook. LDS archives.
Members of the Anointed Quorum, Nauvoo, Illinois—1842–1845. Unpublished manuscripts compiled by Lisle G. Brown from a list of members of the Anointed Quorum contained in the Newel K. Whitney diary and account book (1833–1848). Special Collections and Manuscripts Department, Harold B. Lee Library, Brigham Young University, Provo, UT.
Miller, Henry W. Journal of Henry W. Miller and Elmira Pond Miller, Cherokee Indian Mission, 1855 April–1862 October. Typescript manuscript, 1948. LDS archives. Includes reconverting a number of former Wight colonists living in the Indian Territory in 1856 to the LDS faith.
"The Mormon Colony (Zodiac) Near Fredericksburg, Texas." Unpublished manuscripts compiled by John Cotter and Dorothea (Weinehiemer) Cotter, 1969. Cotter Collection, Pioneer Heritage Memorial Library, Fredericksburg, TX.

Neighbors, Robert Simpson. Robert Simpson Neighbors Papers. Barker Texas History Center, University of Texas.

Porter, Nathan Tanner. "Reminiscences." Unpublished manuscript, ca. 1879. LDS archives.

Pottawatamie High Council Conference Minutes 1848–51. LDS archives.

Pottawatamie High Priest Quorum Minutes 1849. LDS archives.

Richards, Willard. Diary. LDS archives.

Scott, Jess W. "History of the Mormons in Clark County, Wisconsin." Typescript manuscript, n.d. LDS archives. Scott, a local historian of the La Crosse area, cribbed heavily from other histories for this "history."

Smith, Heman C. "Lyman Wight on Succession." Typescript transcript of a document written in the hand of Heman C. Smith. RLDS Archives. Archives notes include: "The following was written en [*sic*] the hand of Heman C. Smith and signed by him. It is in very bad condition—yellow, tissue paper on which the ink ran or blurred as it was copied, possibly as is done in the letter press copy books. This typescript is being made February 17, 1978 by Madelon Brunson." The original was destroyed when copying was completed.

Smith, Heman Hale. "The Lyman Wight Colony in Texas," Manuscript prepared for the Reorganized Church of Jesus Christ of Latter Day Saints, 1920. RLDS Archives. Heman H. Smith (son of Heman C. Smith, grandson of Spencer Smith, and great-grandson of Lyman Wight, all members of Zodiac), an apostle, member of the Seventy, and historian for the Reorganized Church of Jesus Christ of Latter Day Saints, prepared the manuscript from the Lyman Wight Journal, Spencer Smith Journal, and William Leyland Journal, all later destroyed by fire. He insisted polygamy was limited to the families of Lyman Wight, Orange Lysander Wight, and Ezra Chipman.

Snedaker, Morris J. Diary. LDS archives. A journal of LDS missionary travel and experiences in Texas before the Civil War.

Solms-Braunfels Archiv. Original Journals. Bienecke Library, Yale University. Typescript copy at Sophienburg Archives, New Braunsfiels, TX.

Stout, Allen Joseph. Journal of Allen Joseph Stout. Photocopy. Utah State Historical Society archives.

Taylor, John. John Taylor revelation, 27 June 1882. Annie Taylor Hyde notebook. LDS archives.

Thomas, Preston. "Preston Thomas: His Life and Travels," edited by Daniel Hadlond Preston. Photocopy. LDS archives. A handwritten journal and diary of Thomas' six missionary journeys to Texas before the Civil War.

Tickemyer, Garland E. "Lyman Wight (a Description)." Photocopy of reconstructed typescript manuscript, 1961. RLDS archives. A recreation by Tickemyer of lost material given to him by Virginia Hay, ninety-one years of age during the original interview with Tickemyer in 1935 at Bandera County, Texas, recounting her young impressions at the age of twelve of Lyman Wight and his death. A hand-drawn map of Mormon Camp accompanies the recreation.

Turk, Toni R. "The Kingdom of God As a Buffer State: The Mormon Decision for Texas." Photocopy, unpublished graduate manuscript. University of Texas, 1974. LDS archives.

———. "Mormons in Texas: The Lyman Wight Colony." Photocopy, typescript manuscript, 1987. LDS archives.

Voree (WI) Record. Photocopy of pen-written papers, Church of Jesus Christ of Latter Day Saints (Strangites), extracts copied by W. D. Van Dyke Jr., 1909. LDS archives.

Wight, Harriet. Will of Harriet Wight. Iowa State Historical Society Archives.

Wight, Lyman. "Revelation on Baptism for the Dead," 10 February 1851. Iowa State Historical Society Archives. A statement of dedication to the principles of baptism for the dead and a format for recording the administration of the ordinance in the Zodiac temple.

———. Lyman Wight letterbook. RLDS archives.

Wight, Orange Lysander. "Recollections of Orange L. Wight, Son of Lyman Wight," to Joseph I. Earl, 1903, Bunkersville, Nevada. The original was discovered in the St. George Temple, and a typescript copy prepared in 1966 by Winona Wittier and Viola W. Squires. Photocopy. LDS archives. A defense of LDS polygamy, testifying that Wight received the principle from Joseph Smith Jr. as well as from his father, Lyman Wight, and others.

Woodruff, Wilford. Diary. LDS archives.

Young, Brigham. Brigham Young Papers. LDS archives.

———. Manuscript History of Brigham Young. LDS archives.

Books

Allen, James B., Ronald K. Esplin, and David J. Whittaker. *Men With a Mission, 1837–1841: The Quorum of the Twelve Apostles in the British Isles.* Salt Lake City: Deseret Book, 1992. A work that explores the creation of the "inner circle" of the Twelve that dominated the succession crisis of 1844.

Allen, Ruth Alice. *East Texas Lumber Workers: An Economic and Social Picture, 1870–1950.* Austin: University of Texas Press, 1961. Still an important source for the demographic statistics for the world of the East Texas lumberman and his family.

Arrington, Leonard J. and Ronald K. Esplin. *The Role of the Council of the Twelve During Brigham Young's Presidency of the Church of Jesus Christ of Latter-Day Saints.* Task Papers in LDS History No. 31. Salt Lake City: Historical Department, Church of Jesus Christ of Latter-Day Saints, 1979.

Bagley, Will. *Blood of the Prophets: Brigham Young and the Massacre at Mountain Meadows.* Norman: University of Oklahoma Press, 2002.

———, ed. *Scoundrel's Tale: The Samuel Brannan Papers.* Logan: Utah State University Press, 1999. Originally published 1999, Kingdom in the West Series, by Arthur H. Clark, Spokane, WA.

Bandera County History Book Committee. *History of Bandera County, Texas.* Dallas: Curtis Media, 1986. A compilation of genealogical and family histories pertaining to Bandera County, Texas.

Bartlett, John Russell. *Personal Narrative of Explorations and Incidents in Texas, New Mexico, California, Sonora, and Chihuahua Connected with the United States and Mexican Boundary Commission During the Years 1850, '51, '52, and '53.* 2 vols. Chicago: Rio Grande Press, 1965. First published 1854 by D. Appleton, New York.

Bennett, Richard Edmond. *Mormons at the Missouri, 1846–1852: "And Should We Die . . ."* Norman: University of Oklahoma Press, 1987.

Biesele, Rudolph Leopold. *The History of the German Settlements in Texas, 1831–1861.* Austin: Von Boeckmann-Jones, 1930. The first academic to capture realistically the German immigrant experience of the Texas Hill Country.

Bigler, David L. *Forgotten Kingdom: The Mormon Theocracy in the American West, 1847–1896.* Logan: Utah State University Press, 1998. Originally published 1997, Kingdom in the West Series, by Arthur H. Clark, Spokane, WA. The best study at present of the Mormon theo-democratic state in Utah Territory.

———, and Will Bagley, eds. *Army of Israel: Mormon Battalion Narratives.* Logan: Utah State University Press, 2000. Originally published 2000, Kingdom in the West Series, by Arthur H. Clark, Spokane, WA.

Black, Susan Easton, comp. *Early Members of the Reorganized Church of Jesus Christ of Latter Day Saints.* 6 vols. Provo, UT: Religious Studies Center, Department of Church History and Doctrine, Brigham Young University, 1993.

Booker, Helen Hawley. *Life Story of John Pierce Hawley.* Iowa Falls, IA: General Publishing and Binding, 1972.

Brodie, Fawn McKay. *No Man Knows My History: The Life of Joseph Smith, the Mormon Prophet.* 2nd ed., rev. and enl. New York: Alfred A. Knopf, 1971. A psychological history of Joseph Smith Jr., concluding that he suffered from a series of psychotic disorders resulting in hallucinations and megalomania.

Brooks, Juanita. *The Mountain Meadows Massacre.* New ed. Norman: University of Oklahoma Press, 1962–63.

———, ed. *On the Mormon Frontier: The Diary of Hosea Stout, 1844–1861.* Vol. 1: *1844–1848.* Salt Lake City: University of Utah Press / Utah State Historical Society, 1964.

Buenger, Walter L. *Secession and the Union in Texas.* Austin: University of Texas Press, 1984. Opens the modern examination into the disunionist consensus-making movement in antebellum Texas and the various opposition groups to a secessionist South.

Bunnell, Lafayette Houghton. *Winona (We-no-nah) and Its Environs on the Mississippi in Ancient and Modern Days.* For and under the auspices of the Winona County Old Settlers' Association. Winona, MN: Jones and Kroeger, 1897.

Butterfield, Consul Willshire. *History of LaCrosse County, Wisconsin.* Chicago: Western Historical, 1881.

Campbell, Randolph B. *An Empire for Slavery: The Peculiar Institution in Texas, 1821–1865.* Baton Rouge: Louisiana State University Press, 1989. Explores the world of African American slavery and its effects on antebellum Texas.

Cannon, Donald Q. and Lyndon W. Cook, eds. *Far West Record: Minutes of the Church of Jesus Christ of Latter-Day Saints, 1830–1844.* Salt Lake City: Deseret Book, 1983.

Collier, Fred C., comp. *Unpublished Revelations of the Prophets and Presidents of the Church of Jesus Christ of Latter Day Saints.* 2nd ed. Salt Lake City: Collier's, 1981.

Compton, Todd. *In Sacred Loneliness: The Plural Wives of Joseph Smith.* Salt Lake City: Signature Books, 1997.

Cook, Lyndon W. *The Revelations of the Prophet Joseph Smith: A Historical and Biographical Commentary of the Doctrine and Covenants.* Salt Lake City: Deseret Book, 1985.

Corrill, John. *A Brief History of the Church of Jesus Christ of Latter-Day Saints (Commonly Called Mormons): Including an Account of Their Doctrine and Discipline; With the Reasons of the Author for Leaving the Church.* [St. Louis?]: privately printed, 1839.

Debo, Darrell. *Burnet County History.* For the Burnet County Historical Commission. Burnet, TX: Eakin Press, 1979.

Fischer, Ernest G. *Marxists and Utopias in Texas: The Lone Star State's Pioneer Flirtation with Socialism-Communism.* Burnet, TX: Eakin Press, 1980. Popular work detailing various communalistic attempts along the Texas frontier.

Foster, Lawrence. *Religion and Sexuality: Three American Communal Experiments of the Nineteenth Century.* New York: Oxford University Press, 1981.

Reveals the power of regulation of sexuality in polygamous Mormon relationships to create a fusion of the sacred and the secular in their community.

Graves, H. A. *Andrew Jackson Potter, the Fighting Parson of the Texan Frontier: Six Years of Indian Warfare in New Mexico and Arizona; Many Wonderful Events in His Ministerial Life.* Nashville: Southern Methodist Publishing House, 1881. Photocopy in LDS archives. Comments about Noah Smithwick as well as Potter's earlier traveling experiences with the Brewsterites.

Grayson County Frontier Village. *The History of Grayson County, Texas.* Winston-Salem, NC: Grayson County Frontier Village / Hunter, 1979.

Greene, John Portineus. *Facts Relative to the Expusion of the Mormons from the State of Missouri, Uner the "Extermination Order."* Cincinnati: R. P. Brooks, 1839.

Haas, Oscar. *History of New Braunfels and Comal County, Texas, 1844–1946.* 1st ed. Austin: Steck, 1968.

Hampshire, Annette P. *Mormonism in Conflict, the Nauvoo Years.* Studies in Religion and Society Series No. 11. New York: E. Mellen Press, 1985. Presents a macro-sociological analysis of the LDS failure to maintain and extend a closed theocratic system within the pluralistic societies of the American frontier along the Mississippi River.

Hansen, Klaus J. *Quest for Empire: The Political Kingdom of God and the Council of Fifty in Mormon History.* East Lansing: Michigan State University Press, 1967. Details the creation and utilization of the council by Joseph Smith Jr., and later Brigham Young, in furthering the theo-political plans of the LDS leadership.

Hardy, B. Carmon. *Solemn Covenant: The Mormon Polygamous Passage.* Urbana: University of Illinois Press, 1992.

Hartley, William G. *My Best for the Kingdom: History and Autobiography of John Lowe Butler, a Mormon Frontiersman.* Salt Lake City: Aspen Books, 1993.

Hill, Marvin S. *Quest For Refuge: The Mormon Flight from American Pluralism.* Salt Lake City: Signature Books, 1989.

Hunter, J. Marvin. *A Brief History of Bandera County: Covering One Hundred Years of Intrepid History.* Bandera, TX: Frontier Times, 1936.

———, comp. *The Lyman Wight Colony in Texas, Came to Bandera in 1854.* Bandera, TX: Bandera Bulletin / Frontier Times Museum, 1925. Heavily dependent on the work of Heman Hale Smith and Noah Smithwick.

Jackson, A. T. *Mills of Yesteryear.* El Paso: Texas Western Press, 1971.

Jenson, Andrew. *Latter-Day Saint Biographical Encyclopedia: A Compilation of Biographical Sketches of Prominent Men and Women in the Church of Jesus Christ of Latter-Day Saints.* 4 vols. Salt Lake City: A. Jenson History, 1901–1936.

Jordan-Bychkov, Terry G. *German Seed in Texas Soil: Immigrant Farmers in Nineteenth-Century Texas.* Austin: University of Texas Press, 1966. Still the standard work on the demographics of the German immigrant communities in Texas.

Kimball, Stanley Buchholz, ed. *On The Potter's Wheel: The Diaries of Heber C. Kimball.* Salt Lake City: Signature Books / Smith Research Associates, 1987.

Labadie, Joseph H. *Archaeological Investigations at Fort Martin Scott (41 GL 52) in Gillespie County, Texas.* With a contribution by Anne A. Fox; investigator, Thomas R. Hester; and co-principal investigators Jack D. Eaton and Anne A. Fox. Archaeological Survey Report No. 169. San Antonio: Center for Archaeological Research, University of Texas at San Antonio, 1987.

Launius, Roger D. *Alexander William Doniphan: Portrait of a Missouri Moderate.* Missouri Biography Series. Columbia: University of Missouri Press, 1997.

Lee, John Doyle. *Confessions of John D. Lee.* Salt Lake City: Modern Microfilm, 1970. Reprint of 1877 edition titled *Mormonism Unveiled; or, The Life and Confessions of the Late Mormon Bishop, John D. Lee.*

Leone, Mark P. *Roots of Modern Mormonism.* Cambridge, MA: Harvard University Press, 1979. A study of Mormon cooperative settlements in nineteenth-century Arizona.

LeSueur, Stephen C. *The 1838 Mormon War in Missouri.* Columbia: University of Missouri Press, 1987. A well-balanced study of the civil war that ripped apart western Missouri in 1838.

Lucas, Mattie Davis, and Mita Holsapple Hall. *A History of Grayson County, Texas [by] Mattie Davis Lucas (Mrs. W. H. Lucas) and Mita Holsapple Hall (Mrs. H. E. Hall).* Sherman, TX: Scruggs, 1936.

Maxwell, Robert S., and Robert D. Baker. *Sawdust Empire: The Texas Lumber Industry, 1830–1940.* College Station: Texas A&M University Press, 1983.

Miller, A. B. (Andrew Bollinger), John A. Miller, and F. M. Petry. *History of George Miller, Sr., and Catherine, His Wife and Their Descendents.* Genealogy and Local History Series G1555. Dayton, OH: Groneweg, 1926.

Miller, George. *Correspondence of Bishop George Miller with the Northern Islander: From His First Acquaintance with Mormonism up to Near the Close of His Life; Written by Himself in the Year 1855.* Compiled by Wingfield Watson from his file of the *Northern Islander* (Voree, WI). Burlington, WI: [Wingfield Watson?], 1916.

Mohon, Monty, and Michelle Mohon. *Gillespie County, a View of Its Past.* Virginia Beach, VA: Donning, 1996. A popular history of the German immigrant experience in Gillespie County, Texas.

Neighbors, Kenneth F. *Robert Simpson Neighbors and the Texas Frontier, 1836–1859.* Waco, TX: Texian Press, 1975.

Newell, Linda King, and Valeen Tippits Avery. *Mormon Enigma: Emma Hale Smith.* 2nd ed. Urbana: University of Illinois Press, 1994.

Pammel, L. H. *Reminiscences of Early La Crosse, Wisconsin: An Account of the Men and Women Who Lived in La Crosse and Vicinity.* N.p.: Liesenfeld Press, 1928. Reprinted from the *Tribune and Leader Press* (La Crosse, WI).

Pierce, Gerald S. *Texas Under Arms: The Campus, Posts, Forts, and Military Towns of the Republic of Texas, 1836–1846.* Austin: Encino Press, 1969.

Platt, Elsie Hawley, and Robert Hawley. *House of Hawley.* Port Huron, MI: privately printed, 1909.

Quinn, D. Michael. *The Mormon Hierarchy: Origins of Power.* Salt Lake City: Signature Books / Smith Research Associates, 1994. Provocative history of the evolving leadership structure in the LDS Church.

The Reorganized Church of Jesus Christ of Latter Day Saints, Complainant, vs. The Church of Christ at Independence, Missouri; Richard Hill, Trustee; Richard Hill, Mrs. E. Hill, C. A. Hall . . . [et al.] *. . . as Members of and Doing Business Under the Name of the Church of Christ, at Independence, Missouri, Respondents* (Lamoni, IA: Herald House, 1893). James Elliott of Iowa, who has done exhaustive research comparing the interview transcripts of the Temple Lot testimony to the final legal records, notes that the RLDS lawyers did an amazing job in deleting or altering interviewees' comments concerning polygamy and Joseph Smith Jr.'s plural wives.

Richardson, Rupert Norval. *The Comanche Barrier to South Plains Settlement: A Century and a Half of Savage Resistance to the Advancing White Frontier.* Millwood, NY: Kraus Reprint, 1973. First published 1933 by Arthur H. Clark, Glendale, CA.

Roberts, B. H. (Brigham Henry). *A Comprehensive History of the Church of Jesus Christ of Latter-Day Saints.* 6 vols. Salt Lake City: Deseret News, 1930. An *apologia* for the LDS church, a member of the First Presidency calling it good propaganda but not history.

———. *History of the Church of Jesus Christ of Latter-Day Saints.* 7 vols. 2nd ed. Salt Lake City: Deseret News, 1948–52.

Roemer, Ferdinand. *Texas, with Particular Reference to German Immigration and the Physical Appearance of the Country: Described Through Personal Observation.* Translated by Oswald Mueller. San Antonio: Standard, 1935. Reprint of 1845–47 edition. Factual ethnic reflection on the vital importance of the Mormon mills at Sycamore Springs and Zodiac to the material culture of the German colonists in the Hill Country.

Sanford, Albert Hart, and H. J. Hirshheimer. *A History of La Crosse, Wisconsin 1841–1900.* Assisted by Robert F. Fries. La Crosse, WI: La Crosse

County Historical Society, 1951. Includes basic history about early Mormon settlement in La Crosse County, Wisconsin.

Sitton, Thad. *Backwoodsmen: Stockmen and Hunters Along a Big Thicket River Valley.* Norman: University of Oklahoma Press, 1995.

Smith, George D., ed. *An Intimate Chronicle: The Journals of William Clayton.* Salt Lake City: Signature Books / Smith Research Associates, 1991.

Smith, Joseph, III, Heman C. Smith, and F. Henry Edwards. *The History of the Reorganized Church of Jesus Christ of Latter Day Saints.* 8+ vols. Independence, MO: Herald House, 1967–. An *apologia* for the RLDS church.

Smith, Joseph Fielding. *Essentials in Church History: A History of the Church from the Birth of Joseph Smith to the Present Time (1950); With Introductory Chapters on the Antiquity of the Gospel and the "Falling Away."* 13th ed. Salt Lake City: Deseret Book, 1950.

Smithwick, Noah. *Evolution of a State; or, Recollections of Old Texas Days.* Compiled by Nanna Smithwick Donaldson. Barker Texas History Center Series No. 5. Austin: University of Texas Press, 1983. First published 1900 by Gammel Book, Austin.

Swartzell, William. *Mormonism Exposed, Being a Journal of Residence in Missouri from the 28th of May to the 20th of August, 1838: Together with an Appendix, Containing the Revelation Concerning the Golden Bible, with Numerous Extracts from the 'Book of Covenants,' &c., &c.* Pekin, IL: privately printed, 1840.

Taylor, Samuel Woolley. *The Kingdom or Nothing: The Life of John Taylor, Militant Mormon.* New York: MacMillan, 1976. Interesting perspective on the man who succeeded his sometimes foe, Brigham Young, as president of the LDS Church.

Tyler, Ronnie C., Douglas E. Barnett, and Roy R. Barkley, eds. *The New Handbook of Texas.* 6 vols. Austin: Texas State Historical Association, 1996.

Van Wagoner, Richard S. *Mormon Polygamy: A History.* 2nd ed. Salt Lake City: Signature Books, 1989.

———. *Sidney Rigdon: A Portrait of Religious Excess.* Salt Lake City: Signature Books, 1994.

Wight, Jermy Benton. *The Wild Ram of the Mountain: The Story of Lyman Wight.* Star Valley, WY: Llama Star Press, 1996. A compelling and detailed popular biography written from the heart by a great-grandson of Wight.

Wight, Levi Lamoni. *The Reminiscences and Civil War Letters of Levi Lamoni Wight: Life in a Mormon Splinter Colony on the Texas Frontier.* Edited by Davis Bitton. University of Utah Publications in the American West No. 4. Salt Lake City: University of Utah Press, 1970.

Winn, Kenneth H. *Exiles in a Land of Liberty: Mormons in America, 1830–1846.* Studies in Religion Series. Chapel Hill: University of North Carolina Press, 1989.

Woodruff, Wilford. *The Discourses of Wilford Woodruff.* Edited by G. Homer Durham. Salt Lake City: Bookcraft, 1969. Reprint of 1946 edition.

Young, Brigham. *Journal of Discourses.* Delivered by Brigham Young, his two counsellors, the twelve apostles, and others, reported by G[eorge] D. Watt. 27 vols. [Salt Lake City: Deseret Book], 1966. Reprint of 1854–86 edition by E. D. and S. W. Richards, Liverpool.

Young, Frank J., comp. *Strangite Mormons: A Finding Aid; A Listing of the Followers of the Mormon Prophet James Jesse Strang at Voree, Beaver Island, and Other Locations, Including Notes of Genealogical Interest.* Vancouver, WA: privately printed, 1996.

Articles and Pamphlets

Abernethy, Francis Edward. "*Deutschtum* in Texas: A Look at Texas-German Folklore." In *German Culture in Texas: A Free Earth; Essays from the 1978 Southwest Symposium,* edited by Glen E. Lich and Dona B. Reeves-Marquardt, 203–28. Immigrant Heritage of America Series. Boston: Twayne, 1980.

Alexander, Thomas G. "A New and Everlasting Covenant: An Approach to the Theology of Joseph Smith." In *New Views of Mormon History: A Collection of Essays in Honor of Leonard J. Arrington,* edited by Davis Bitton and Maureen Ursenbach Beecher, 47. Salt Lake City: University of Utah Press, 1987.

Baggett, James A. "The Constitutional Union Party in Texas." *Southwestern Historical Quarterly* 82, no. 1 (January 1979): 233–64.

Banks, C. Stanley. "The Mormon Migration into Texas." *Southwestern Historical Quarterly* 49, no. 2 (October 1945): 233–44.

Bennett, Richard Edmond. "'A Samaritan has passed by': George Miller—Mormon Bishop, Trailblazer, and Brigham Young Antagonist." *Illinois Historical Journal* 82, no. 1 (Spring 1989): 2–16.

———. "Lamanism, Lymanism, and Cornfields." *Journal of Mormon History* (1986–87): 44–59.

Bitton, Davis. "Mormons in Texas: The Ill-Fated Lyman Wight Colony, 1844–1858." *Arizona and the West* 11, no. 1 (Spring 1969): 5–26.

Blair, Alma R. "RLDS Views of Polygamy: Some Historiographical Notes." *John Whitmer Historical Association Journal* 5 (1985): 16–28.

Booth, C. C. "Lyman Wight—in Early Texas." *Improvement Era* 62 (January 1954): 26–27, 62–63.

Butterfield, Consul Willshire. "The Mormon Invasion." In *History of La Crosse County, Wisconsin.* Chicago: Western Historical Co., 1881. An antagonistic portrayal of early Mormon settlement in the Black River Falls region.

Campbell, Randolph B. "Family History from Local Record: A Case Study from Nineteenth Century Texas." *East Texas Historical Journal* 29, no. 2 (1991): 13–23.

Coker, Caleb, and Janet G. Humphrey. "The Texas Frontier in 1850: Dr. Ebenezer Swift and the View from Fort Martin Scott." *Southwestern Historical Quarterly* 96, no. 3 (January 1993): 393–414.

Compton, Todd. "Fanny Alger Smith Custer: Mormonism's First Plural Wife." *Journal of Mormon History* 22, no. 1 (Spring 1996): 174–207.

Ehat, Andrew F. "'It seems like heaven began on earth': Joseph Smith and the Constitution of the Kingdom of God." *Brigham Young University Studies* 20, no. 3 (Spring 1980): 253–79.

———. "'They might have known he was not a fallen prophet'—the Nauvoo Journal of Joseph Fielding." *Brigham Young University Studies* 19, no. 2 (Winter 1979): 141–66. Joseph Fielding Diary (1843–46), transcribed and edited by Andrew F. Ehat.

Ghost Towns of Texas. Pamphlet, ca. 1933 or 1934. Copy at Chamber of Commerce, Marble Falls, Texas.

Gilbert, Glenn S. "Origin and Location of German Speakers." In *Texas and Germany: Crosscurrents,* edited by Joseph Wilson, 21–34. Rice University Studies 63, No. 3. Houston: Rice University, 1977.

Harby, Lee C. *Magazine of American History* (November 1888). This issue includes a romantic description, although factual, of the idyllic community of Zodiac more than thirty years after the Wightites departed for Burnet County, Texas.

Howard, Richard P. "The Evolving RLDS Identity." *John Whitmer Historical Association Journal* 14 (1994): 3–10.

Hunter, J. Marvin. "A Bandera County Pioneer." *Frontier Times* (Bandera, TX) (July 1924): 12–13.

Hyde, Orson. *To The Saints Scattered Abroad—Greeting: Beloved Brethren and Friends.* Pamphlet, 1 August 1848. RLDS archives. Compare copy in Journal History of the Church 69:1 August 1848.

Jesse, Dean C., and David J. Whittaker. "The Last Months of Mormonism in Missouri: The Albert Perry Rockwood Journal." *Brigham Young University Studies* 29, no. 2 (Winter 1988): 5–41.

Jordan, Gilbert J. "Excerpts From My 'Hill Country' Talk." *Journal (German-Texan Heritage Society)* 8, no. 3 (Fall 1986): 1–3.

Jorgensen, Danny L. "The Fiery Darts of the Adversary: An Interpretation of Early Cutlerism." *John Whitmer Historical Association Journal* 10 (1990): 67–83.

LeSueur, Stephen C. "The Danites Reconsidered: Were They Vigilantes or Just the Mormons' Version of the Elks Club?" *John Whitmer Historical Association Journal* 14 (1994): 32–52.

Lewis, David Rich. "'For life, the resurrection, and life everlasting': James J. Strang and Strangite Mormon Polygamy." *Wisconsin Magazine of History* 66 (Summer 1983): 274–91.

Mills, H. W. "De Tal Palo Astilla" [edited version of *The Life of George Miller, Written By Himself*]. *Annual Publications of the Southern Historical Society* (1917): 88–156.

Montague, George. "Reminiscences." *Autumn Leaves* 9, no. 9 (September 1896): 387–89.

———. "Reminiscences No. 2." *Autumn Leaves* 10, no. 1 (January 1897): 73.

Newell, Linda King. "Emma Hale Smith and the Polygamy Question." *John Whitmer Historical Association Journal* 4 (1984): 3–15.

Pierce, Gerald S. "The Military Road Expedition of 1840–41." *Texas Military History* 6 (Summer 1967).

Quinn, D. Michael. "The Council of Fifty and Its Members, 1844–1945." *Brigham Young University Studies* 20, no. 2 (Fall 1979): 163–97.

Quist, John. "Polygamy Among James Strang and His Followers." *John Whitmer Historical Association Journal* 9 (1989): 31–48.

Rowley, Dennis. "The Mormon Experience in the Wisconsin Pineries, 1841–1845." *Brigham Young University Studies* 32, nos. 1–2 (1991): 119–48.

Sanford, Albert Hart. "The Mormons of Mormon Coulee." *Wisconsin Magazine of History* 24 (December 1940): 129–42.

Smith, Heman C. "Newell K. Whitney." *Journal of History* 2, no. 1 (January 1909): 70–77.

———. "Pioneer Trails Across Iowa." *Journal of History* 10, no. 1 (January 1917): 47–59.

———. "Succession in the Presidency." *Journal of History* 2, no. 1 (January 1909): 3–14.

Smith, Heman Hale. "George Miller." *Journal of History* 2, no. 2 (April 1909): 225–32.

Smith, Joseph, III. "Statements of Joseph Smith." *Journal of History* 12, no. 4 (October 1919): 400–447.

Smith, Thomas T. "Fort Inge and the Texas Economy." *Military History of the Southwest* 21 (Fall 1991): 135–56.

Smith, Vida E. "Two Widows of the Brick Row." *Journal of History* 3, no. 2 (April 1910): 202–12.

Taylor, Thomas U. "Lyman Wight and the Mormons in Texas." *Frontier Times* (Bandera, TX) 18, no. 9 (June 1941): 385–87.

Timmons, Joe E. "The Referendum in Texas on the Ordinance of Secession, February 23, 1861: The Vote." *East Texas Historical Society* 11 (February 1973): 12–28.

Wight, Levi Lamoni. "Autobiography of L. L. Wight." *Journal of History* 9, no. 3 (July 1916): 259–99.

———. "Memories of Other Days." *Autumn Leaves* 5, no. 6 (June 1892): 253–56. Photocopy. LDS Archives. Wight, under the name "Lamoni," writes about a trip to the ruins of Mountain Valley, Burnet County, Texas.

Wight, Lyman. *An Address by Way of an Abridged Account and Journal of My Life from February 1844 up to April 1848, with an Appeal to the Latter Day Saints.* Pamphlet. Iowa State Historical Society Archives. A defense for his leadership of the Mormon colony in Texas in defiance of the guidance of Brigham Young and the Quorum of the Twelve of the LDS church. Annotated with the symbol "No. 183 A8" and inscribed with the notation "Read to the Branch at Zodiac on April 30, 1848. Endorsed on May 1, 1848 and G. Miller, J. Young, W. P. Eldridge, O. L. Wight, and S. Curtis appointed by committee to have it published."

Dissertations and Theses

Bowden, M. G. "History of Burnet County." Master's thesis, University of Texas, 1940.

Cates, Charlotte H. "The History of Bandera County." Master's thesis, St. Mary's University, 1942.

Cunningham, Michael C. "The Historic-Geographic Principles of the Mormon Migration and Colonization of Texas." Master's thesis, East Texas State University, 1985.

Curtis, Sarah Kay. "A History of Gillespie County, Texas, 1846–1900." Master's thesis, University of Texas, 1943.

Durning, Bonnie Means. "A History of the Mormon Church in Texas, 1843–1906." Master's thesis, East Texas State University, 1964.

Ehat, Andrew F. "Joseph Smith's Introduction of Temple Ordinances and the 1844 Mormon Succession Question." Master's thesis, Brigham Young University, 1982.

Hearne, Carl H. "The History of the Mormon Colony at Kelsey, Upshur County." Master's thesis, East Texas State Teachers College, 1949.

Hormachea, Carroll Randolph. "The Mormon Migration to Texas Under Lyman Wight." Master's thesis, Trinity University, 1930.

Johnson, Melvin C. "A New Perspective for the Antebellum and Civil War Texas German Community." Master's thesis, Stephen F. Austin State University, 1993.

Larche, Douglas Wayne. "The Mantle of the Prophet: A Rhetorical Analysis of the Quest for Mormon Post-Martyrdom Leadership, 1844–1860." PhD diss., Indiana University, 1977.

Neighbors, Alice Atkinson. "Life and Public Work of Robert S. Neighbors." Master's thesis, University of Texas, 1936.

Van Wagenen, Michael. "The Texas Republic and the Mormon Kingdom of God: The Attempt to Establish a Theocratic Nation in the Texas-Mexico Borderlands in 1844." Master's thesis, University of Texas at Brownsville and Texas Southmost College, 2000.

Wightman, Philip C. "The Life and Contributions of Lyman Wight." Master's thesis, University of Texas, 1970.

Newspapers

Beaver Island (MI) Record

Burnet (TX) Bulletin

Dallas Morning News

Democratic Telegraph and Texas Register (Houston)

Deseret News (Salt Lake City)

Dubuque (IA) Transcript

Eldorado (TX) Success

Evening and Morning Star (Independence, MO)

Frontier Times (Bandera, TX)

Gospel Herald (Voree, WI)

Iowa Standard (Cedar Rapids)

Latter-Day Saints' Millennial Star (Liverpool, England)

Liberal Democrat (La Crosse, WI)

Melchizedek and Aaronic Herald (Covington, KY)

Morning Chronicle (La Crosse, WI)

Neu Braunfels Zeitung (New Braunfels, TX)

New York Sun

Northern Islander (Beaver Island, MI)

Saint's Herald (True Latter-Day Saints' Herald) (Lamoni, IA)

San Antonio Express

Texas Democrat (Austin)

Times and Seasons (Nauvoo, IL)

Tribune and Leader Press (La Crosse, WI)

Weekly News (Galveston, TX)

Zeitung (Galveston, TX)

Index

The index contains a great majority of the individuals that appear in the Wight Colony during a period covering more than twenty years. Each personal name that has variant spellings in historical documents is listed here only under the most common, widely accepted, or likely spelling. Variants of names are included, in parentheses. All married members of the Wight colonies listed in this index are cross-referenced to their spouses. The letter *p* following a page number denotes a photograph.

A

An Address, by Way of an abridged Account and Journal of My Life from February 1844 up to April 1848, with an Appeal to the Latter Day Saints, 68n29, 112–15, 118, 120–21, 124, 149n26
Anderson, Lewis, 92, 93
Andrews, Abigail Emma, 80, 190. *See also* Ballantyne, James
Andrews, Ann Elizabeth, 80, 190. *See also* Hawley, Aaron
Andrews, Margaret Francis, 81, 82, 146, 153, 154, 155, 201. *See also* Miller, John F.; Montague, George Jr.
Andrews, Marion, 187

B

Badham (Badlam), Alexander, 34, 35n6
Bailey, George, 78, 127, 127n6, 128
Ballantyne, Andrew, 63, 78, 79, 80, 128, 131, 146, 151, 152, 172, 202. *See also* Connyers, Rebecca Jane
Ballantyne, Ellen (Hellen), 76, 78, 79, 155, 156, 187, 188, 201. *See also* Bell, William; Moncur, Abram
Ballantyne, James 80, 190. *See also* Andrews, Abigail Emma
Ballantyne, Jane Margaret, 39–40, 49, 57, 156, 190, 201. *See also* Wight, Lyman
Ballantyne, Jane V., 76, 78, 83, 155, 156, 201. *See also* Moncur, Abram
Ballantyne, John, 57, 63, 202. *See also* Ballantyne, Janet Turnball
Ballantyne, Robert, 79, 195. *See also* Minear, Marinda
Ballantyne, Thomas, 84
Ballantyne, William, 57, 58, 146, 159, 185, 186, 187
Bandera hanging tree, 196
Banks, C. Stanley, 86, 157
Bartlett, John, 103–4, 165
Baye, Henry, 117
Bell, William, 82, 83, 155. *See also* Ballantyne, Ellen
Bell, William (First non-Wightite Bandera County Commissioner), 185
Bennett, Richard E., 2, 110
Benson, Ezra Taft, 109n1, 110, 114, 118, 119, 123, 123n28
Bent, Samuel, 12, 35n6, 55
Benton, Harriet, 9, 93, 145, 159, 181p, 190, 192, 201. *See also* Wight, Lyman
Biesele, Rudolph Leopold, 89
Biggers, Don H., 89, 157–158, 164
Bird, Benjamin F., 78, 80, 159, 186, 188. *See also* Bird, Mary
Bird, Charles, 57, 80, 152, 159, 186. *See also* Monroe, Bernice
Bird, George W., 57, 66, 78, 80, 83, 93, 146, 152, 190. *See also* Curtis, Eliza
Bird, Mary, 78, 80. *See also* Bird, Benjamin F.

Bird, Millicent (Polly), 78. *See also* Bird, Phineas
Bird, Phineas, 26, 28, 45, 78, 202. *See also* Bird, Millicent
Bird, Richard, 79, 83, 195, 196. *See also* Moncur, Jenemie
Bird, Samuel H., 79
Bitton, Davis, 38, 40n17, 191
Black River Pine Company 21–26. *See also* Wisconsin logging camps
Blair, Alma R., 200
blood oaths, 143, 144
Boggs, Lilburn, 18
Boland & McKee, 166
Book of Commandments, 14, 128
Boughton, Elizabeth, 153, 201. *See also* Miller, George
Brace (Bray), Rodney, 80, 146, 172, 194. *See also* Curtis, Sarah
Brace, Truman, 15, 57, 58, 78
Brace, Veronica, 78, 80, 146. *See also* Jenkins, Ralph
Bracht, Viktor, 60, 64
Briggs, E. C., 198
Bromme, Tr., 65
Brooks, Juanita H., 91
Brown, Captain James, 143n13. *See also* blood oaths
Buffalo Hump, 5, 62, 86, 178
Bunnell, Lafayette Houghton, 32, 45, 46, 48, 51

C

Cadwell, Edwin, 128
Cahoon, Pulaski, 50. *See also Maid of Iowa*
Caldwell, Silas, 127, 127n6, 128
Camp Houston, 96
Camp Verde, 196
Campbell, Alexander, 9
Campbell, Robert, 118
Carl, Herrin (Grafen zu Castell), 66, 187, 188
Carter, Gideon, 48, 149, 157, 158, 159, 185, 186, 187, 202
Carter, Irwin (Irvin) F., 128, 146, 159, 162, 185, 186. *See also* Six, Mary Ann
Carter, Matilda, 26, 46, 47, 78, 80, 83, 149, 152, 153, 201. *See also* Wight, Orange Lysander
Carter, Rosilla, 78, 80, 153, 154, 155, 186, 201. *See also* Wight, Orange Lysander
Chatfield, Martha, 76, 80, 82, 83, 156. *See also* Miller, John F.
Chatfield, Silas Porter, 79, 80. *See also* Howard, Rosetta Jane
Chipman, Ezra Alpheus, 7, 76, 77, 78, 79, 81, 83, 93p, 106, 153, 154, 155, 158, 159, 165, 169–71, 180, 185–87, 190, 192, 195, 200, 201. *See also* Porter, Malinda; Sutherland, Janette; Sutherland, Marian
Chipman, Heber N., 79
Chipman, Malinda M., 79. *See also* Johnson, Oscar D.
Claren, Oscar, 85
Clark, Amasa, 187, 196, 202
Clark, Frances, 202
Clayton, David, 49–50, 151
Clayton, William, 30n41, 35n6, 50, 52, 151
Comanche, 84–85, 96, 119n21, 130, 175, 178–79, 182, 184, 189
Connyers, Rebecca Jane, 19, 79, 80, 130–31, 172. *See also* Ballantyne, Andrew; patrilineal succession
Coon, L. W., 169
Cornet, Edward, 184
Corrill, John, 14, 16
Council of Fifty, 5, 20, 29–31, 33–36, 38, 42, 51, 52, 55, 90, 91, 93, 95n13, 112–13, 118, 122–23, 126, 137, 167, 204
Cowdery, Oliver, 10, 13n12, 111
Croft, Jacob, 173
Curtis, Eliza, 57, 78, 80, 152, 159, 190. *See also* Bird, Charles W.
Curtis, Emeline, 78, 80, 154. *See also* Curtis, Meacham
Curtis, Jeremiah Sr., 63, 76, 78, 202
Curtis, Joseph Smith, 79, 80. *See also* Vicero, Mary
Curtis, Meacham, 12, 65, 78, 80, 154, 165, 179, 185. *See also* Curtis, Emeline

Curtis, Patience, 57, 80, 151, 152, 201. *See also* Miles, Joel S.
Curtis, Sarah, 80, 194. *See also* Brace, Rodney
Curtis, Sarah Kay, 88, 101
Curtis, Stephen Zeloutus, 127, 128, 145, 146, 165
Curtis, William, 57, 77, 78, 80, 81, 84, 106p, 152, 154, 159, 171, 190. *See also* Minear, Lydia P.; Racig, Maria Henrietta; Sutherland, Marian
Cutler, Alpheus, 23, 30n41, 35, 93, 137–38

D

Daniels, Nancy Anderson, 76, 80, 83, 153, 154, 155, 201. *See also* Montague, George, Sr.
Davis, Joseph, 136
DeMontel, Charles, 179, 195
Dixon, Herschell Harry (Dickie), Jr., 1
Dixon, W. H., 166
Doctrine and Covenants, 14, 36n9, 128, 150
Doniphan, Alexander, 12, 18–19
Drake, Daniel, 92
Drake, Newell, 92, 148, 148n24. *See also* Johnson, Cynthia Parker
Duggans, S. A., 173
Duncan, Homer, 6, 7n8, 117, 118n19

E

Earl, Wilbur Bradley, 174, 202. *See also* Langley, Mary; Wight, Harriet Martensia
Eldridge, Nancy A., 78, 83. *See also* Eldridge, William P.
Eldridge, William P., 20n26, 55, 57, 78, 82, 83, 128, 162. *See also* Eldridge, Nancy
Eldorado, Texas, 1
Emmett, James, 90, 91
extermination order, 18

F

"the Family," 3, 9–10, 87. *See also* Wight, Lyman
Fielding, Joseph, 30n41, 43, 47, 95n13
Fischer, Ernest G., 86
Fort Belknap, 175, 184
Fort Crawford, 24
Fort Croghan (Croggin), 166, 175
Fort Gibson, 175
Fort Johnston, 4, 57, 59, 59n11 *See also* Mormon Grove
Fort Martin Scott, 84, 89, 96, 98, 99
Foster, Lawrence, 74–75, 147
Fry, Mary Catherine, 153, 201. *See also* Miller, George
Fundamentalist Latter Day Saints (FLDS), 1, 207

G

Garland, Virginia Minear Hay, 190
Gartner, Christian, 163
Gaylord, Lyman, 172
Gaylord, Sydney, 172
Gaylord, William, 172, 187
Gibbs, Alta Holland, 161, 175
Goodale, Elvira Kay, 78. *See also* Goodale, John D.
Goodale, John D., 78. *See also* Goodale, Elvira K.
Goodale, Joseph Dwight, 78, 87, 100, 127, 128, 145, 146, 165, 172, 178, 179. *See also* Johnson, Sally
Goudie, James, 127, 127n6
Goudie, Jeannette, 174. *See also* Hadfield, Joseph
Grant, Jedediah M., 144. *See also* blood oaths
Grape Creek, 66, 93, 95, 96, 101n24, 125, 154
Green, John A., 176
Gressman, Asher, 44, 45, 78, 83, 181. *See also* Gressman, Effelinda
Gressman, Effelinda (Essilinda), 44, 45, 78, 83, 181. *See also* Gressman, Asher
Graves, H. A., 72

H

Hadfield, Ann, 78, 79, 80, 82, 141, 148, 154, 156, 170, 200. *See also* Hawley, George

Hadfield, Joseph, 174. *See also* Goudie, Jeannette
Hadfield, Sarah, 63, 80, 82, 148, 152, 156, 170, 200. *See also* Hawley, George; Wight, Orange Lysander
Hamilton Creek or Mills or Valley, 4, 7, 70, 107p, 133, 156, 158, 161, 163, 165–67, 169–73, 175–77, 179
Harmon, William, 81, 201. *See also* Sutherland, Marian
Haun's Mill, 18
Hawley, Aaron, 80, 187, 190. *See also* Andrews, Ann Elizabeth
Hawley, George, 63, 78, 79, 80, 82, 142, 145, 146, 148, 149, 152, 154, 156, 170, 170n24, 173, 174. *See also* Hadfield, Ann; Hadfield, Sarah
Hawley, Gideon, 195, 196
Hawley, John, 47, 48, 50, 54, 56, 57, 59, 63, 66, 78, 80, 81, 82, 87, 94, 108p, 112n7, 116, 129, 140n8, 141n10, 142, 142n12, 148, 151, 152, 154, 158, 161, 171, 171n24, 172, 173, 198, 202, 143; Pine Valley (UT) church and public offices, 174, 174n35; Texas and Utah temple ceremonies, 143. *See also* Hobart, Harriet; Johnson, Sylvia
Hawley, Mary, 57, 78, 80, 83, 148, 152, 155, 158, 201. *See also* Wight, Lyman
Hawley, Pierce, 26, 28, 44, 45, 48, 56, 57, 63, 74, 78, 95, 142, 145, 146, 151, 152, 170, 172, 173, 202. *See also* Schroeder, Sarah
Hawley, Priscilla, 63, 78, 80, 83, 142, 146, 152. *See also* Young, John
Haws, Peter, 23, 24, 35
Hay, George, 79, 106p, 159, 179, 185, 186, 187, 195, 196. *See also* Minear, Amanda; Minear, Virginia
Hay, Jeanette (Jenet, Jennet), 187, 188. *See also* Hoffman, Andrew
Henderson, James, 61
Hewitt, E. B., 77, 78, 80, 93, 154. *See also* Hewitt, Elizabeth
Hewitt, Elizabeth, 77, 78, 80, 154. *See also* Hewitt, E. B.
Hewitt, Richard, 93, 97, 97n17, 150
Higbee, John, 151
Higbee, Isaac, 151
Hinckson, John, 57, 58
Hobart, Harriett, 63, 80, 81, 141n10. *See also* Hawley, John
Hobart, Mary Ann, 57, 63, 78, 80, 155, 190, 201. *See also* Wight, Lyman
Hobart, Otis, 44, 55, 56, 57, 80, 82, 83, 127, 142, 152, 155
Hoffman, Andrew, 79, 80, 129, 159, 178, 179, 185, 186, 187, 196, 197. *See also* Hay, Jeanette
Hoffman, August, 85
Holland, Samuel E., 71, 157, 169
Hook, Aaron, 129n8
Hopkins, Abijah, 170
Houston, Sam, 4, 22, 29, 37n11, 42
Howard, Rosetta Jane, 79, 80. *See also* Chatfield, Silas Porter
Hunter, J. Marvin, 157, 158, 196
Hyde, Orson, 49, 60, 94n11, 109, 112n8, 113–14, 121, 122, 123, 124, 134, 137, 204

I

Isom, Richard Lamb, 62

J

James, Nathaniel T., 128
Jeffs, Warren, 1, 207
Jenkins, Ralph, 78, 80, 145, 154, 162. *See also* Brace, Veronica
Johnson, Cynthia Parker, 92, 148. *See also* Drake, Newell
Johnson, Heber (Eber), 82, 83, 92, 146. *See also* Goodale, Sally
Johnson, Lucy Matilda, 92. *See also* Kelting, Joseph
Johnson, Oscar D., 79. *See also* Chipman, Malinda M.
Johnson, Sally, 82, 83, 92. *See also* Johnson, Heber
Johnson, Sylvia, 80, 81, 92, 106p, 141, 142, 148, 154. *See also* Hawley, John
Johnston, Colonel Albert Sydney, 134

Jordan, Terry G., 96, 99

K

Kane, Thomas D., 60
Kelting, Joseph, 92, 93. *See also* Johnson, Lucy Matilda
Kimball, Heber C., 30n41, 31, 39, 59, 110, 119n21, 134, 205
Kindla, John, 187
Kindla, Petronella, 187–88
Kinser, Nannie Mae, 169
Kirtland Temple, 13, 14

L

Langley, Mary, 174. *See also* Bradley, Earl Wilbur
Lee, John D., 16, 47
Leyland, Eliza, 165, 182, 183. *See also* Wight, Orange Lysander
Leyland, Sarah, 140
Leyland, Sarah Wallace, 83, 97. *See also* Miller, George
Leyland, Sophia, 140, 181, 182. *See also* Wight, Levi Lamoni
Leyland, William, 79, 82, 86, 93, 94, 95, 98, 113n10, 124, 125, 139–40, 146, 157, 206; journal, 10n2
Lyman, Amasa, 39, 110, 122, 136, 139, 187, 196
Lyman Wight & Co, 100, 102, 103, 104, 186
Lytle, Hugh, 197, 198

M

Magill (McGill), William, 166, 176
Maid of Iowa, 34, 50, 56, 62, 199
Martindale, William, 113n10, 117–18, 120–22, 124, 125
McCord, Alexander, 198
McGaw, James, 190
Meusebach, John, 65, 85
Miles, Delia, 153, 201. *See also* Miles, Joel S.
Miles, Ira, 50, 55
Miles, Joel S., 15, 57, 80, 101n24, 116, 149, 152, 153, 154, 159, 201. *See also* Curtis, Patience F.; Miles, Delia
Miles, Orlando B., 159, 185, 187
Miller, George, 22, 24–28, 30, 34–35, 37, 42, 44, 56, 73, 83, 84, 90, 93, 96, 97, 104, 112, 114, 118, 119–120, 124–25, 137, 139, 148n24, 150, 152–53, 158, 162, 182, 201. *See also* Boughton, Elizabeth; Fry, Mary Catherine; Leyland, Sarah Wallace
Miller, Henry W., 24, 27, 38n8, 90n1, 118, 172
Miller, John F., 26, 66, 76, 76n9, 78, 80, 81, 82, 83, 93, 94, 95, 98, 146, 152, 153, 154, 158, 162, 163, 172, 194, 201. *See also* Andrews, Margaret Francis; Chatfield, Martha; Wight, Rosina Minerva
Minear, Amanda, 79. *See also* Hay, George
Minear, Emma, 79. *See also* Sutherland, Joseph L.
Minear, Lydia P., 106p, 179. *See also* Curtis, William
Minear, Marinda, 79. *See also* Ballantyne, Robert
Minear, Virginia, 79, 106p, 190, 212. *See also* Hay, George
Miner, Jarvis G., 98
Missouri-Mormon Civil War, 14–19. *See also* Wight, Lyman: Colonel, 56th Missouri Militia Regiment.
Mohon, Marty, 88
Mohon, Michelle, 88
Moncur, Abram (Abraham), 26, 76, 78, 79, 80, 83, 154, 155, 156, 169, 179, 186, 187, 188, 201. *See also* Ballantyne, Hellen; Ballantyne, Jane V.
Moncur, Jenemie, 79, 83, 196. *See also* Bird, Richard
Monroe, Bernice, 57, 80, 83, 152. *See also* Bird, Charles
Monroe, David, 57, 66, 186, 188
Monroe Bird & Co, 186
Montague, George Jr., 56, 76n9, 80, 82, 186, 187, 201. *See also* Andrews, Margaret Francis
Montague, George Sr., 78, 80, 146, 153, 154, 186. *See also* Daniels, Nancy Anderson; Segar, Eliza

Montague, Mercy Lincoln, 73
Mormon Coulee, 43–45
Mormon Grove, 57
Morris, Jacob, 49, 50
Morrison, Arthur, 50
Mountain Valley, 4, 7, 70, 80–81, 180–82, 184, 185–87, 190, 203
Myrick & Miller, 43, 46, 54

N

Nauvoo Temple, 49–50, 52, 146
Nisonger, Henry, 128

O

Oeler's sawmill, 43
Ostler, John, 118n19

P

Page, John E., 34, 35, 115, 122
patrilineal succession: Hawley, Pierce, 21; Hyde, Orson, 113; Strang, James, 129; Wight, Lyman, 19, 33, 36, 41, 130, 131; Young, Brigham, 36, 199; Zodiac community, 126, 199
Pond, Elmira, 27, 28, 156. *See also* Miller, Henry W.
Porter, Malinda (Matilda), 78, 81, 83, 153, 200, 201. *See also* Chipman, Ezra Alpheus
Porter, Sanford, 133, 180, 200
Potter, Andrew A., 72–73
Pratt, Orson, 30n41, 60, 110–11, 113n9, 122n25, 125
Pratt, Parley, 10, 12, 30n41, 39, 110, 113, 120, 205, 206n21
Prindle, Jacob, 172

Q

Quinn, D. Michael, 14, 18, 20, 20n26, 29n40, 34n4, 37n11, 111, 113n10, 136n1

R

Ramsdell, Charles W., 159, 160
Richards, Willard, 30n41, 34, 35n6, 37, 39, 57, 91, 110, 111, 189
Rigdon, Sydney 9, 10, 20, 21, 22, 36, 41, 44, 75, 109n1, 118, 147
Roberts, Brigham H., 149, 157, 202
Roemer, Ferdinand, 60, 65
Rosig, Henrietta Maria Rosig (Racig), 78, 80, 81, 84, 154. *See also* Curtis, Meacham

S

Schmidtzensky, John, 68, 100, 163
Schroeder, Sarah 78, 145, 146. *See also* Hawley, Pierce
Schubbert, F., 66, 67, 88–89
Scott, Major Martin, 96
Scovil, Lucius, 120
Segar, Eliza, 78, 146. *See also* Montague, George, Sr.
Sheen, Isaac, 127n6, 128, 199–200
Simpson, Major Robert Neighbors, 183, 184
Six, Mary Ann, 78, 83, 146. *See also* Carter, Irwin
Slade, William, 173
slavery, 11, 15, 67, 68n29
Smith, Alva, 128
Smith, George A., 30n41, 34, 109, 110, 113, 113n10, 114, 118, 119, 123, 134
Smith, Heman C., 35n6, 41, 58, 81n13, 83, 131, 157, 160, 211
Smith, Heman H., 10n2, 67, 81n13, 125, 157, 158, 159, 160
Smith, Hyrum, 20, 30, 33, 37n11, 40, 143. *See also* blood oaths
Smith, John, 20, 112, 122
Smith, Joseph, Jr., 3, 5, 7, 9, 10, 12–15, 18–22, 29–31, 32–40, 45–46, 49–50, 52, 87, 91, 92, 96, 97, 109, 111–12, 114–16, 118, 122, 123, 125, 127–28, 130, 132–33, 134, 136–37, 140, 145, 146, 147, 149, 151, 159, 160, 167, 169, 173, 181, 183, 198, 199, 202, 204–5, 207
Smith, Joseph, III, 7, 10, 19, 33, 125, 128, 129n8, 130–31, 135, 136n1, 151, 160n45, 167, 189, 197–200, 204
Smith, Spencer, 26, 63, 78, 81, 83, 128, 130–31, 146, 152, 157, 159–60, 178–79, 181, 190, 197, 198;

journal, 10n2. *See also* Wright, Anna Christina
Smith, William A., 34, 35, 113, 114, 118, 122, 124, 126, 127, 127n6, 128, 129n8, 131, 137, 167, 199, 204
Smithwick, Noah, 61–62, 68, 71, 72–73, 157, 158, 166, 168, 170, 171, 172, 175–76, 194, 195, 196
Snedaker, Morris, 7n8, 118n19
Snow, Erastus, 30n41, 92
Spaulding, Jacob, 24
Spencer, Orson, 60,
Staniford, Brevet Lieutenant-Colonel Thomas, 98
Steffey, William, 57
Stout, Allan, 25–28, 44, 144
Stout, Hosea, 91–92, 174, 198
Strang, James, 35, 96–98, 115–16, 118, 129, 131, 137, 150, 167, 182, 183, 200, 204
Stratton, Ruth, 63, 76, 78. *See also* Curtis, Jeremiah Sr.
Sutherland, David, 58
Sutherland, Donald, 57, 58
Sutherland, Jane Menzies, 58
Sutherland, Janette (Jenette), 78, 155. *See also* Chipman, Ezra Alpheus
Sutherland, Joseph D., 186
Sutherland, Joseph L., 79, 195. *See also* Minear, Emma
Sutherland, Marian (Marion), 57, 78, 79, 80, 81, 146, 152, 153, 154, 155, 159, 171, 187. *See also* Chipman, Ezra Alpheus; Curtis, William; Harmon, William
Swartznell, William, 16
Swift, Ebenezer, 102, 103
Sycamore Springs, 4, 60–62, 65, 67, 80, 89, 98

T

Taylor, Eleanor, 59, 83. *See also* Taylor, John
Taylor, John, 59, 83, 65, 66, 174, 198, 199, 200. *See also* Taylor, Eleanor
Taylor, John (apostle), 29, 30, 34, 39, 60, 110
"Texas Epidemic", 23, 114.
Thomas, Preston, 35, 84, 113, 120–22, 125
Thomas, W. G., 163
Turk, Toni R., 147
Turnbull, Janet, 76, 156, 179. *See also* Ballantyne, John
Twohig, John, 96
Tyson, James, 59

U

Urie, Barbara, 78. *See also* Bailey, George

V

Vandeever, Logan, 166
Vicero, Mary, 79, 80. *See also* Curtis, Joseph Smith
von Solms-Braunfels, Prince Carl, 85
von Wrede, Friedrich, 85

W

Walton, John, 33
Wight, Anna Christina, 63, 78, 152, 159, 190. *See also* Smith, Spencer
Wight, Harriet Martensia, 174, 202. *See also* Earl, Wilbur Bradley
Wight, Levi, 9, 145
Wight, Levi Lamoni, 27–28, 58, 63, 67, 79, 80, 86, 90, 95, 139, 149, 160, 178, 181, 182, 187, 190, 192, 194, 195, 207. *See also* Leyland, Sophia
Wight, Loami Limhi, 79, 187, 195
Wight, Lyman, 105p; alcoholism, 25, 44; Baneemy, military office of, 15; *Book of Commandments*, 14; Colonel, 56th Missouri Militia Regiment, 15–19; common-stock philosophy, 9, 44, 45, 66, 86, 87, 88, 90, 94, 101–2, 114, 115, 116, 121, 125, 128, 134, 138, 164, 185, 207; Council of Fifty, 20, 30, 52, 55, 90–91, 93, 95, 112–13, 118, 122–23, 126, 137, 167, 181, 204; coward, called by Brigham Young, 52; excommunication of, 112–13, 122, 134; faith healing and illness, 13–14, 72–73; "the Family," 9, 10, 87; high priest,

10; Kirtland Temple, 13; LDS Quorum of Twelve Apostles, ordained, 20; Liberty jail, 19; Nauvoo temple, 13, 25, 43, 50, 52, 102, 146; Ohio (Cincinnati) mission, 11; patrilineal succession, 19, 36, 41, 126, 129, 131, 167, 199; polygamy, 13, 39, 47, 49, 51, 62, 76, 127, 141, 147–51, 155, 157–58, 160, 169, 200, 202; Pontiac branch, St. Clair, Michigan, 12; Quorum of the Anointed, 20, 32–34, 36; succession crisis, 33–36, 40–42; succession struggle, 37–41, 49, 50, 52–53, 55, 56, 58–59, 87, 112, 114–15, 119, 120–23, 134, 204, 206; Smith, Joseph, III, 19, 36, 91, 109–10, 126, 129, 130, 131, 167, 199; Thomas, Preston and Martindale, William, 120–22; Wisconsin lumber missions (Black River), 21–28; women, attitude toward, 47–48

Wight, Lyman Lehi, 80, 187, 190. *See also* Leyland, Eliza

Wight, Orange Lysander, 11, 26, 46, 47, 49, 66, 76, 78, 80–81, 82, 83, 93, 95, 99p, 115, 116n14, 128, 148–49, 150–51, 152–53, 154, 155, 156–59, 165, 169, 174, 178, 182, 186, 187, 190, 192, 195, 201, 202, 206. *See also* Carter, Matilda; Carter, Rosilla; Hadfield, Sarah

Wight, Rosina Minerva, 26, 76, 80, 82, 84, 152, 153, 201, 206. *See also* Miller, John F.

Wight, Susanna, 9

Woodruff, Wilford, 110, 143, 206

Woodworth, Flora, 46

Woodworth, Lucien, 4, 5, 29, 30, 32n1, 35, 37, 112–13, 120, 123n28, 189

Y

Young, Brigham, 5, 6, 20, 23, 32, 35–36, 40–41, 45, 49–53, 55–56, 60, 87, 146, 148, 151, 160, 165, 167, 172, 174, 177, 181, 183, 189, 195, 198, 200, 202, 204; assumption of LDS Church President, 109–12, 149; blood oath, 143; *Maid of Iowa,* 50, 56; Miller, George, 90–91, 96–99, 112; Second Anointing, priests and kings, 28; Texas mission, 32–37, 41–42; Venn diagram and inner circle of the Twelve, 37–38; Wight, Lyman, moderation toward, 59, 134, 137; Wightite antipathy to, 56, 124, 127, 131, 134, 173, 199

Young, John, 28, 28n39, 63, 75, 78, 80, 142, 145, 152, 162, 170, 175. *See also* Hawley, Priscilla

Young, Joseph, 110, 118, 119n20, 123n28, 134

Z

Zodiac, 4, 5, 7, 58, 65, 67–68, 70–73, 76, 80–84, 86–104, 109, 112–13, 115–18, 120–21, 124–31, 136–50, 153–61, 168–69, 175, 185–86, 191, 204, 206, 207

Zodiac Temple, 125, 127, 128, 137, 139–42, 146–47, 207; Endowment House, comparison, 138–45; Ordinances, 1850 to 1851, 145–47